Gen Ed

Social Fictions Series

Gen Ed

By

D. G. Mulcahy

BRILL

SENSE

LEIDEN | BOSTON

All chapters in this book have undergone peer review.

The Library of Congress Cataloging-in-Publication Data is available online at
http://catalog.loc.gov

ISSN 2542-8799
ISBN 978-90-04-45934-2 (paperback)
ISBN 978-90-04-45935-9 (hardback)
ISBN 978-90-04-45936-6 (e-book)

This book is printed on acid-free paper and produced in a sustainable manner.

ADVANCE PRAISE FOR
GEN ED

"In *Gen Ed*, D. G. Mulcahy provides us with a fascinating insight into the politics of university life. The story is gritty, moving and riveting, holding the reader's attention from the very outset. The fictitious Metropolitan Atlantic University provides a convincing platform for the exploration of a range of themes and ideas, and while the idea of education is at the core, the various themes and sub-themes which emanate and are advanced capture the reader's imagination and curiosity. The novel is unique in that while it can be read by educationalists as a novel about education, its reach and impact are both broader and deeper, treating perennial issues such as gender equality, leadership, power and the meaning of education. The emergence of a virus towards the end of the novel provides a timely and apt closing to a complex and spellbinding world."
– Judith Harford, FRHistS, University College Dublin

"*Gen Ed* is a remarkable work. It follows in the long tradition of the academic novel, and is a delightful tale of life and politics on a small university campus. It is far more than this, though, because it also addresses a number of important topics about liberal arts and general education in higher education, and does so in a thoughtful way without overwhelming the reader with the complexities of the debates taking place on many college campuses. As a professor and former university administrator who has also served on a local board of education, I can vouch for much of the reality of *Gen Ed*. The main characters in the book may seem like caricatures, but for anyone in higher education, they have more than a touch of authenticity."
– Timothy Reagan, The University of Maine

"Some aspects of university politics are universal and some are country and even college-type specific. That is particularly so in relation to the United States and we get a great sense of how it can manifest itself throughout this most engaging book set in the fictitious Metropolitan Atlantic University. Thus, while the work contains lots of good humour, it is also insightful for the academic reader both in the United States and elsewhere in terms of the detailed day-to-day infighting that takes place. For me the most engaging aspect of the book is the many Socratic dialogues on general education – the site of so much contestation at 'The Metro'. Time after times I had vicarious experience, feeling I was in the seminar room and partaking with the students. These scenes alone should make it compulsory reading for would-be undergraduates, graduates, schoolteachers, academics, and the general reader."

– Tom O'Donoghue, The University of Western Australia, Fellow of the Academy of the Social Sciences in Australia, Fellow of the Royal Historical Society

"*Gen Ed* is a profound and cutting-edge book for everyone; especially those trying to find meaning during the pandemic and hope for the future of education in America. Just as the COVID pandemic is ready to force the timely, gutsy, and provocative characters in Mulcahy's latest book into quarantine, a fierce GEN ED curriculum debate is raging at the METRO. Mulcahy takes us on a labyrinth full of diverse characters that will instantly remind you of people you know; including graduate and undergrad students, administrators, politicians, and professors. Mulcahy expertly juxtaposes the complexities of university life with the local board of education 'hidden' agenda. The political forces and intricacies surrounding those that believe they found the Holy Grail of GEN ED are expertly woven amidst the daily life of the characters. Mulcahy is a creative force bringing the characters to life within the dance of politics and the narrow-minded aspirations of university professors and politicians. Fasten your seat belt as you enter GEN ED's political circus and ride a roller coaster of enlightenment. Mulcahy weaves a much needed and creative portrait of general education philosophy and pedagogy; the first of its kind in years. Professor Patrick Kelly (who brews his own Guinness) will make you wish you were in his class as he challenges his students to

think deeply and critically about their life and what is an educated person after-all. You will find yourself laughing one minute and frowning the next, when politics, back stabbing, and overall crude and dangerous behavior meet at the Metro GEN ED arena as COVID 19 appears on the scene."
– Barbara Clark, Central Connecticut State University

"Welcome to the world of academe, and the ever-so-bitter struggle to reform general education at Metro University. Who would think something as simple as curriculum revision would be a mirror for the folly and absurdity of our world? Here, we see protests and battles rage. There are no swords and blood, but the battles are as captivating as if we were watching zombies take over our backyard.

In the tradition of some of our finest satirists, *Gen Ed* is overflowing with endearing and infuriating characters: contrarians, intellectuals, Polly-annas, sycophants, radicals, cynics, and blowhards. In addition to the flesh-and-blood characters who promenade along its stage, various philosophers make appearances in the classroom ruminations of our hero, Professor Kelly, who draws students into the captivating world of Cicero, John Dewey, Horace Mann, and Paulo Freire. Even William Butler Yeats make a figurative appearance, reminding us that 'education is not the filling of a pail, but the lighting of a fire.'

And what a fire it is!

With heavy doses of snappy dialogue and chuckles throughout, *Gen Ed* is its own course in both the inanity and gravity of human behavior. Political intrigue, backroom deals, and bureaucratic jockeying are as prevalent as midterm exams. We see debates involving the nature of education, religion, the rights of parents – all played out amid the hum of administrative gears that grind in often hilarious and illuminating ways. We meet student radicals in the making, especially the endearing Filomena, as well as whistle-blowers, radio talk show hosts, and tweedy hustlers. In crossing paths, these characters create a microcosm of our world where personal vendetta, idealism, and human absurdity clash. To the credit of Mulcahy, all this is done without ever judging the characters. We love these characters, mostly because we see a bit of ourselves in them.

The book starts with the beginning of a typical semester at a non-descript city university and ends in a shocking and all-to-real finale, reminding us that we are mere players in a larger game of which we have no control. *Gen Ed* is a social critique. It is also a philosophical treatise. It is a lampoon that exposes the underbelly of our madcap lives. It lets us laugh at the silliness of its characters. It also lets us laugh, and learn to love again, the goodness in people around us, who are flawed and infuriating but never broken."
– Ronnie Casella, Associate Dean of Education, SUNY Cortland

"I am delighted to have been invited to review this novel which explores the nature and purpose of education and general education in particular in higher education in the US. This fictional work is both entertaining and light hearted but also addresses so many issues which are fundamental in education, locally and internationally. The arguments of the value of public versus private education/universities, the definition and purpose of education, what counts as curriculum and who selects curriculum, the role of politics on the policies and the role of the media in shaping policies are just examples of the matters raised. The debate within Prof Kelly's classroom reveals the best of socratic teaching and the capacity of a good teacher to enable students from a variety of backgrounds to express themselves and to engage in authentic and challenging conversations on matters which they had not previously considered. The engagement of students in real debates and their inclusion in university committees, promoted their ownership of learning, gave them a voice and created opportunities to break down barriers between social classes. Some of the universal issues about status and gender are highlighted throughout the text; the education school is undervalued within the university and while the business school is described as 'plush', the conditions within the education school are described as 'appalling', reflecting the hierarchy within disciplines on university campuses. The text brilliantly portrays the mini-politics of life on campuses and in particular the sexualisation of female students and the undermining of female leaders is very real; the traditional male voices advocating the status quo are very dismissive of the new female academics who have alternative views and who are seeking to revise and reform programmes which have legendary status within the academy.

This work is humorous and at the same time has the capacity to stimulate conversations around very serious, deep and pervasive cultural issues in education. This is a very worthwhile and useful text and I commend the author for his imaginative and at the same time, wholly realistic approach to initiating discourse in education. This is a great piece of literature as well – the characters are well-defined and the reader is easily hooked, and constantly wondering 'what will happen next?' I know that if I were teaching a postgraduate program, or indeed working with a team of staff involved in the review of a course/curriculum, I would use this text to provoke critical conversations and to analyse the contextual layers which influence decision-making on education campuses. I look forward to seeing this book published and know that it will be a most useful resource in education."
– Teresa O'Doherty, President, Marino Institute of Education, Dublin, Ireland

To Mary, with love

CONTENTS

PREFACE

The concept of general education has had a profound impact on the understanding of higher education, at least since the emergence of the medieval university, and a substantial amount of scholarly literature has grown up around it. Over the centuries, it has been spoken of with reverence and seen as a highly academic form of education, at times viewed as one befitting leaders of government. All of this notwithstanding, the fate of this hallowed ideal at Metropolitan Atlantic University (aka the Metro) is at the mercy of an assorted collection of ordinary souls when the battle for control of its program of general education is set in motion. It is around the account of the sometimes-errant behavior of key players and unpredictable developments in the unfolding drama at the Metro that the more consequential and conceptual themes of *Gen Ed* are explored. There are two essential elements here: the meaning of general education and how it is best implemented.

In challenging the stranglehold of the conservative faction that controls the general education program at the Metro, newly appointed Vice President Valerie Sainsbury strikes up an unlikely partnership with Marilyn, a carefree and self-described redneck majoring in surveillance services, and Filomena, a recent graduate of Swasser, now pursuing teacher certification. Alongside the oft-pugnacious policy debate among the faculty regarding the program to which Marilyn and Filomena are given privileged access, Professor Kelly directs a parallel and more lighthearted discussion of related questions as he aims to model Socratic teaching in his upper-level undergraduate class for prospective teachers. Reforming general education at the Metro is not free of the vanities and vulgarities of ambitious men and women and self-serving politicians, of course, nor those who poke fun at them. Arnie Smatter, the irrepressible and inquisitive chat show host of Radio YOY, ensures that this does not go unnoticed.

In the debate regarding the meaning and merits of general education and the shape it takes at the Metro, typical issues to which attention is usually given, such as a core of arts and science subjects for all students, form the centerpiece of the discussion. The second element that arises is explored by looking at the skillful approach to Socratic teaching employed by Professor Kelly and the range of issues he addresses. To move the action along smoothly, many of the matters discussed among faculty merge with (rather than overlap) those dealt with in Socratic fashion in Kelly's class. In these conversations, attention is given to the consideration of fundamental issues often overlooked in public debates on education: What is education? What is an educated person? Should there be moral education in school? What about the teaching of religion? Does the curriculum respond adequately to the educational needs of female students? How well does the curriculum deal with issues of social and racial justice? Should general education include a practical component? Should home economics and progressive education really be consigned to the rubbish dump? What about health education? What should we do about testing?

Although *Gen Ed* is a work of fiction with an element of humor, the substantive issues involved in general education are treated seriously; it is the behavior of those involved, the broader media, and the political context in which events take place, including the involvement of Radio YOY, that become the object of the humorous treatment. At the same time, Professor Kelly's approach in the classroom is portrayed in such a way as to demonstrate that Socratic teaching may be conducted in an easygoing and lighthearted manner that facilitates rather than hinders the consideration of demanding conceptual issues.

Even if there may appear to be a favored perspective presented by Professor Kelly, in the discussions that take place throughout the novel, an attempt is made to convey a balanced view, allowing readers to come to their own conclusions on the merits of the various issues considered. This is accentuated by the ending of the novel; with the sudden and unexpected emergence of a virus, life is utterly changed just before final exams. Almost overnight, the campus is evacuated and goes into indefinite lockdown. By bringing ongoing discussions and activities to an abrupt end, readers do not see how the various matters under debate are resolved, leaving it up to them—in pure Socratic form—to resolve outstanding issues for themselves.

While the topic of education is widely examined in a sober and scholarly manner, other notable treatments also exist. *Emile* by Jean-Jacques Rousseau, for example, is probably the most influential novel ever written on education. Other literary treatments of the subject are also highly regarded, including *The Republic* by Plato, *Utopia* by Thomas More, and numerous others. Many exhibit sophisticated humor, such as *Lucky Jim* by Kingsley Amis, *The History Man* by Malcolm Bradbury, and *Changing Places* by David Lodge. The classic by C. P. Snow, *The Masters*, strikes a more somber tone. There are also a small number of books that may not be considered novels, yet treat education in a fictional way, including *The Saber-Tooth Curriculum,* written by Harold Benjamin under the pseudonym J. Abner Peddiwell, which has a timeless quality; more recently, there is *The Pedagodfathers*, by Doug Simpson. While the writing style displayed in these works varies in their humorous dimension and the insights they articulate, they are the inspiration behind *Gen Ed*. Although entirely fictional, *Gen Ed* also builds upon a body of scholarship and personal experience working in universities and other educational settings.

Gen Ed can be used in faculty development programs and faculty discussion groups. It can be utilized as core or supplemental reading in honors courses, as well as a variety of graduate and undergraduate courses in teacher education, curriculum, foundations of education, philosophy of education, higher education, education policy, educational leadership, women's studies, gender studies, creative writing, media education, and communications. In addition to the many questions for discussion raised in the text itself, an appendix presents further questions and suggested topics for term papers and research projects. *Gen Ed* can also be read entirely for diversion and pleasure.

ACKNOWLEDGEMENTS

It is impossible to adequately acknowledge the many family members, friends, and colleagues, some no longer with us and others who have contributed in one way or another to the creation of this book. A listing of those to whom I am indebted would inevitably result in crucial omissions, so I will refrain from creating such a list. Yet I must say thanks to Patricia Leavy, Shalen Lowell, Katie Lowery, and John Bennett for accepting my work and helping in bringing it to completion in published form. I also wish to thank Ronnie Casella, Barbara Clark, Judith Harford, Teresa O'Doherty, Tom O'Donoghue, and Tim Reagan for taking time from their busy schedules to write in support of *Gen Ed*. Of course, I say special thanks to my greatest fans—my family—for their patience and undying interest in and support for what at times must have seemed like pointless endeavors. And lastly, as in all things, I am thankful for and indebted to my wife, Mary.

Gen Ed is a work of fiction. Any similarity between fictional characters, places, events, works, and institutions created and actual persons, places, events, works, and institutions is coincidental.

CHAPTER 1

"What are goody-goody courses, Mom?" asked little Rachel curiously, tugging gently at her mother's skirt.

She had heard her mother mention them before, but not with the enthusiastic disdain shown by Marilyn as they stood to register for classes in a line that inched its way along the sun-drenched limestone corridor and up the broad staircase to the registrar's office.

"I'm taking two this semester, myself. A friggin' waste of time. At least one of them is given by a really cool guy," said Marilyn.

"You might get him to hang out with you," chimed in a classmate, uninvited and to general laughter.

"You're friggin' jealous," came Marilyn's response. "Can you guys think about nothing else?" Turning away, she said, "I'm almost finished with 'em. Just a couple more business org classes and my business proposal in the spring, and then I'm done. Phew, it's warm!" she finished, taking a gulp of Coke, perspiration running down her forehead and midriff as her blouse crept over the top of her denim shorts.

Marilyn had never met Rachel nor her mother, but she felt comfortable in announcing to them and to anyone nearby, "This must be your kid. You are..."

"Filomena. I'm new here."

"Yeah, I'm Marilyn. I'm a business major in the Department of Surveillance Services. Pleased to meet ya. Goody-goody courses fill out our gen-ed forms. You know, history and that stuff," Marilyn continued, turning to Rachel, who marveled at her less for what she said than what she was and how she kept going.

At once, Filomena realized it was time for Rachel to visit the ladies' room, or anywhere else on campus away from Marilyn, and she excused herself politely.

"Who was that human, mom?" asked Rachel, looking back over her shoulder as she was swept away.

"Oh, she's a student here, darling. Now, where's the ladies' room?"

"This place sure is crowded and hot, Mom."

"Let's avoid the crowd, and just head home. I'll come back tomorrow by myself," responded Filomena, thinking it best to restrict her daughter to preschool for the time being.

"Well, good afternoon! Filomena, isn't it?" came a voice toward them as the pair made their way toward a large car park in the distance. "This must be your daughter. Hello there, I'll be looking after your mom this year," said the friendly gentleman with a smile, reaching out to shake hands with Rachel. It was Dr. Terry Johnson, director of the student teaching office.

Unsettled by the interaction with Marilyn, Filomena scarcely recognized Johnson, even though she had met him only the day before to have her amended program of studies approved.

"Oh, good afternoon, Dr. Johnson," responded Filomena, calming herself. "Do you think I could meet with you tomorrow?" she added to his surprise. "It's a rather philosophical concern," she continued to a bemused Dr. Johnson, even though she was still a little flustered and uncertain of precisely what she had in mind.

She didn't have any such concerns yesterday, he thought to himself. Of course, he was not a great judge, if any at all, in such matters. Nonetheless, he had been impressed that she affirmed her allegiance to the epistemological and ethical underpinnings of the university's ideal of a general education, as she had put it, without ever being queried on the matter by anyone in his office. Unaware of her happenstance encounter with Marilyn, Johnson couldn't have known that she was beginning to doubt the efficacy of any such underpinnings, at least at Metropolitan Atlantic University.

"Tomorrow? Thursday... Well, my calendar is pretty full tomorrow, but let's see," he added, checking his diary. "If you'd like to come along for a few minutes before 9:30, I could fit you in between appointments."

"Thank you," replied Filomena with a half-smile. "See you then."

On the drive home, she thought back the few short years to her own undergraduate education at Swasser, a well-regarded private college on the West Coast where she had majored in English literature, with a minor in art history. She also thought about what lay ahead of her at the Metro, as people insisted on calling it. The moniker made it sound like it was a train station, although she had to agree that it was crowded, with people rushing to and fro and showing little appetite for reflection. As she drove the five-mile journey home, the traffic still free-flowing before the onset of rush hour, Filomena's head began to fill up with questions for Dr. Johnson. Once home, she made out a long list, thought about it for a few minutes, and then went about preparing dinner.

***

"This is not how general education was viewed at Swasser. It leaned toward a 'less is more' philosophy," Filomena remarked to Johnson, as if setting out to defend a lengthy thesis in his neat but drab and vacant office early on Thursday morning.

Carefully groomed and dressed in well-fitted, white slacks and a bright sea-blue top, Filomena had fully regained her usual composure and showed no trace of her temporary uncertainties. To make matters worse, she seemed to have forgotten that the meeting was squeezed in between appointments and would not allow for the exhaustive evaluation of issues that her attitude conveyed. This was to say nothing of the sheet-long list of "topics for consideration" that she laid out in front of Johnson. Nor did it align with his personal disinclination toward protracted and, as far as his contribution would be concerned, vacuous discourse on the sorts of sociocultural and metaphysical issues that the list threatened to unearth. He began to question the wisdom of such an early-morning meeting or any meeting at all.

"The university catalog speaks eloquently of general education," Filomena was saying, crossing her legs to make herself comfortable on a visitor's chair never intended for that purpose. Johnson sneaked a peek at his watch and realized that time was already almost up.

Filomena's monologue left little opportunity for Johnson to be heard. "This is one of the reasons I chose Metropolitan Atlantic University, although I've got to admit the intricate system of form courses and area studies that all undergraduates must take irrespective of their major is a rather fanciful approach," she continued, inattentive to time constraints.

The student teaching office catered to the certification needs of all prospective teachers at the Metro, so Filomena had dealings with the office even though she had already graduated from Swasser. As a graduate student working toward a master's degree in combination with teacher certification, the Metro's undergraduate general education requirements did not affect Filomena directly; consequently, she had been prepared to overlook these requirements until now. She adopted a similar stance toward the university's mission to "serve the unique needs of an urban population in an age of rapid economic and technological change, which calls for a new-age response to the universal human and societal quest for relevant higher education in the 21st century." This, too, appeared to stray from the meaning of general education as she had come to know it. Now as she got to know some of the new-age students, such as Marilyn, she grew less forgiving of the curriculum mandates and the assertions of the mission statement. She needed an explanation.

Filomena was not alone in her concerns. At least one other new member of the university community sought changes as well as explanations: the recently appointed vice president for academic affairs, Dr. Valerie Sainsbury. Unlike Filomena, Sainsbury was a graduate and a champion of state universities. Yet she had gained her appointment at the Metro only when the deeply divided search committee split hopelessly between two internal candidates for the job, both of whom favored the existing approach to general education. Many had misgivings about Sainsbury as an outsider. For that reason, her appointment at so high a level was considered a daring experiment in the administration of the university. It would not have been smiled upon by the new chair of the board, who was appointed shortly after Sainsbury took office. Some thought she was doomed to fail anyway, and they planned to see that she did.

***

"The time has come to revisit the 19th-century spokesman for liberal education, John Henry Newman, and his celebrated work, *The Idea of University*, as we prepare our university to move more confidently through the 21st century," intoned Sainsbury. She waded through her partially prepared script, seated on a slightly elevated platform alongside the committee chair at the first and possibly only meeting of the university curriculum committee to which she would be invited. This year, the chair happened to be Dr. George Lukas, chair of the Department of Curriculum and Teaching. Together, they sat behind an old office clerk's desk that doubled as a barricade between faculty members and the committee chair when discussions became heated.

As the attitude of those present affirmed, the invitation to be heard by the committee was more out of courtesy than a sincere interest in Sainsbury's views on general education. Truthfully, the courtesy was to the president, Jim Beame, rather than to the vice president herself. Eventually, in a high-pitched, warbling voice that reverberated throughout the cavernous, wood-paneled, 19th-century university council room, Sainsbury concluded her presentation to the committee. Oblivious to the behind-the-scenes maneuvering needed to arrange this hearing, she announced, "To put it in the words of a notable Ivy Leaguer of late, 'Less is more.'"

No one at the Metro took kindly to invoking the Ivy League, even in the austere surroundings of the university council room, yet all were agog at the 'less is more' proclamation. Some were keen to take issue with the vice president who, by now, had been talking for more than 50 minutes and seemed unaware of the scheduled time for the first pitch in the televised ball game that evening.

Sensing the mood of the meeting, someone quipped, "I agree. A shot of whiskey beats a six-pack any day," to scattered laughter. "Less bulk, more bang!"

"But how can that possibly be, Dr. Sainsbury?" intervened a severe and tense Dr. Joseph M. Edwards from mathematics, president of the faculty union and one of the unsuccessful and now bitter internal candidates for her job. He was also the long-serving secretary of the university curriculum committee. "For many years now, we at the Metro have had oversight of a well-regulated and balanced set of general education requirements that all undergraduates are required to study, ensuring a breadth of knowledge that leads to a round person upon graduation from our university. For us at the Metro, more is more. Simple and straightforward," he added, looking around at his colleagues to earn their agreement.

"Keep it simple for the simpleminded, if you will," came the retort from Sainsbury, smarting from the wisecrack about whiskey and adding sharpness to her earlier measured tones. "It's not our mission to clothe the undergraduates in a straitjacket of information masquerading as enlightenment," she continued in a huff and rising to her feet to make her way out. "I'd ask you to give some serious thought to this," she added, addressing Lukas. To the growing murmur of discontent around the room, she said, "I'll be happy to provide my remarks in writing in a few days." With that, she was off, to the amazement of all.

"I've heard those words before," volunteered Lukas, as he attempted to bring some order back to the meeting in the wake of Sainsbury's sudden departure. "Quiet, please, everyone," he pleaded. "Why, just last week, Terry and I had a young graduate student from Swasser in our offices going on about this very point, less is more. I don't think I agree with her, but she made me listen. It sure sounds catchy, I'll give her that."

"Hey, George, every cause has a crank or two," responded Edwards without absolving himself from the charge. He raised his voice as other members of the committee decided they had heard enough and began to shuffle out. "But I'll be darned if we're going to let some woman from the Big Ten come in here and dump our elaborate gen ed scheme with this catchphrase or that. Our system has been working for over 20 years now," Edwards continued as intensely as ever. "It protects students who come from lousy high schools where they're taught nothing; it shields them from schools in our own university that are specialization crazy, and it parcels out gen ed fair and square, whether these kids want it or not. And a few of them do, let it be said!"

This time, Edwards got a better show of support now that the guest had departed: "Well said, Joe," "I second that," and "Go get 'er!"

"You've got to have regulations in place to govern what students take in their gen ed. While math is a special case, who would possibly choose all of our form courses and area studies if we didn't enforce them?" the mathematician concluded, feeling he was evenhanded.

Then, as so often before, not wishing any one subject to gain an edge over the other competitors for academic space on the timetables of all those who swarmed to the Metro, there was another general outburst of eagerness. The claims of all subjects, from anthropology to zoology, were asserted with enough fervor to enable the chair to ask for a motion of adjournment, following an hour of hell-raising rhetoric. Faculty members felt good about themselves again, and even Edwards allowed himself a grin of satisfaction as the meeting broke up. The status quo is secure, he thought.

Back in her office, meanwhile, Sainsbury had finished scripting its demise.

***

Shortly afterward, Sainsbury's assistant entered her office to say that a gentleman from Radio YOY was on the phone and wished to interview her for the late-afternoon edition of his chat show. "Dr. Edwards just joined him in his truck in the parking lot out front," she added.

"Let me speak to him," said Sainsbury, walking to the window without being noticed from the outside. She was on the radio show right away.

"Thank you, Dr. Sainsbury, for speaking to me and my listeners today. The news is getting out that the Metro's gen ed program is being dumped," said Arnie Smatter, the host of the show calling from his broadcasting truck parked outside her office.

"Nonsense. Anything else?"

"Well, why are we receiving these reports, then? Can you explain?" Smatter replied.

"Despite the efforts of TVViews to convey otherwise, there is a difference between news and views, Mr. Smatter," countered Sainsbury. "Now, who did you hear this silly talk from?"

"Can you give me a quote to put a stop to this nonsense, as you call it?" asked Smatter.

"Here's a suggestion: Bring your source for this nonsense on the show," said Sainsbury.

"That would be tricky. I keep my sources confidential."

"Well sir, that should tell you all you need to know about your so-called source. And you can tell him I said so since he's right there in your truck with you. Feel free to wave if you like. I can see both of you," she said, putting down the phone.

CHAPTER 2

"Me? I dunno. You tell us…"

Caught off guard by being asked a question on the first day of the semester, the young man was already hoping he was in the wrong classroom. He had no such luck. This was EDUC 401, all right, "Foundations of Educational Innovation," a requirement for everyone in the teacher education program at the Metro. To make matters worse, the professor, Dr. Patrick J. Kelly, seemed to be serious about having students speak. It meant he'd have to come up with answers for a change, instead of just listening to them. It was also warm and humid, the classroom stuffy, shabby, and ill-designed for anything other than one-way communication.

"Come on, you can do better than that," said Professor Kelly. He stepped around a dusty overhead projector that lay at his feet and emerged from behind the lectern that separated him from the class. "Yes, you, in the back row," he said, pointing as a few people raised their hands.

"I'm Jean. Education is learning," she announced with assurance and a hint of nervousness.

"Learning!" exclaimed Kelly, as if the thought had never occurred to him. "How can that be?"

Surprised at his response and more self-conscious than before, Jean replied, "It just is, sir."

"Of course it is," said Miguel. He sat beside the large window that overlooked the sun-drenched quad, now mostly cleared of students who had made their way to class, but not yet free from the hum of lawnmowers, busy as ever.

"No, it's not," charged Filomena, two rows ahead of him. "I learned to tie my shoelaces at home. That's not education."

"Oh, yes, it is," claimed Anette from the front row, aggrieved and looking straight ahead. "As a parent, I'm an educator, even if the state thinks I'm not a teacher just because I'm not yet certified."

"OK, just a minute," said Kelly, quieting down the class, which was beginning to find its wind. "It is, or it isn't—which is it? And why? Declarations are OK, in their place. But as I explained just a minute ago, Foundations of Educational Innovation is not one of those places. Here, we need reasons for our opinions. So, let me see. Yes, Jean, you got us into this mess."

"OK. When my parents sent me to college, they sent me to be educated. They wanted me to get a job, and to do that, I needed to learn things. So, that's why I came to school, to be educated. So, education is learning," she said. She wasn't nervous anymore, but she was also less sure of herself. "Right?" she added.

"But you didn't have to come to school to learn," said Filomena, and she brought up the example of tying one's shoelaces again. "You learned to do that at home, didn't you?"

"Yes, but I didn't say you couldn't learn at home."

"True, but you did say that your parents sent you to school to be educated, and now you seem to be unsure if learning to tie your shoelaces is being educated."

"Maybe it is if you learn it at school."

"OK. Let me see if I can follow this," interrupted Kelly. "You both seem to agree that you can learn at home: tying your shoelaces is an example of that. But for one of you, learning to tie your shoelaces is not education. If you learn it at school, according to Jean, maybe it is. Have I got that right?"

"Yeah," said somebody, wishing he would get on with it.

"Now we have two new questions. One is whether learning to tie your shoelaces is ever education, and the second is whether it is only education if you learn it at school." He looked around for illumination.

"Wherever you learn it, it's the same thing," said Miguel. "So, if it's education at school, it's education at home."

"Then let me ask you, Miguel," replied Kelly, "is it education at school?"

"I suppose so. That's why we go to school, isn't it?" Miguel answered, less than enthralled with the proceedings.

Filomena was having none of it. "Not everything you do at school is education. There sure isn't much education in the study hall. Or at lunch. I don't go to the cafeteria to be educated; I go there to eat."

"Yeah, but you learn a lot there, too," said Jean.

"Maybe. But it's not education," said Filomena. "You can even learn things by accident. Is that education, too?"

"Ugh, we're back to square one," Miguel declared, growing restless and showing it. He was already wondering if he was going to learn anything in EDUC 401. "This is only just words, anyway. What difference does it make what we call it if you learn something?" he added, unaccustomed to hearing himself say so much in one class and turning to his buddy to mutter as much.

"Why don't you call it square two?" inquired Kelly, as Miguel looked away.

"Oh, no," he thought, fed up with what he viewed to be a silly discussion. He had foolishly allowed himself to be dragged into that very silliness, and to his embarrassment, he was beginning to sound like a scholar himself. But having to justify which square he was on was something else. He was nonplussed, presumably because it was square one. After all, that was where all this pointless talk had started, wasn't it, with, "What is education?"

"Why not square two, or seven, or whatever?" asked Kelly, who was a little more exacting in what he required of students in the early days of class. As other students who were also perplexed began to chuckle about it, Miguel decided it was best to say something. Anything.

"Because square one is where we started."

"I agree that's where we started, but why call it square one? Why not call it square five or the round square or simply the North Pole?"

"Because it was the first square, not the fifth square or one of those other stupid names," Miguel replied quickly, getting serious about the matter, though unsure of where this was heading.

"Oh! So, it does make a difference what we call it?" asked Kelly, sounding a little surprised.

"Of course it does."

"But you said a minute ago that it didn't. Now, don't get me wrong, I agree it's square one," added Kelly. "So, what we call things is important?"

"Yes."

"OK," said Kelly, turning to the class as a whole, "if it does matter what we call it, what is education?" He paused to look at his watch. "Oh, we're out of time. Let's continue this in our next session."

"Jeez, what a waste of time," someone griped as the class filed out.

"No, it's not," insisted another. "At least he listens and lets you say something if you want to. I'm looking forward to this class."

"Get a life," chimed in another.

"He got us talking, didn't he? That's what it's all about, man. I like it. Imagine someone getting excited about what education is! Cool!"

"Not so cool if it's the chair of my department," thought Kelly as he overheard the brief exchange. He left the classroom and made his way to yet another argument with Lukas in what was undoubtedly the bleakest office on campus. The subject, once more, would be the appalling teaching conditions in his department, the Department of Curriculum and Teaching, which claimed to specialize in teaching.

***

"Look, George," said Kelly, "I know this is not entirely your fault. You inherited much of it. But our teaching conditions would be subpar even if we weren't involved in the education of teachers. We really need to get our act together. I know we're making some headway in high-tech connectivity and the like, but the same cannot be said for the learning environment. Classroom layout, esthetic appeal, space, and accessibility all need attention. At a minimum, please try to get the classrooms cleaned up regularly and made more pleasant for our students. Like it or not, we are modeling what their future classrooms in schools are going to look like. As it is, it's the schools that are showing *us* the way forward. We should be setting the standard!"

"Yes, Pat, I did inherit a wreck, and I'll try to get after these issues again," said Lukas, standing up and looking out the window. "Nothing has been attended to since Jim Beame was our chair," he added wistfully.

Kelly continued in a more positive tone. "Despite the antediluvian conditions in our building, our faculty does some excellent work, as can be seen in the spirit and pedagogical skills demonstrated by our young teachers in their schools. Yet, I wish more emphasis were placed on classroom dialogue—you know, less teacher talk. Come to think of it, that's needed across all the undergraduate programs on campus. I mean, students coming into my classes often appear never to have experienced much in the way of class discussion, and nearly all of them are seniors supposedly whipped into intellectual shape through the form courses and area studies.

"Good point, Pat," agreed Lukas. "And don't think I don't know that the classrooms are lousy. When I go to our dean to tell him that, I get two answers in one. First, he says, 'I am the dean of the entire school, and in this school, your department is just one of many.' Then, he always says something like, 'We started out as a teachers college run by the state Department of Education, and they still think they are the ones in charge. I'm not going to waste my time challenging them. I've got the whole School of Professional Studies to spend my time on.' I never get anywhere with him, but I'll try."

"A fat lot of help he is to us," said Kelly.

"Look, Pat. I'll do what I can about the classrooms, but here's a thought: Go talk to Terry Johnson. He's the state Department of Ed's man on campus, and even though he's not a regular faculty member here, he sure enjoys the benefits. More like a plant," Lukas suggested.

"But he's an open-minded kind of fellow, isn't he?"

"Oh, yes, and easy to work with, too," continued Lukas as Kelly got up to leave. "He's highly regarded in the state Department of Education. He also serves on the Midleton school board with Butch Conners, that dimwit who was just appointed chair of the Metro board—another well-connected party-political fundraiser. Terry probably has more contact with Conners than most of us here, and he seems to find him more obnoxious and domineering than helpful. According to Terry, he lives in a state of perpetual agitation and fancies himself to be a ladies' man."

Back in his office, Kelly was on the phone to Johnson right away to see if they could meet.

"Hi, Pat," Johnson replied. "I'm busy with Filomena right now. She's a student in your 401 class, you know. She loves it already, she tells me." And then, "I could see you tomorrow morning."

The next morning suited Kelly. Previously unaware that Johnson was not a regular faculty member, he was looking forward to learning more about his role on campus and his connection to the state Department of Education.

He also wondered who Filomena was.

***

"How would you like to serve on a committee with our illustrious vice president for academic affairs, Marilyn?" inquired Dr. Wang, the associate dean of business, as he eased back in his leather swivel chair in the plush surrounds of his office. "She talks like an Ivy Leaguer, an innocent abroad in the real world. You know, a gen-ed type and all that."

"Gen ed! Jeez, I loathe the stuff. You know that," Marilyn answered with a grin.

"Yes, but the vice president doesn't know it, Marilyn. She's looking for some student input on gen ed; you could hobnob with the top brass and get your view out there. It won't prepare you for the corporate world, but surveillance services has been good to you, and I was hoping that maybe you could do us a favor. I have confidence in your view, Marilyn," he said, taking her by surprise. "You're a senior now, and I'd like you to represent us."

Few at the university had expressed such faith in Marilyn in her years at the Metro, and she was flattered.

"Well, I'll give it a try. It won't get me into trouble now, will it?"

"That will be up to you, Marilyn. But we're on your side. Just watch the obscenities and speak properly—not proper. And, of course, push that good old services perspective of yours," Wang responded, rising from his chair and leading her to the doorway. "Go kick butt!" he whispered in the vernacular of the business school, shaking her hand and reminding her to report back.

"Will do," she said.

***

The next day, in the student teaching office, a similar scenario was playing out in a more frugal setting.

Having explained to Filomena in some detail that Sainsbury had established a committee to examine the general education program at the university and was looking for students from different schools across campus to participate in it, Johnson asked her if she would like to join the committee. After discussing what was involved, she agreed to join.

"Yes, Dr. Johnson, I think I would find that fulfilling. I will be happy to participate."

"I'm pleased you've agreed to do this for us, Filomena. We may not see eye to eye on general education, but I've been impressed by how you articulate your thoughts on the subject. I am confident that the position of the student teaching office will still be well represented on the new committee by the deputy commissioner from the state Department of Education and myself."

Johnson did not give any hint that he had earlier pleaded with Lukas and the dean to provide Filomena with an outlet other than the student teaching office to carry on the discussion of her list of "topics for consideration," freeing up some time for him to meet with other students. He also did not consider it necessary to mention that, as chair of the Metro board and member of the Midleton school board, Conners was keen on the general education program of the Metro retaining its traditional character and remaining closely aligned with Midleton schools. After all, it was from there that the Metro drew many of its freshmen. Neither did Johnson explain that, in his opinion, the deputy commissioner from the state Department of Education, controlled the "autonomous" decision-making of the university on general education. The state's requirements for teacher certification and the university's dependence on the teacher education program for a substantial share of its student intake each year saw to it that this mechanism of control remained in place.

By now, Filomena knew well the view of the student teaching office on a range of education issues, and she was also quickly getting a sense of the state's position. She just could not discern which came first, and she knew even less than Kelly did about the connection between the state Department of Education and Johnson's office.

Johnson assumed that Filomena was not aware of the rough and tumble nature of faculty meetings. This was especially true at the

Metro, as Vice President Sainsbury was beginning to discover. Here, faculty and even board meetings proudly dispensed with the formal niceties and etiquette of deliberative bodies, in favor of a free-wheeling mode of interaction and even a no-holds-barred protocol.

Filomena seemed unconcerned, and besides, she was hoping for better things from the new vice president for academic affairs. "I understand. I'm confident I can convey my views as forcefully as the others on the committee," she responded, unaware of the behavioral tendencies of combatants such as Edwards.

"I hope you can," Johnson replied without elaborating.

As Filomena prepared to leave, Johnson thought of asking her to report back, but decided to leave well enough alone. Yet, before she left, he wanted to pass on the good news regarding the concerns she had expressed regarding the teaching conditions in the building. Following meetings with Kelly and the deputy commissioner, Johnson received assurances that the state Department of Education would be upgrading the classrooms as soon as possible.

***

Johnson received the same assurances again during a conversation with Butch Conners. Conners had called him to discuss the classrooms after the deputy commissioner had sought his agreement for the state Department of Education to expedite upgrading the classrooms in what was known as the education building. But in reality, the call had very little to do with upgrading the classrooms, in which Conners had no interest. Instead, he sought inside information on the improvement plan that the Midleton school district was preparing to submit to the U.S. Department of Education.

Being new to the school board and knowing that Johnson was a long-time member, Conners wanted guidance on how he might coax the superintendent to buy into his scheme to get a computer into the hands of every student in the Midleton schools. Given his financial interest in a small computer company run by his son, it would be quite a lucrative achievement for this "Music Man" turned "Komputer King," as he imagined himself. Not wishing to become entangled in anything to do with Conners, Johnson suggested that he speak with Wayne Singleton and Brett Burnett, two influential members of the Midleton school board.

***

Progress would be slow on the reform of general education at the Metro, Sainsbury surmised as she turned her thoughts over in her mind while awaiting her first appointment of the day in her swanky office on the second floor of the administration building. Her memo to the chair of the university curriculum committee summarizing her recent presentation was disturbing to some who received it, and indicated to her which way the wind was blowing. The memo also explained that the new committee she was creating would be known as the Committee on General Education and the Major, or COGEM for short. She hoped that the opened-ended nature of the broad agenda she sent for the new committee conveyed that her thoughts were as much process-oriented as content-oriented at this stage.

Sainsbury still did not have a firm idea as to program content, and was hoping for guidance from the faculty on that score. The several rancorous responses generated by her inclusion of four students on the committee cast some doubts on that possibility, even if they did show that her intentions were having an impact. That, at least, was reassuring. It needed to be—Marilyn had just arrived.

"Hi, ma'am," came the bright salutation. "I'm Marilyn."

"Hi," echoed Sainsbury uncharacteristically. "Do take a seat," she added as Marilyn sat down, managing to bend without ripping her skin-tight shorts at the seams.

"Thanks. Phew, it's warm outside."

"Well, Marilyn, I understand you have an interest in general education," said Sainsbury, mesmerized as Marilyn caught her breath, and she herself hurriedly tried to refocus on the familiar.

"Jeez, I find a lot of things more interesting than gen ed. But, yeah, I suppose, kinda," Marilyn said, settling down quickly. "My interest is in finding out what bloomin' use is it, do ya know what I'm sayin'? All those bloomin' courses, and for what? They all cost the same dollars. See my point?"

Sainsbury saw curves as well as points, some she had never noticed at Michigan, and she didn't quite know where to begin. "But how can you put a price on education?" she chanced. "How can anyone?"

"The Metro puts a price on it," Marilyn shot back. "It's $2,000 per three-credit course."

"So, it does," Sainsbury agreed unexcitedly, belatedly realizing that it was her office that had justified the price tag. No less comfortable than before and still quite unable to get the hang of Marilyn, she pondered the cost of a priceless education as Marilyn continued.

"But, Dr. Sainsbury, cost isn't the only issue. It's not just that it's a waste of money; it's a freakin' waste of time. I mean to say, for most of us kids, it's all those courses. Fifty percent gen ed courses. Stuff like history, poly sci, earth science, art appreciation, and if you're not lucky, two semesters of a foreign language. I mean, that's more courses than I need for my major. I came here to go into surveillance services, not to be an archaeologist or a ventriloquist."

Sainsbury could not comprehend how anyone would view general education as a waste of time. Although she was not going to admit it to Marilyn, at least not yet, there might be common ground between them on the major. "You think the major is important?" she asked as she considered her position on that question. "Are you telling me that it is more important than your general education?"

"You betcha," said Marilyn seriously, putting it more succinctly than Sainsbury thought possible.

"Why?"

"It's my major!"

"I see. Any other reason beyond that circular argument?"

"Circular argument? Well, I do want to get a job when I'm done here, if that's what you mean."

"Of course. But how good is your major for you as a person, Marilyn? Does it make you a better citizen, a better human being?" added Sainsbury, hoping to find some further agreement between them but to no avail.

"I'm not too bad as I am, ma'am."

"I didn't mean to suggest otherwise, Marilyn, but educators have argued that a general education makes better people of us," added

Sainsbury with the first hint of a smile. "I've enjoyed meeting you, Marilyn. I look forward to having you on the committee," Sainsbury continued, as she came out from behind her desk to shake her hand and walk her to the door.

That was quick and easy, Marilyn thought as she gathered her books and headed out.

***

"Haven't you noticed, Dr. Edwards? This is not a meeting of the university curriculum committee," said Sainsbury in response to the mathematician's observation that most of the issues she had listed on the agenda for the first meeting of her new committee had already received full consideration from the faculty on the university curriculum committee. "This is an independent committee with an open agenda, Dr. Edwards."

Having reminded him that she would be chairing the committee herself, with Lukas agreeing to act as secretary, she continued, "This is the Committee on General Education and the Major. Here, you are expected to embrace the universal community of scholars, Dr. Edwards, not just a clique of your like-minded friends. Your contribution will be evaluated on the educational merits of your arguments, not what it means for pension benefits or job protection."

Following a tense silence, Lukas loudly cleared his throat and volunteered, "I move we adopt the agenda."

"Have we a second?" asked Sainsbury calmly.

"Heck, why not?" thought Marilyn. "Seconded."

"Thank you, Marilyn. The question of 'what is a major' is on the floor," added Sainsbury, turning to the main item on the agenda.

***

"Friggin' control freak," said Edwards angrily, as signs of strain on the faculty invaded the vocabulary of the ordinarily staid faculty lounge later that afternoon.

"She's ahead of us, Joe," replied Vic Torino, also a member of both the university curriculum committee and the faculty union executive committee. Unaccustomed to such a show of strength from the occupant of the vice president's office, he was now a member of the new Sainsbury committee as well. "And she's confident she can execute her plan." He finished a welcome cold beer and motioned to the bar attendant for another.

"What the hell does she want? She sure as hell isn't getting it out of my hide," Edwards insisted.

"She wants to be the boss, Joe, what else? Between you and me, I guess that's the price of getting a self-respecting VP. Anyway, we have ourselves to thank for this one. When we couldn't decide between you and Garcia for VP, we passed the choice to Jim, and he jumped at it. I guess I would too if I were in his shoes. Our buddies on the Metro board should've hung tough, but they didn't. Your strike threat irritated them, Joe, and they swung to Sainsbury," Torino said.

"Some good that is to us now. Where does Sainsbury stand on gen ed, anyway? Or, as you suggest, is that just a decoy?" asked Edwards. "She's a crafty virago to pack the committee with students. Christ, half of them shouldn't even be here. Punks," he added in disgust.

"Gen ed's her thing, all right, Joe," replied Lukas. "And she's determined to leave her mark."

"Damn woman. If this keeps up, I'm outta here in two years," said Edwards. "Why put up with this crap and pay taxes too? I think it's time for us to pay Jim another visit. Remind him who his friends are."

"Count me in," agreed Torino.

"Changing the subject," Edwards said to a burst of laughter from his pals before swallowing another beer. "Hey, George, what's with that smart-ass from Swasser and her brand of less is more shit?"

***

In class a few days later, Kelly posed his question once more: "What is education?" banishing from his mind the state of the classroom, which was yet to be upgraded.

Anette, who had consulted with her husband, a lawyer, since the previous class meeting, felt obliged to make a constitutional point:

"The federal government has no constitutional authority in education. Education is a state responsibility, and as parents, my husband and I intend to see that it stays that way and that Midleton maintains control of education where we live," she announced, sullen faced.

"Good for you," quipped Miguel, smiling. "But what does that have to do with anything?" Miguel was acquainted with Anette from an earlier class they had taken together. Hearing so much about her husband in that other class, he had come to know the fellow better than he wished to without ever laying eyes on him.

"It has everything to do with it," responded Anette sharply as she paged quickly through her yellow legal notepad to an appointed spot. "It means that we parents decide what education is."

"So, what is it then?" asked Miguel.

"It's whatever we tell the schools to do. Some of us here pay taxes, you know," Anette responded heatedly. "Have you ever heard of delegating responsibility?"

While Anette craved authority yet needed direction, other students waited impatiently for answers, thought Kelly to himself.

"What do you say education is, Dr. Kelly?" asked one, who had been waiting to find something he could write in his own notepad.

"What I think isn't very important," replied Kelly with a smile. "Besides, I'm much more interested in what you think." Turning to open a more specific and hopefully more fruitful line of inquiry, he continued, "Let's step back for a moment and let me ask you all this: If learning and education are one and the same, as was said in our last class, and if you can learn even by accident, as Filomena says, why do we pay teachers?"

The class was silent for a moment as if confronted by the first real question of the semester.

"Because it's their job to get children to learn, and not just wait for it to happen by accident," observed Levi.

"You mean to have it happen on purpose rather than by accident?" asked Kelly.

"Yeah, I guess so," replied Levi.

"I can tell anyone here who doesn't know any better," added Anette, trying to stare down Filomena, "that my daughter didn't learn to tie her shoelaces by accident. That took a parent to teach."

"And that's why you still say it was education?" asked Kelly.

"Of course. I would have thought that was obvious," came the snooty reply from Anette, who didn't feel the need for any assistance in making her argument and disliked being singled out.

"If it's obvious," inquired Kelly, "why didn't everyone realize it sooner?"

"Don't ask me that. Why don't you ask them?"

"It wasn't obvious to me at first," said Mark as mutterings of agreement spread around the room.

"I like the way Levi put it," said Jean. "If education isn't exactly the same as learning, then it tries to bring about learning. I think I can agree to that. And of course, you can still learn by accident."

"But where does that leave the school of hard knocks that my dad talks about?" asked Miguel, only halfway paying attention to the discussion. "He says that's where he was educated—learning from life. Don't we get lots of education from life experiences?"

"Would you say that he was educated but not a learned man?" asked Jean.

"Or that he was a learned man but not educated?" interjected Kelly.

This led to a general puzzlement once more, so Kelly decided to elaborate. "OK, let's take the example of Abraham Lincoln. Was he a learned man? Was he an educated person?"

"He didn't go to school for long as a kid, like Benjamin Franklin, but they knew a lot from reading. At least that's what we learned in history class," volunteered Mark.

"So, they weren't very schooled?" asked Kelly.

"Right, but does that mean they weren't educated?" asked Miguel.

"Or learned?" asked Kelly quickly. "Which is it, or does it matter?"

"I give up," said Miguel.

"I get it," said Jean, raising her hand excitedly but not waiting to be called on. "He was learned but not educated. He learned by himself. That's why the lady up there thinks her kid was educated about her shoelaces."

"The name's Anette, thank you.," interjected Anette, thinking she should be getting the credit for any advances made in the discussion.

Ignoring the remark, Jean continued, "And now I see that's what I had in mind when I said maybe it was education if you learned something in school, meaning if someone intended you learn it or taught it to you. Yeah, that's it. Is that what you're getting at?"

"Are you saying that learning may be accidental or unplanned, but education must be intentional?" asked Kelly.

"Yes, that's better," said Jean. "And there must be someone else involved. I learn, and someone else educates me. They do the educating; I do the learning. Got it! Got it!" she exclaimed. "Right?"

Whether Jean was right or wrong, she was not told. As luck would have it, the lesson was running over again, and she had to rush away to volleyball practice the minute the professor called class to a halt, leaving her no time for a word with him afterward. Anyway, it wasn't exactly his style to say yes or no. It was frustrating, but there always seemed to be other possibilities, and the next day's class would surely be no exception.

CHAPTER 3

Conners moved quickly to promote his plan for computers in the classroom by approaching the two school board members that Johnson had mentioned. His "Komputer a Kid" program would require all students in Midleton schools to have a computer in the classroom every day. Unsurprisingly, the two urged him to have a word with the superintendent about it.

"Hi, Brett! Butch here. I finally got a call back from the superintendent. She wants out of the computer deal. She's hung up on the improvement plan and other junk."

"So what?"

"Well, this computer deal is a plan too, Brett. Can't we have a change of plan or have a second plan in the works too? Is there a law against that?"

"What's your point, Butch? I've got a client coming in."

"Oh. Will you be at the Mon Field this evening? Talk to you then over a beer. Yeah, cheers."

As a newcomer to the Midleton school board, Conners was enjoying reconnecting with the town where he grew up. He didn't realize that Burnett had strongly supported the improvement plan as a way to make his own mark, and in quite a lucrative way, since he was the consultant architect. Since President Allcott came to the White House, school improvement plans across the country were encouraged to broaden their scope beyond the bricks and mortar to dovetail with new legislation at the federal level. So, Burnett was now reading up on that, too.

He had also come to appreciate the views of Dr. Margaret Price, the new superintendent as he referred to her, having been rather impatient with her two predecessors and an activist in assuring their removal. He had learned a little about education policy since joining the board, and recognized that he had been wrong about the previous superintendents. In fact, Burnett had mellowed to such a degree that he might be considered for chair of the board one day. He had even gotten to know one or two of the teachers.

***

"Hi, Wayne! Butch again. I just got a call from the superintendent. She wants out of the computer deal."

"Oh, yeah?" said Wayne Singleton.

"She's on about that school improvement garbage again, you know, the Allcott stuff that she's excited about. Look Wayne, I'm getting a little worried about this. I mean, we make school policy, right?"

"You bet!"

"And she's sort of the CEO, right? In a skirt?"

"Yeah. And colored, too."

"I know the chamber favors computers," said Conners.

"And the state's a big consumer, sure. Who else have you spoken to?"

"Only Brett so far. I just talked to him after the call from Price."

"Feel out Dick Blair. You saw him in action last month. As a chair of the board, he will at least listen to you," said Singleton, eager to bring the chat to an end.

"Yeah. Maybe he's listening to Price now," said Conners, anxiously.

"Look, Butch, I've gotta get back to the campaign. Just a few weeks to go."

"You're in no danger, Wayne. Nobody in Midleton takes the Nationalist Party seriously. When is the election, anyway?

"November 19."

"Well, you'll breeze in. No sweat there, future Congressman Singleton," Conners added enviously. "Good luck."

"Thanks. Get back to me before the board meeting, Butch."

***

Blair was listening all right, following his late-afternoon arrival in the superintendent's modest but attractively appointed and spotlessly clean office. It was situated in the Midleton school district suite in the town hall, right in the center of the leafy Mount Farran section of Midleton.

Joined by the superintendent and Johnson from the Metro, who sat on the school board as the representative of the state Department of Education, all three were going over the business on the agenda for the upcoming meeting of the board.

"As you can see, Dick and Terry, we've got an usual kind of mixed agenda shaping up for the September meeting," the superintendent observed as she finished a quick overview of the main items and settled in for a closer look at each of them in preparation for the board meeting. They included the first test of the district's expulsion policy, which arose out of a controversial weapons incident in one of the town's two high schools; a vote on the appointment of a new principal for Blackrock Middle School; and a new proposal by several residents for establishing a charter school in Midleton. "The main item, of course, is approval of the Midleton school district improvement plan aimed at getting federal support for the district's grant application under the terms of President Allcott's National Education Goodies 2020 Act."

"In addition to hearing board member sentiment on each of those items," said Price, "there are a few other matters not on the agenda that I expect will come up at the meeting."

"Butch is getting rather worked up about his so-called computer plan and wants it on the agenda again. You remember he brought it up at the last meeting. I wouldn't call it a plan, really, but he wants to have the schools outfitted with new computers. 'A Komputer a Kid' is his slogan."

"Oh, yes, I remember that," said Johnson. "We don't have anything on paper from him, do we? If not, it's a nonstarter with the Department of Education."

"We've nothing on paper to this point," said Price.

"I suppose it's the kind of thing no one would be against if it came for free," added Blair with a shrug.

"I guess so. I told him we don't have that kind of money, but maybe we can roll out a first phase if we win a Goodies 2020 grant," Price remarked.

"Anything else, Margaret?" asked Blair.

"There are the minor repairs to Rochestown High, roof damage from the storm. We can deal with that from within budget by reapportioning some from Bishopstown High. And we might be asked to give formal approval to the name change for the combined schools' orchestra. That costs nothing, thankfully. I think that's about it."

"We're all set then," said Blair. "See you both at the meeting."

"Oh, there is one more thing I want to mention." said Price as they began to break up. "You will remember that before Butch joined the board, I explained that President Allcott's National Education Goodies 2020 Act was so named because he wanted it to build upon the Goals 2000 Act signed into law by President Clinton. President Yankovitch did the same when he introduced the National Education Goods Act of 2012. So, let's be prepared to explain that to Butch should the question come up at the board meeting."

***

Following the familiar words of introduction from the chair, the September meeting of the Midleton school board got off to a promising start. There was a lively and good-natured discussion of the weapons incident. While the board was initially divided on the matter, the majority of members eventually agreed with the superintendent that the new discipline policy should be strictly enforced and the guilty student suspended; there was unanimity in the vote for the new principal of Blackrock Middle School. After that, on the very issue the superintendent had targeted to put her stamp on the Midleton school system—the district's school improvement plan—the proceedings quickly turned disagreeable.

Eager to make his mark, Conners attempted to set the ball rolling, although he had little involvement in school matters up to now. It was only because of the long-standing practice in which the chair of the Midleton school board sat on the board of governors of the Metro, and vice versa, that Conners became a member of the school board less than two months earlier.

"Partisan politics aside," Conners began ominously, "what we need is support from the superintendent for local school initiatives, not directives from President Allcott and his buffoons in Congress. This whole school improvement plan idea…"

"Ahem. If I may speak, Mr. Chair," cut in Singleton, now running hard for election to the Fourth Congressional District, which included Midleton. Singleton served the same party and the same end of the political spectrum as Conners, except that Conners valued himself and his own interests above the party. As the presumptive next congressman in the district, Singleton expected that he had the prerogative to spearhead opposition to the district's improvement plan, as Conners was finding out. He also feared that Conners needed to be more delicate in scuttling the plan, since Singleton had been a strong supporter of many of the policies it contained when he was a state representative. That was while President Yankovitch, representing the Patriot Party, advocated for the National Education Goods Act of 2012 during his term.

"Like my good friend and colleague Butch Conners, I wish to keep politics out of this, and I recognize that we have worked hard on this for some time. At times we have been more at one about it, at others less so, and we seem to be moving in that direction again," Singleton continued, beginning to backpedal, leaving a few to wonder to which direction he was referring.

"But I thought you were a strong supporter, Wayne," said Burnett, who was seemingly out of touch with the evolving policy on national control of local affairs in Singleton's Patriot Party. This policy was quietly being discussed at headquarters ever since the party lost the White House and both houses of Congress, and was now being tested on the ground in advance of the special election.

"I don't think we're being completely fair to the superintendent," Burnett continued. "We've been fine-tuning this plan for months. Now that it's almost ready for submission—and it's a solid grant proposal, in my view—suddenly, some of you want to back off of it. Heck, this is a way of getting federal monies to support the kind of curriculum and learning reform that Margaret has been working toward since she got here. Please, let's get on with it."

"Not so fast there, Brett," Conners responded sharply. "I haven't been working on fine-tuning this for months. This is only the second time it's been discussed here since I joined this board. I see other priorities. Why, I can't even get the superintendent to get moving on a program to computerize our schools. Now, if that's not a priority in this day and age, tell me something that is. It sure as hell ain't Goodies 2020," he added, his modified yet unfamiliar wrong-side-of-the-tracks, east Midleton style of communication showing through.

"I think you put your finger on the problem, Brett, but you're coming up with the wrong way forward," Singleton interjected, completely ignoring Conners and his pet project of computerization. "Many of the townspeople are unhappy and nervous about encroachment by the feds. This improvement plan is Washington policy, not local policy. That's the problem," said Singleton.

"If Washington policy suits us locally, that's OK with me," Burnett replied.

"Yes, that's what I'm for, the local policy side of it," Singleton claimed, thinking that the generals in Washington who were in charge of local control wouldn't object to his putting it that way.

"But I also know where the Nationalists are leading us. Folks, this is the thin edge of their wedge," Singleton charged, glad of the opportunity to slowly unveil his revised position. Surely, he thought to himself, these were reservations he had held all along but which somehow went unnoticed by other members.

With Allcott's 'National School Board,' as he called it, "there won't be much of a need for us as a school board anymore," intimating to the silent members they might not be town bully for much longer if President Allcott got his way.

"Where's the thin edge of the wedge in all this, Wayne?" asked Blair gently, not wishing to offend a likely new member of Congress. "Do you mean to imply that we're unwittingly playing into the hands of some monster in Washington, just because we want to improve our schools? After all, the improvements in the plan are all our ideas. All that's coming from Washington is the cash to pay for them. I must say it still seems like a good deal to me."

"In fact, Wayne," added Burnett, "if your party becomes the majority the next time around, you should be able to lobby more powerfully for us. Midleton has given you its loyal support for years. You owe us."

Finding this to be an awkward perspective, Singleton thought it best to back off for a while and see what else came up. If someone with Burnett's political savvy was at odds with him, he should be careful. Who knows, Conners might even help him out, whatever about helping himself. If Conners became sufficiently strident, God willing, Singleton himself could always let on that he was just seeking the middle ground.

"I'm beginning to think this is more confusing than it ought to be," said Mr. Bartley when Burnett had finished speaking. "As the longest-serving member of the school board and president of the Midleton Savings and Loan Association, I don't agree at all with Washington telling us what to do in the Midleton schools. President Reagan was right when he wanted to give the government back to the people. I never did care for Yankovitch's idea of National Education Goods 2012. Education is a local matter. It has been a local matter for as long as I've been on this board, and I don't plan on changing that. I'd like to think some more on the improvement plan. We have until December to make a decision."

"Agreed," announced an animated Conners.

"I'm sorry, but I'm opposed to waiting," said Burnett, showing further impatience. "Look, we've been working on this nonstop for over a year now. We've paid a consultant to assist us, and we've been told by the state Department of Education that we've got an excellent chance, that our proposal is maybe the best one in the state. I realize that Butch is a newcomer to the board, but with all due respect, we can't hold up business every time a new member joins us. I came here tonight expecting to vote on this. Butch can abstain in the vote, I respect that. And believe me, I'm no more a fan of big government than anyone else here, but let's not be frightened off by talk. We know what we're doing. This is Midleton policy, not Washington policy, not Allcott policy. Why, they're just picking up the tab."

"But Brett, what's the rush?" Singleton responded, seeing the opinion shift among the members. Many of them knew little about Yankovitch policy or Allcott policy, or any education policy if the truth were known, but they were usually steered by those who spoke out against federal encroachment and by the town's business leaders, meaning themselves. As Bartley liked to put it from time to time, "noblesse oblige, and all that." Besides, if the teachers favored the plan, as the superintendent herself had to admit they did whenever she was asked, it was surely suspect.

"Teachers should be focused on increasing SAT scores for our college-bound kids and maintaining stricter discipline over the undesirables on the east side of town who are growing more numerous and looking to move westward," Singleton maintained. "Policy is the domain of the school board; teachers are hired to execute it, not think about it," he concluded while behaving as though it was nobody's job in particular to think much about it.

Mr. Blair could see that Burnett was not making much headway in the face of the opposition, a resistance that neither he nor Price had anticipated. Rather than inviting the superintendent to speak, he felt it would be best if she had some time to think about it, and he asked the members whether they wished to proceed with a vote or postpone it for a month or two. If delayed, Price would be asked to confer with anyone wanting to provide fresh input. That would leave over two months to meet the December 15 deadline. With two additional board meetings scheduled before that date, postponing the vote should be manageable. When Price indicated that she would be ready to vote at the November meeting (since there was no meeting scheduled for October), somebody suggested December to avoid clashing with the special election and Thanksgiving. Without much further discussion, the board agreed to a December vote, at which point Singleton asked to be excused, and he rushed off to stonewall elsewhere.

***

It was a challenge to find a Nationalist politician with name recognition in Midleton, but Price knew she should develop a relationship with one soon. The next day, she tracked down the nearest thing: Singleton's opponent in the November special election, Frank Mobilo. They met for lunch out of town and away from prying eyes.

"Singleton started out as an advocate for local control of schooling and remained so until President Yankovitch began promoting his own version of national education goodies," Mobilo began as he started into a rare leisurely meal at The Rib-Off. "Then he did a flip and fell in line behind Yankovitch and the Patriot Party policy of National Education Goods 2012. This policy favored national goodies and the like, but tried to conceal it in the title of the Act by dropping the word 'Goodies.' But now his crowd has new marching orders from their generals: 'Say no to Nationalist education goodies.' So Singleton's doing another flip flop to oppose the Nationalist and Allcott policy of Goodies 2020. Yet the new policy is much the same as the policies promoted by Yankovitch. In practice, that means Singleton opposes Allcott's Goodies 2020-related initiatives at the constituency level just because it's party policy. So, he's back to the rhetoric of 'local control.' It's just a pretext," Mobilo continued.

"How do you know all this, Frank?" asked Price.

"Look, the last thing they want is for Allcott to get Goodies 2020 implemented successfully. To hell with education. Opposing Goodies 2020 helps them build a case against Allcott, and they've made the loss of local control into a straw man to do the job. Go read the record, the *Congressional Record*, if you don't believe me. Go read the Goodies 2020 Act itself. Even though it aims to promote national education goodies, it's the most pro-local control piece of education legislation to survive Congress—ever! Now, Singleton's party will try to scotch it in the name of the people, even though some 45 states have decided to participate in it. With a Patriot Party governor here in our state, guess where we're headed?"

After a deep sigh, Mobilo changed his emphasis. "To be truthful, Margaret, if you want to know what I think, your best bet is to bring your improvement plan to the airwaves. I served on the Midleton school board for years; Singleton and his crowd will just play Follow the Patriot Leader in Congress, and for now, that's going to be the Patriot Speaker-in-Waiting."

This is potent stuff from a likely loser in the upcoming election, Price thought on her way back to the Metro for a chinwag with Johnson. She trusted him, regarding him as somewhat of a mentor, especially in regard to state-related business. Mobilo's point of view seemed to explain the unexpected turn of events surrounding the sudden lack of support for the improvement plan, especially Singleton's change of tack. But did she dare bring it to Arnie Smatter at Radio YOY, Midleton's loudest chat station? She wouldn't share Mobilo's complete line, of course, just the issue of school improvement. She or Johnson, or perhaps Burnett, could lay out the position outlined in the draft plan and let opponents shoot it down if they dared.

***

"See you tomorrow," said Johnson to a graduate student with her young daughter in tow, and then he turned to welcome Price to the student teaching office. This office was not her favorite place for a meeting, but she did like to be seen around the university from time to time, and right now, she wasn't choosy about which part.

"That's an intriguing idea, Margaret," he said, after Price had steadied herself on the visitor's chair and raised the idea of the chat show. "I'm not the best at these sorts of PR ventures myself, but Brett Burnett would be good, especially in presenting what he knows. Unfortunately, I don't think he has sufficient grasp of the educational issues. Brett's still only learning, though I must admit he's covered more ground than others who've been on the board for decades. And he's excellent on the improvement plan, you know, costings, technology, data, that sort of thing."

"I'm not the best on the radio myself, either," admitted Price, showing reluctance. "Yet I do agree our spokesperson has to know something about the broader educational issues. If we were to go on air, we'd need to be ready for anything." Then, to double-check, she asked, "But you don't object to the idea that someone should go on, do you, Terry?"

"We've never done it before, Margaret, but these sorts of public relations strategies are more commonplace nowadays than when I joined the board."

"Another problem would be if Smatter wanted to bring on someone to present the opposing side."

"Actually, I think that would work to our advantage. We have the stronger case," Johnson surmised.

"Even if he brought Wayne Singleton on?" Price wondered.

"No point in asking Frank Mobilo for our side, I suppose?" asked Johnson.

"Not much," Price admitted grudgingly. "He's surely going to lose to Singleton in the special election. Let me think about it. I'll also feel out Brett. Maybe the two of us could show up, he and I, I mean." She steadied herself to get up off the chair to leave. "Do you think I should let Wayne know about this?"

"Might as well; he'll find out anyway. Maybe you should even set him up for the other side if you can. At least he's a known entity!"

***

"A warm welcome from myself, Arnie Smatter, host of our midday edition of *The Chat Show* on Radio YOY. Our guests today are Wayne Singleton, local candidate for Congress, Dr. Margaret Price, superintendent of Midleton schools, Mr. Brett Cutler (for whom he should have said Brett Burnett), a member of the Midleton school board, and a special guest all the way from Washington, D.C., Mr. Harvey Broadshaw, national director of local control operations for the Patriot Party. Our topic today is local versus national control of education. Many of you have been reading about President Allcott's proposal for a national curriculum and national examinations. Even President Yankovitch, one of our great education presidents, was big on national goodies and uniform standards for all Americans. Yet not all Americans agree about that.

"These are the issues for today's debate," announced Smatter to the consternation of Burnett and the superintendent, for whom this was quite the news flash. Not a word on the district's improvement plan, which was supposed to be the purpose of the debate, and he left no opportunity to counter all the errors he made in the introduction. And then, as if to give the out-of-town guest time to catch his breath, Smatter inquired, "What do you think of our lovely weather in this beautiful part of our country, Harry?"

"That's Harvey!" said Broadshaw, correcting Smatter.

"Oh, I'm sorry, I thought you were he. Then you must be Brett," Smatter said, misunderstanding. "Well, Brett, what have you got to say for yourself?"

"Hi. I'm Brett, over on this side. His name is Harvey, not Harry," said Burnett, wondering if this would pass for slapstick on TV. "What I've got to say is that it's time to get the show on the road."

"I'm sorry, Brett," said Smatter, turning toward Burnett. "This is a studio show. We haven't been able…"

"No, no," said Burnett, rolling his eyes. "I mean we, that is, the school board needs to get its show on the road. We have got to lay out the benefits of our district improvement plan…"

"District improvement plan? I don't remember hearing anything about that. Can you tell us a smidgen about it?"

"Be happy to. That's why I've come here."

Smatter interrupted again. "Hold that thought, Brett. First, a few words from Shealy's Shoe Polish."

No spits! No spots! No splatter! That's Shealy's Shoe Polish!
Some shoes! Some shine! Some Shealy's Shoe Polish!
For shoes, it's Shhhhheeeeeeeeeaaaaaaaaaly's!

"OK, now you were about to say, Brett."

Instead, Singleton cut in. "Ahem, Arnie. Hi. Wayne Singleton here. Perhaps I could have a few words, you know, to set the background."

"Sure, Wayne. You're always a welcome guest at Radio YOY."

"It's the old tax and spend story all over again, Arnie. Their Goodies 2020 is an Allcott plan to take control of the public schools. Mr. Burnett and Superintendent Price here are regretfully willing to do his bidding on the Midleton school board. The plan that Mr. Burnett wants to push through will mean that Washington money will flow right into Midleton to tell us what to teach our children and how to do it. I'm as willing as any to accept money for the people, and especially the students of Midleton. But I also have my principles. Read the Goodies 2020 legislation, Arnie. Line after line, it says 'You shall do this, you shall do that.' Go read it in full, and you'll see," he finished, confident that nobody would actually bother, himself included.

And then, remembering the sentence that Mr. Broadshaw had added to his script just before the show started, he declared, "They want to replace the Midleton school board with a national school board. Not me, I can tell you. Count me out."

"Is that really what the Midleton school board hired you to do, Superintendent Price?" asked Smatter. "I remember when I was a student here, teachers were in charge of their own curriculum. They didn't have to teach anything they didn't want to…"

"Or weren't able to," interjected Burnett before the superintendent spoke up.

"I don't know if this can be put delicately," said Price, unsure of herself. It did not help that Singleton was still beaming from the high five Broadshaw gave him following his opening statement.

"Come on, Dr. Price," said Smatter. "Out with it. We don't have all day. Out with it."

"Mr. Singleton is a hypocrite," Price finally blurted out. "Everything he's just said is the complete opposite of what he told me when I interviewed for the superintendent's job."

"Christ!" exclaimed Singleton, incredulous and choking on his ice water, his smile a thing of the past. "Doesn't the woman realize we're live on the radio?" he whispered to Broadshaw.

Then, "cut, cut," he shouted only to be reined in by Smatter. "What the heck are you doing, Wayne? We're still on the air, and we have a caller on the line."

With no time for Smatter to get the Shealy's Shoe Polish advertising ditty back up and running, he instead put the caller on the air.

"Hi. I'm Frank Mobilo," said the caller. "I'm running against Wayne Singleton for the seat in the Fourth Congressional District. You surely don't need a double-dealer like him as your representative. Vote for me, Frank Mobilo. Head over to my website to subscribe to my newsletter. And thanks for listening," said Mobilo, suppressing his laughter until he was off the air.

Appalled by his loss of control over his own program, Smatter quickly apologized to his listeners and cut to somber music. He hurriedly shunted the guests out of his studio, leaving Singleton to do damage control on his cell phone. The apology did little to placate radio listeners, as the call screener who doubled as producer made abundantly clear to Smatter.

***

The next morning, Johnson was first on the phone to congratulate Price at home for a great day's work for on behalf of the school board. At the same time, Smatter's early-bird edition of his show on Radio YOY was inundated with Saturday morning callers demanding that listeners support Price, and vote for Mobilo in the upcoming election. Even Conners called in to say that under the distressing circumstances, he would be willing to run for the vacant seat as an Independent.

CHAPTER 4

Unaware of or paying no attention to the excitement on Radio YOY a few days earlier, Filomena was more invested in a special meeting of COGEM that was held toward the end of September.

"It's really not a tricky concept at all, Dr. Edwards," replied Filomena when he asked what she meant by less is more, though he phrased it more delicately than he had for his buddies in the faculty lounge.

"Except that it's self-contradictory, young lady," Edwards responded in his usual pedagogical style, expecting that to be the end of the exchange. But it was Sainsbury who was running this particular class, not Edwards, and by the looks of things, she was giving out the grades as well.

"Well, Filomena, what do you think of that? How's the professor of mathematics doing?" she inquired.

"I think he's wrong, to be truthful. He's stuck at the literal level of interpretation that smacks of the form courses and area studies mentality as the basis for general education at Metropolitan Atlantic University."

"I beg your pardon..." started Edwards, only to be silenced again by Sainsbury, who had already been treated to Filomena's epistemological perspective on general education at the Metro. Sainsbury felt it would be suitable for her cause if the committee also had to endure it.

Much to the dismay of Johnson who had a good idea of what was coming, the vice president asked her to elaborate. "Thank you, Dr. Sainsbury," continued Filomena in her confident Swasserlike tone. "On paper, maybe 'form courses and area studies' have an illusory appeal, but what does that really mean?" Filomena went on, mentally adding Edwards to the group of conceptually impaired professors she had encountered over the years. "In practice, notions such as 'form courses and area studies' fall asunder, being nothing more than a sort of cut-and-paste approach to curriculum design, incapable of accommodating the epistemological and pedagogical nuances inherent in a process as highly personal as education. They're OK, I suppose, for pigeonholing."

"This is an outrage," thundered Edwards, rising to his feet more determined than ever to have his say.

But it was not to be.

"An outrage, indeed," added Sainsbury. "With your assistance, Filomena, we'll put an end to it. Why, even Dr. Edwards is already coming around!" she said before finally letting him have his say if he still felt so inclined.

Edwards was incensed and took a moment to choose his words carefully. "Dr. Sainsbury, the Metro was here long before me. It was even here for a while before you," he said, casting his eyes around the room in search of a thumbs up. They were few and fleeting.

"You can cut the history lesson, Dr. Edwards," said Sainsbury. "If you've lived through it, you've no need to suffer it again—nor we."

"So much for institutional history," began the makeshift response from Edwards. In the absence of the usual supportive guffaws he had come to expect in the university curriculum committee, he suffered a sudden attack of flagging self-confidence and leaned on antiquated formality to aid his argument. "You see, Madam Chair, at this esteemed university…"

"I've heard these dreary words before," Sainsbury interjected with an air of resignation. "Let's hope you have something new to add," she continued as her apathetic attitude kept him off balance.

"Me, too," piped up Dr. Arlene Jackson, a young associate professor of political science who was highly regarded in her field. "Next, we'll have to hear a treatise on general education."

"Young woman," replied Edwards, "the university, not just the Metro, but the universal idea of a university in its Platonic sense is our touchstone here. That university is a place of sacred tradition, and no part of it is more sacred than gen ed," he continued, wading in beyond his depth.

"Then I guess Vice President Sainsbury is to be congratulated in wanting to put the Metro back on track, so to speak," said Marilyn.

"Thank you, Marilyn," replied Sainsbury. "Now, before Dr. Edwards spends another five minutes dragging us in no particular direction, I'd like to return to what Filomena was saying before he brought us on this little detour. But first, does anyone else wish to comment?"

"Yes, I do," Jackson responded. "In my experience, structures such as form courses and area studies lack any intrinsic coherence, hence their reliance on a cumbersome bureaucratic support system, one that puts a premium on impersonalization and stymies student initiative. These schemes also undermine the role of individualized faculty-student interaction, and they minimize the opportunity for student choice. I contend that we should consider relaxing imposed curricular controls and encourage exploration, not just the absorption of mere information as per the form courses and area studies model. By exploration, I mean delving deeply and on one's own, under some guidance, if necessary. This bears heavily on the issue of the major, and it raises important questions regarding its relationship to general education, all of which makes this committee's formation so timely."

"It looks to me as if this lady professor isn't satisfied to just do away with curriculum rigor in the university; she wishes to dispense with the professoriate as well," replied Edwards, fearing that a several members of the faculty were beginning to tilt toward the vice president's way of thinking. "What do you imagine your old friend Cardinal Newman would think of that, Dr. Vice President?" he added, his voice quivering with determination and rage.

Not one to brush off a challenge, Sainsbury was taken by the possibilities opened up by the question. "Oh, what an intriguing question," she replied calmly, recalling that it was none other than the cardinal himself who had once opined that in certain circumstances, even professors might be done without if students would continue to gather and debate among themselves. Troubled by what she learned from Marilyn about the price per course of education at the Metro, any decent scheme that might enable her to cut costs was worthy of consideration. Newman's view needed closer study, she thought. "Well, Dr. Edwards, I'd like you to follow up on that question if you would.

It's precisely the sort of question you can explore in a subcommittee. I'm going to ask Marilyn to join you, and one or two more if anyone is interested."

Immediately, Filomena shot her hand up, having learned at Swasser how Newman dealt with the issue; she had also learned how to exert leadership and influence people.

"If I may, Dr. Sainsbury, I'd like to join the subcommittee," she said with her understated brand of aggression. "I'm especially interested in Newman's views on religion in the university, matters to which we've not yet given any attention."

Sainsbury nodded her agreement and declared that the subcommittee could include one additional faculty member, and that Dr. Edwards, who allegedly came up with the idea, would chair the group. Jackson was nominated to fill the remaining faculty slot, and gladly agreed to join. Edwards seethed in stony silence. Sainsbury ordered him to have a report from the Newman subcommittee prepared for the next meeting of the full committee, and then brought the meeting to a close.

As the group dispersed, some of the disgruntled faculty grumbled that they had again been outwitted, and a few began to complain that even the students were becoming heavy-handed. For Edwards, who was more accustomed to giving orders than receiving them, it was time for that visit to the president and another to his old school chum, the new chair of the Metro board of governors, Butch Conners.

For their part, the students displayed an air of enthusiasm as they headed for The Pizza Pan, not far from campus. They were delighted that the vice president was prepared to let them have their say, even though, unlike the faculty who were all on the payroll, they had to pay for the privilege. All agreed that this had never before happened at the Metro and, according to Rajiv Singh, a graduate student in history, most likely hadn't happened since the days of the medieval university. When Marilyn learned that some of the earliest universities were established by or were to some degree controlled by students, her entrepreneurial inclinations began to take hold. She wondered if someone from surveillance services might make a notable contribution to higher education one day. Perhaps she could make that breakthrough and establish a university of her own.

***

The new-found optimism of the students over the vice president's initiative was dealt a blow the next day when Sainsbury received a short, hand-delivered note from the president. It said:

> Dear Dr. Sainsbury,
>
> Please come see me right away.
>
> The chair of the board of governors has instructed me to report on your deliberations regarding the reform of general education in the university.
>
> Additionally, Chair Conners wishes you to appear before a special meeting of the board to justify your committee, COGEM. I expect he will inform you of his request in due course.
>
> Sincerely,
> Jim Beame
> President

***

It was not Smatter's style to pass up an opportunity to bring a political figure on his show. Following his recent broadcast that ended in chaos, listeners were wondering who this Mobilo fellow was. Was he really a congressional candidate? Why had almost no one heard of him? He would be less of an unknown once he appeared on Smatter's Radio YOY chat show.

"Welcome, Mr. Mobilo. By the way, may I call you Frank?" began Smatter on the early afternoon show.

"Please do, Arnie."

"I must say, Frank, you sure made a colorful entrance to my show and to the election campaign last Friday."

"Happy to do so, Arnie."

"Tell me, was it all preplanned?"

"Come off it, Arnie! How could I have set that up in advance? It all just happened because of the way your show evolved, or should I say dissolved, right before our ears."

"So, you're a regular listener, I take it? You have an ear for the good stuff, eh?"

"Yeah, I listen for the good stuff, but that's not to say I'm a regular listener of your show."

"Surely, you think this is a good show, Frank."

"Well, what can I say, Arnie? I mean, … on your show"

"You could say it's a great show."

"Look, I'm running for Congress. My mission is to beat Wayne Singleton, that two-timer who you threw out of your studio last week. So, yes, it's good to be on your show."

"Now that you're running, what do you think of the media, besides me, that is?

"You know, Arnie, you could be the most powerful man in the state. You've got a studio, a microphone, and room to expand. I mean, just listen to the nonsense being spouted off every night on TVViews. Nothing but hogwash, deceitful hogwash. And people listen to it and actually believe it, can you imagine? They would've believed Singleton too, if it weren't for Superintendent Price. Boy, did she stick it to him!"

"So you think the media is fake news, do you?"

"Some of it sure is. At least TVViews has the dignity not to call itself TVNews. And no offense intended, but just look at what took place on your show the other day. That Singleton fellow tried to pull one over on the good people of Midleton. Tell me, Arnie, was he drunk? He's sure shown his true colors. Good work by the superintendent, I must say."

"You came out of it pretty well yourself, Frank. I mean, people have been asking me to have you on the show ever since you called in. So, if you win, you owe me big time! By the way, did you hear me interview the VP of the Metro some time back? They say she's trying to disrupt gen ed at the Metro. Have you heard that?"

"I hear lots of things about the Metro, but I hadn't heard that," said Mobilo.

"Really? So do you think I should have interviewed her?"

"Did she think you should have?"

"Well, I didn't ask her that. But she didn't feel like staying on too long. Anyway, I guess the Metro will survive her?"

"I don't know her well enough to say. Is she out now?"

"Not yet, but from what I hear from my source, it won't be too long. And again, just as you have, I think I will have done a service to the listening public."

Mobilo's attention was drawn to his cell phone. "Excuse me, Arnie," he said. "I've got to go. I've just received a text from TV Views. They seem angry about something I said, and they want to interview me. Thanks for having me; it's been a pleasure. Vote Frank Mobilo!"

CHAPTER 5

Several weeks into the semester, Kelly began his Tuesday class by saying, "Let's turn our attention to what some people consider to be the real issue here: the content of education, as opposed to the process of education."

Jean was incredulous. "Were the previous classes all for naught?" she wondered aloud before gaining the courage to ask, "You mean we've been way off-track this whole time?"

Miguel, who was beginning to get the hang of Kelly's approach, was uncertain of what to think, and he shifted uneasily in his seat. A few in the class looked politely at their nails.

"No, no, Jean. Not at all. It's just that most people do not find the discussion of education as a process as interesting as talking about the content of education—that is, what it means to have a good education or to be an educated person. But, as future teachers, we needed to compare the process of education with the process of learning because people often confuse the two. I think you drew an important distinction between education and learning in our previous class."

Happy to hear this, Jean was ready with another question. "Thank you, Professor. So, what question are we considering this morning?"

"Let's start with this: What does it mean to be an educated person? Or, to put it differently, are you an educated person simply because you can tie your shoelaces or because you are an excellent car mechanic?

"I don't believe you are," said Mark decisively.

"And why not?" asked Kelly.

"There's more to being educated than tying your shoes. You need to be educated for gainful employment. There isn't much use in going to school if you don't get at least that much out of it," Mark added.

"And you need to be able to relate to other people," said Filomena.

"My dad is one of the most educated people I know," said Jean, stepping back into the conversation, "and he happens to be a car mechanic. He may not have a great deal of school knowledge or book learning; he left school when he was 16, but he knows an awful lot about a great many things. Even though I'm getting a college degree, I still go to him for advice on all sorts of questions. He's also kind and caring. In the evenings, he volunteers with a little league team in my town and gives hours of his time to those young kids for free. We need more people like him. And… and I don't think it's just because he's my dad," she concluded as her voice became a little shaky.

"No offense," Anette was quick to add, "but I don't think being a car mechanic or being kind and caring is enough."

"I didn't say it was enough," Jean replied, composing herself quickly. "I said we needed more people like that. What good is education without that?"

"Now you seem to be implying that education is more than that, more than the warm and fuzzy," Anette persisted, turning to Jean. When Jean remained silent, Anette continued, "I don't want to harp on your father. He's probably a good man."

"There's no probably about it," Jean observed sternly, as Anette persisted.

"But it's one thing to be good and another to be educated. It's not enough to be good or even to be a skilled mechanic, in my view. It needs more, and the car mechanics that I know don't seem to have it. It's a certain kind of quality, you know, that they don't have." As an afterthought, she added, "Some professors have it, and lawyers."

Jean was upset, so Miguel took up the running. "So, now you're saying that education is a kind of quality? Not something you learn? You mean knowing the law, like you seem to think your husband does, is a kind of quality?"

"You could look at it that way, yes. Ambiance is a better term, perhaps," Anette replied, beginning to wonder but not showing any outward signs of it.

There was another silence, longer than usual. Kelly was about to say something, but then Filomena spoke up. "I don't mean any disrespect to your father, Jean, whom I admire from the account you gave of him, but I agree somewhat with Anette. I do think that there is something about educated people. Yes, maybe it is partly a quality. Some of my teachers at school had it, but I wouldn't say all," she added, pausing as if searching for the right words.

"Would you say it's about being wise?" asked an older woman, almost inaudibly. Sitting near the front of the classroom, she had first raised her hand for permission to speak.

Here is someone in need of support, thought Kelly. Now that she had built up the courage to venture an utterance, he would provide some by probing further.

"Why did you choose that word?" he asked, addressing the lady and pointing toward her.

"Well, when I think of an educated person, I imagine someone who thinks before he speaks, if you know what I mean," she replied almost apologetically and no more audibly. Then, to scattered laughter that took her by surprise, she added, "The words don't just fall out of his mouth, you know." She joined in with a little chuckle of her own.

"Well," continued Kelly, smiling himself, "that leads me to my next question. Which comes first, the wisdom or the education?"

"They come together," the lady replied smartly. "The more educated you become, the more you know, and the more you know, the more you think. That's what makes a wise person, knowing and thinking. It's also what makes an educated person, if you ask me."

"I see," said Kelly, and he turned to address the rest of the class. "What do you all think of that?"

"Surely it also depends on *what* you know," Filomena suggested.

Before she could continue, the older lady interjected enthusiastically, "Oh, I agree entirely. Any old knowledge is not good enough. By the way, my name is Christine. Pleased to meet you all," she added with a smile.

"I disagree," declared Miguel loudly, causing heads to turn toward the window.

"That's emphatic," said Kelly.

"How right! 'One person's medicine is another person's poison.' It's the same in education," Miguel continued, gaining the attention of all. "No one is going to tell me how I should be educated. It's for me to decide what knowledge is good enough for me."

"I agree," said Mark. "Some people think that education is simply the stuff you learn in school, like history and math. I know people who dropped out of school and are now millionaires. They didn't get their education in school. My brother-in-law started out as a bricklayer, and now he owns his own construction company. He made three million dollars last year, and his wife doesn't have to work. As a teacher, I won't make that much in a lifetime."

"Right," said Miguel. "Education is a personal matter. If you can make a living doing one thing, it doesn't matter whether you're good at history and poetry. That's the bottom line. Some people think they're better than others because they have a college degree. I know people with a degree who are the biggest racists and who couldn't fix a flat tire if their lives depended on it. Why do you need history if you can make a living without it? It's obvious to me! Same goes for calculus and all that other stuff."

Christine wished to speak again, urgently. "Please," said Kelly, inviting her to continue the dialogue.

"I'm afraid I can't agree with any of these young men."

Elena, the student next to her, interrupted. "By the way, this isn't just a man's thing. I agree with them," she said.

"Regardless, I still can't agree," said Christine. "I raised my children to have a well-rounded education. Even though I had not finished my own degree, we sent them all to college because my husband and I recognized the value of that. Today, they are all married with young children of their own, and they all have good jobs. But there's more to education than getting a good job. I agree with Jean that the world needs good people. Education can do that."

"But some of the most notorious people in history have been highly educated. What about the Unabomber guy? He was a math professor, and even all these years later, he has followers," Mark said. "And wasn't Nathan Leopold considered a genius, who also taught mathematics at university?"

"But they don't all turn out like that," Christine responded, beginning to enjoy the interaction.

"Yes, but if some do and some don't, what does that prove about education having anything to do with it?" asked Mark.

Christine turned to the professor with a bit of a smile and said she still thought it had a lot to do with it. Maybe he can help me out, she thought. He surely knows the answer.

Others in the class followed her cue and looked to Kelly. It seemed it was his turn to say something.

"OK," he started. "Now let's see, where are we? Miguel, you say anything goes?"

"Right on!" said Miguel, raising his beaten-up baseball cap. "One thing is as good as the next. It really doesn't matter what we learn, as long as we learn something that will enable us to make a few bucks."

"As for our neighbor, if he wants us to be good to him, that might cost a few too. That's life. Do I have it right?" asked Kelly.

"I like it!" said Miguel, laughing.

"One thing is not as good as the next," Filomena asserted. "Education, and especially general education, does stand for something, not just *anything*. A few days ago, I insisted that tying your shoelaces is not education. That's not to say it's useless or that you might not have to learn it. It's just not sufficient. Education means you have to know certain things, such as reading and history and math and the like. It's not quite enough just to say it's a type of quality."

Miguel nodded in agreement. "All right, I'll go that far. There are some basics, like reading and writing and basic math. You need those to do most things, like being a bricklayer or an accountant. But not all that other stuff."

"But surely there's more to life than being a bricklayer, with all due respect to Mark's brother-in-law," insisted Christine.

"If I were a bricklayer or an accountant," Filomena said, "I'd want to be more than just that. I'd want my voice to be heard. I'd want to vote for president. I'd also want to better myself. There's more to life than just making money."

"Yeah, but you can't be 'all that you can be' without it," Mark said, determined to have his say.

"Well, that implies that there's more to life than money," Jean added.

"So maybe education should prepare you for getting a job, and your job should help you make yourself a better person," surmised Mark.

"And a voter," Jean added.

"Yeah, as if big business cares. They're only interested in the bottom line," Miguel shot back. "God help our country if we depended on big business."

"Even if they wanted to do that, I don't think the business world is the place to make yourself into a full person. Their job is to create things, provide services, and make money. Why do you think we have schools? The job of the school is to make us rounded human beings. That's why we associate being a rounded person with education," said Anette, even if it meant agreeing with someone else.

Seeing that the class was beginning to drift away from the core question he wanted to address, and realizing that the time was almost up, Kelly decided to refocus the discussion by reframing the subject a little differently. "If the federal government or school boards—or in other countries, state departments of education—are willing to pay teachers, spend money on buildings, and require children to go to school, they surely have something specific in mind that they want those kids to learn. I can't imagine they pay out all the money they do in the belief that anything goes. So, my question is not so much what do they want to teach young people, but what *should* they teach them if they are to be considered educated? In other words, what is an educated person?"

"That's not a fair question," said Miguel immediately. "It's based on the assumption that there is such a thing, and I don't agree with that at all."

"But I'd still like us to address the question and how it relates to general education. It might open up some interesting avenues for discussion," Kelly responded. "We might not do so all in one class session, but I expect that the question will continue to crop up from time to time as we move forward through the rest of the semester." Several hands were raised, but he looked at his watch and said, "I'm afraid we'll have to leave it there for today. Our time is up."

***

Enthusiastic and feeling honored to be working with the vice president and other members of COGEM, Marilyn wanted to hear her friends' opinions on what the committee was discussing. Over breakfast one morning, she excitedly began to express her thoughts to them.

"Jeez, guys, Sainsbury's real cool. I get to give my input. Dr. Jackson from poly sci is pretty awesome, too. She's from Memphis, and she does research on Martin Luther King. But then there's this clunky guy there from the math department. He's the worst. Anyway, I'm beginning to think I might even open up a university myself when I'm done here. I'm going to make it part of my business proposal requirement for graduation. Rajiv Singh says that was done in the Middle Ages."

"Why don't you start right now? Sign me up for a degree. How much?" asked one of Marilyn's buddies. "Sure beats hanging around here waiting to fill up on gen ed."

"I'll get to that later. Anyone have any suggestions on gen ed?" asked Marilyn.

"Yeah. Get rid of it!"

"Get a life, man. That's no solution. Our committee is looking for solutions, not 'death by committee,' if you see what I mean," replied Marilyn, trying to moderate her language and come across more like Filomena in the way she spoke.

"You're the one on the committee. Do *you* have any suggestions?" asked another.

"Yeah, I've got plenty. First step is to make it interesting and useful," said Marilyn.

"But we're told it's not supposed to be useful, just that it makes us better," chimed in another.

"We'll all be better off if we're interested in what we're studying; that's my answer to that. So, how do we make it interesting?" Marilyn asked again but felt she was not getting much help. "Anyway, call me if you get any brilliant ideas. I've got a class to go to now," she said before heading off.

After class, Marilyn bumped into Filomena, who had just come from EDUC 401. Following their lengthy discussion in class that day, she was still trying to figure out if she was an educated person herself.

"Hey Filomena! Care to join me for lunch? I was going to text you anyway."

"Sure, Marilyn. I'd love to."

In the student cafeteria, they found a quiet spot. Once seated, Filomena explained that in her EDUC 401 class, many of the issues they were discussing coincided with topics related to the two committees she was a part of. "It sure makes class really interesting, although I find it interesting anyway," she said, raising the very issue Marilyn wanted to talk about.

"Gee, I wish I could say that about some of my classes, especially the ones in gen ed. One of my professors says we should be interested in them whether we like it or not. That's very uninformed of him, if you ask me. So, that's my question for our committees. What do you think, Filomena? You seem to find all this theory interesting, but what about those of us who don't?" asked Marilyn.

"That's what Dr. Kelly, my professor for EDUC 401, would call a pedagogical problem, I think. I'm beginning to think that some if not much of the challenge with general education is just that. That is to say, how do we make it relevant for students? How do we make it interesting to students? Regarding schooling, I know some scholars I read say we should try to meet the students where they are. Maybe it's the same in college."

"That's all well and good, Filomena, but if the students are all in different places, as indeed they are, can there really be anything as rigid as gen ed?" asked Marilyn eagerly.

"Gosh, Marilyn, that's a great question. It reminds me of the question we were just discussing in Dr. Kelly class today, 'What is an educated person?'"

"An educated person needs to be able to do something. I don't buy this shit—oh, pardon my French, Filomena—that it's all about thinking and knowing stuff like philosophy and literature. We also need to know stuff like how to work, cook, look after our health and well-being, and that sort of thing. One of my gen ed profs walked into a door the other day. What a dope! We need to be able to handle ourselves. We used to learn so many fundamental tasks in home ec, but they cut it from the curriculum to have more testing and all that. They also cut my favorite theory course, social studies. Funny, they replaced it with business studies, and that's where I am now."

Trying to be constructive, Filomena said, "Well, maybe it's a good idea that Dr. Jackson from political science is joining our subcommittee. I don't disagree with you about an educated person being able to do things, I just never thought of it that way. Yet, Plato was no fool, I'm sure. I never heard of him walking into doors."

"Yeah, but what about his pal, the guy who drank poison? Sounds kinda stupid to me."

Changing the subject, Filomena inquired, "Tell me, Marilyn, are you enjoying this committee work, or do you find it to be a waste of time?"

"I love it! How about you?"

"Yes, I do enjoy it. It reminds me of what we used to do at Swasser, and also do now in Dr. Kelly's class. He's good, I can tell you. And cute too."

"Gee, maybe you can coax him into joining the committee?" said Marilyn as she got ready to leave for another class.

"Gosh, I never thought of that. Maybe I'll try it. Thanks, and thanks for the chat," said Filomena as she headed off to pick up Rachel from preschool and as her assessment of Marilyn continued to evolve.

CHAPTER 6

Concerned that Kelly's class had not yet touched on moral and religious issues during the first month of classes, Filomena sought him out to see what could be done about it. "The same issues are being overlooked in Dr. Sainsbury's committee," Filomena told him when she went to visit him in his office a few days after her meeting with Marilyn. Having explained how she was a member of the committee, she continued, "I am very much enjoying your class, Professor Kelly, but I'm a little troubled that the religious and moral dimensions of education have not come up for discussion."

"Dr. Sainsbury's committee? I thought that had been disbanded when she was…"

"Oh, not at all. The committee has been suspended for now, and Dr. Sainsbury may have been quieted a little, so to speak, but the project has not been terminated. The students on the committee have met with the president twice during this suspension. Some dedicated faculty members have also joined us. Well, one has: Dr. Jackson from political science. The president said he'd like to keep the committee in existence, but sees no one fit to lead it. Still, the president said there's a possibility Dr. Sainsbury will return if he could do anything about it."

"Interesting."

"Yes, but that's not why I came to see you."

"Of course. Susan, is it?"

"Filomena."

"I'm sorry, Filomena. What is it then? You're upset by the omission of the moral and religious content of education from our class discussion. Is that it?"

"Well, maybe upset is too strong. I'm concerned."

"OK."

"You did say you might come back later in the semester to some topics we had not discussed up to this point in the course. That's really why I'm here. You see, at the last meeting of Dr. Sainsbury's committee, I was appointed to a small group to examine some issues that arose because Dr. Edwards mentioned Cardinal Newman."

"Edwards! Newman! That's Edwards from mathematics?

"Yes."

"I didn't know he could read."

"Well, I think you might be right there," Filomena said with a chuckle. "He certainly hasn't read Newman carefully, and the vice president walked him right into a trap of his own making. He is to be the chair of this Newman subcommittee."

"That's hilarious."

"Even more than hilarious; I think it'll cause him problems.," Filomena added, feeling more at ease. "Anyway, that's all beside the point," she continued, becoming serious once more. "Do you think it would be possible to take up these questions in class sometime soon? I mean the question of moral education. And religious education. If you have any thoughts on Newman, they would also be welcome."

"I'd love to. You see, it links into the question I raised in class the other day and that I expect will crop up from time to time as we go forward: What is an educated person or what is the proper content of a good education?" said Kelly. Opening a drawer in his desk, he took out the rough class schedule he used as a guide for himself. "Let's see now," he said, mumbling half to himself and half to Filomena. "I could follow our discussion of Cicero and the emergence of the medieval university. That should take about another week. Doing it sooner rather than later isn't a problem…"

As he mumbled these words in between glancing at her and at his diary, Filomena began to admire his bright blue eyes, light brown hair, and sturdy but athletic body, not to mention his perpetually pleasant demeanor, which she knew from class.

"Yeah," he said finally, turning to Filomena with a smile. "That should be no problem. I hope you'll find it worthwhile."

"I'm sure I will." She returned his smile and rose to her feet. "Boy, he's nice," she thought, as she leaned over to pick up her books.

"I'll tell you what, Filomena. Would you remind me to mention it in class next time? and I'll rearrange the reading schedule," he said, standing up and holding the door for her.

"Be glad to, Dr. Kelly," said Filomena, looking directly at him, casting her spell, and unavoidably drawing closer to him as she left the office.

"My God, I like her," he thought, instinctively looking her up and down as she left.

Toward the end of class a few days later, Kelly introduced the topic of moral education. "I'm going to ask you all to do a new reading for this upcoming segment of the course, starting on Tuesday. The article I'd like you to read is called 'In Loco Parentis.' With the few minutes we have remaining today, I just want to indicate the scope of the topic. The reading addresses wide-ranging issues, such as the place of religion, caring, ethics, and civic education in the curriculum. The article also raises questions of gender and the unmooring of the young, that is, the de-skilling of our young people regarding the customs of civilized society by failing to educate them in the knowledge, attitude, and skills of socialization. These topics are not often found in the curriculum, are not tested in the SAT, and some contend that they have been banished from schools that are too academic or institutionally incapable of dealing with them. In the past, these issues were often taken care of in the home, but this is less so nowadays. So, these are the kinds of issues that we'll be discussing, and they tie in with the idea of a general education and the question of what an educated person is, which will be a recurring question for us. The range is well captured in 'In Loco Parentis,' so please be sure to read it before our next class. See you then."

***

Come Tuesday, Kelly began class as open-endedly as he could. "Well, what did you all think of 'In Loco Parentis?'"

"I must say, Dr. Kelly, speaking as a parent, I strongly object to the tenor and direction of the argument. In fact, I'm disturbed that you have made it required reading for this class," Anette announced sharply.

"And what did you think of it as a student?" he responded calmly, leaving her nonplussed and momentarily caught for words.

Out of the silence, Filomena spoke up. "I disagree, both as a parent and as a student. I think it's a wonderful piece."

On hearing her reveal that she was a parent, suddenly it was Kelly's turn to feel nonplussed, never suspecting that Filomena was a mother and likely a married woman. It didn't help that she now seemed to smile at him freely, as she had during her visit to his office.

"OK.," he said, trying to get his mind back on track and having missed the rest of what she had said. "Anyone else?" Looking toward Filomena as if to admit he didn't catch everything, he asked, "… and why do you disagree?"

There was no shortage of takers for the question, so Filomena just smiled.

"I'm in between," said Jean, "if that helps."

"It does and it doesn't," said Kelly. "You mean you favor teaching the right morals but not the wrong, the right values, religion, caring, and so on, but not the wrong?"

"Yeah, I guess so. But then again, who wouldn't?"

"I'm not against teaching the right values to my own children," said Anette, having regrouped. "As long as I do that teaching and not the school. My point is that teaching values is not the business of a school. That's for the home, for parents. Period. I don't buy this in loco parentis bit at all. If you have kids, it's your job to look after them."

"If you don't buy into in loco parentis, then why do you send your children to school at all?" asked Filomena.

"I can't teach them everything, can I?"

"So, you have the school teach them in loco parentis. Right?"

"I leave it to the school to teach them math and science and the other academic subjects. I'm no Einstein, you know."

"I'm not saying any of us is. That's why we need schools to do what parents cannot do on their own. That's in loco parentis. It's not the only kind, but it is one example, and it does establish the principle, in my opinion," Filomena responded.

"Would you like to give your professor your reasons for that now?" said Anette.

"I just did."

"OK, OK," said Kelly, not wanting it to come to fisticuffs, especially with Filomena in the middle of it. "Is that your position also, Jean? You agree with the schools teaching academics, but not values and the like?"

"Oh, no. I just said I favor the school teaching the right values."

"My apologies. You did say that," said Kelly, still a little distracted and less sharp than usual.

Jean clarified her thoughts. "But the school also exists to teach other things, not just values and the like. I'm not so sure about religion. I'm not a religious person myself, so I don't think I'd want the school teaching my kids religion. If I were a religious person, I don't think I would want it teaching them someone else's faith."

"Again, you favor the right, not the wrong, be it religion or values. Is that so?"

"I guess it is. I suppose that I'm more consistent than I thought."

"This is all poppycock," declared the voice near the window. "What's right and what's wrong? Who's to say?"

Looking toward Miguel by the window, Filomena quickly answered, "Two and two equals four is right. Two and two equals five is wrong."

"Sure, there are some true facts, which are different from alternative facts," Miguel replied, altering his stance. "Anyway, I did agree before that I favor the school teaching the basics. But morals and religion and this caring stuff, that's not the basics, not in my opinion. That's the part of in loco parentis that I disagree with completely. No teacher is going to tell my kid not to strike back if they're hit. Better still, my philosophy is you have to strike first! You gotta earn respect. Maybe they should teach real basic values, like parental respect."

There was an awkward lull in the conversation, so Kelly asked if anyone besides Anette and Miguel, who had already expressed strong reservations, did not accept at least some part of in loco parentis. No hands were showing. Drawing the lines more sharply, he asked if anyone rejected it entirely. There were no hands. "OK," he said. "Anyone accept it without qualification?"

This caused a few feet to shuffle and heads to look around. Christine raised her hand with a question mark on her face. "I can't say yes or no to that yet. It depends on several factors. The biggest factor, of course, is what is morally right and morally wrong. In our reading from Plato earlier, he seemed to think there was a right and a wrong, but never really told us what it was. Jesus received a similar question when Pontius Pilate asked him, 'What is truth?' But he didn't live to give us the answer."

"It's wrong if it's against the law," said Serena firmly.

"But who says the law is right?" asked Christine, reflecting an acute transformation. She had never in her life had such a thought nor asked such a question.

"The law is right if it's based on the Constitution," Serena replied. "I suppose one can have an incorrect interpretation of the Constitution, so a law based on an incorrect interpretation may be wrong. I guess that's why we have the Supreme Court, and why it should respect the views of the people in interpreting the Constitution. But a law correctly based on the Constitution is right, at least it is in this country."

"So, morality has geographic or political boundaries? Something might be wrong in the U.S., but it was all right for Hitler to do the outrageous things he did in Germany or Stalin in Russia?" asked Miguel. "Maybe that's why they didn't live here. Anyway, as far as I'm concerned, there's no such thing as a universal moral truth. Plato was way off the mark to think there was, and so are we if we agree with him, if that's what we're trying to say."

"I think you're taking it to extremes, Miguel," said Christine, continuing her transformation.

"Let's take a closer look at that," interjected Kelly. "Surely, something is either right or wrong. It's not whether it's extremely right or extremely wrong," he added.

Filomena disagreed. "Oh, no. I'm a Catholic, and in my religion, there's venial sin and there's mortal sin. We certainly recognize degrees of wrong."

"OK, that may be true. But it's also true, is it not, that no number of venial sins adds up to a mortal sin? There is a difference of kind, right? It's not just that a mortal sin is an extremely wrong venial sin. It's a different type of sin, right?" asked Kelly.

Christine was stumped. What Kelly was saying was in line with what had been imprinted on her mind by the parish priest many years ago. (As she remembered, it went like this: She could steal up to $20 worth of something 10 times a day, and that was just 10 venial sins. But stealing $200 even once, that was a mortal sin!) But at least the professor was looking increasingly like a Catholic himself. Who else would have consumed such theological minutiae? That made three of them, she figured, for whom these things mattered, especially in a state school like the Metro: Filomena, who had told her directly, the professor, and herself, and maybe others as yet unidentified. Their presence made Christine feel more comfortable. It's nice to have a professor who knows where the truth is, she thought, even if he sometimes makes fun of getting there.

"All right, I can live with that," Miguel agreed, cutting across the finer points. "The U.S. Constitution is the measure. I couldn't give a hoot about other countries anyway. Yeah, I can live with that."

"Then let me ask you this, Miguel, seeing as you are prepared to change your mind when the evidence warrants," said Kelly. "Should the school teach values? I mean specific values, such as 'Love your neighbor?'"

"Jeez, no!" proclaimed Anette loudly before Miguel had a chance to open his mouth again, indignant yet maintaining the hint of a Christian theme. "What on earth is this class coming to? Some kind of Woodstock all over again, full of hippies?"

"Professor, I have to say I take strong offense to the woman up front with the lawyer husband," said Levi, annoyed. "I know we don't all have the same point of view, but we don't have to make everything into an attack. Can you throw her out or anything like that?"

"Hear, hear," came a few brave voices.

"Some days are easier than others," Kelly thought, observing the time. Most were easy, in fact, but this was not one of them. For sure, none in the life of this professor was very demanding. Yet, he had to admit that Anette was a nuisance, although perhaps he could have been more careful in how he dealt with Levi's request to throw her out.

"OK," said Kelly, "Let's call it a day; it's almost 12:30." He approached Anette to have a word with her, but she turned away. Best to tread carefully, he thought. This could be a matter for the law, and that depended on her husband.

Following the class, Filomena had the urge to stop by Kelly's office. She wasn't sure why, but had a feeling she should.

"God, she's stunning," Kelly thought as she entered, her loose ponytail falling long over her shoulder. Slender and graceful.

"Hi, Dr. Kelly. May I come in?" she asked.

"Hi, Filomena," he replied. "Of course. Take a seat," he added, needing the other chair for himself in the face of the bewildering contradictions confronting him.

"I want to thank you for dealing with the topics I asked about in class today," she said, sitting down.

Hearing no more, Kelly said to think nothing of it, and following an awkward silence, he asked how the Sainsbury committee was going.

"Very well, thank you." Then, out of the blue, she said, "Would you like to join us?"

"Join you?" he asked, incredulous, as she wondered how on earth that came out of her mouth.

"Yes, I did," she replied, scrambling for what to say next. "Dr. Beame did ask us if we knew of a full professor who might be willing to join or maybe lead the committee. If you're willing, I'd love to propose your name."

"I'm supposed to be writing a book, Filomena. I'm sorry, but I don't think I have that kind of time."

"If you'd like to think about it, I'll be glad to wait for an answer," she said, feeling more at ease again and knowing from a Google search that his book was already in press. The title: *The Academic Major*.

Meanwhile, Kelly was trying to factor in the implications of an unanticipated and possibly illicit relationship growing out of this.

"Why don't I do that," he said, tumbling to an answer, and then, "do you have any objection to me calling Jim, I mean President Beame, about it?"

"None at all," Filomena replied, wishing she were answering if she had any objection to joining him for dinner some evening. It would be her first date since Rachel arrived, and she was still only 24. But

Kelly didn't know any of that, and it would be tricky for her to supply the information then and there. It would have to wait. Anyway, his fingers were still bare, if not his CV.

***

"Hi, Jim. Good to hear from you," said Kelly on the phone a couple of days later when the president returned his call as Kelly was preparing for class.

"It's this bloody European Union thing, Pat," Beame said. "It's a bloomin' waste of time. If you're looking for a junket for yourself and a few graduate students anytime soon, let me know. Get that bloody book of yours finished, and I'll be glad to share the burden with you."

"Sounds interesting. I might just do that."

"Please do. Would you believe I've been to Ireland, England, France, and Belgium four times in the past three months? I'm more like president of the Aero than the Metro nowadays. At least they've got real Guinness in Dublin. Boy, that's a treat."

"Sure is, but you know I make a better brew myself. I call it 'Kelly.'"

"Christ, I forgot about that. Anyway, let me get to the point. You don't want to become VP, do you? Valerie isn't the problem. It's that asshead Edwards and his cronies. Thankfully, there aren't as many of them on the board as on the faculty. What did you want anyway?"

"Actually, it is about a grad student."

"Not you, too? Gosh, she's pretty for sure."

"What the heck are you talking about, Jim?"

"You know who I'm talking about. She's in your 401 class. You know, the kid with the curves."

"You mean Filomena?"

"Yeah, I think that's it. She'd send anyone nuts. She has a young kid, can you believe it?"

"Yeah. I just learned that in class recently!"

"You did? Anyway, Pat, my boy, what do you want? I haven't all day to waste on you."

"Actually, it is Filomena related…"

"Of course, it is. I've got your number, young man."

"But it's also about the Metro. Gen ed at the Metro. She wanted to know if I'd serve on Valerie's new committee. She said you prompted the question in a general sort of way. How did that come about, and what's the issue?"

"Yeah, I told her group about maybe having to replace Valerie on the committee, and asked if they could suggest anyone in her place. By the way, this committee is big on the major. Isn't that what your bloomin' book is on about? Look, Pat, I'm serious about this. You really could help me out here."

"You're running ahead of yourself again, Jim."

"For Christ's sake Pat, gimme a break. Can you come over some day next week? I'd like to chat with you anyway. We can set the time later. I've got that freakin' chair of the board coming in this morning to complain about Valerie again. That's Conners. Have you met him yet? What a pain. As you probably know, he's instructed Valerie to suspend her new committee, pending a review."

"Yeah, I heard about the suspension. But what kind of a review?"

"Who knows, Pat? I don't think even he knows at this point. Anyway, what about a day to meet?"

"Fridays are good for me, any Friday that you can manage. You can call me back with a date and a time later on."

"Yeah, Pat. That's good. Thanks a million. I'll be in touch."

***

In his class that day, Kelly wanted to focus on the points raised the previous day, hoping that Anette would behave herself.

"OK, last time, some of you expressed reservations about the teaching of values in school. The article I asked you to read, 'In Loco Parentis,' takes the position that the school must delve into the moral and civic domains because there is inadequate education in those areas in many homes today. Society needs its members to hold some shared values, and so the author of the article maintains that it is entitled, as a matter of survival, to have them taught in school. What do you think of that? To preserve and sustain itself, society, through a program of general education in its schools, has the right to teach values not taught in the home?"

"I agree fully," said Filomena quickly, as eye-catching as ever. "We may have individual freedoms, but we also have social and civic responsibilities. Bridging the gulf between freedom and obligation is the challenge. If the balance is lost, we could end up with totalitarian rule or anarchy. The trick is to keep it somewhere in the middle. If the home does not teach the values and skills society has deemed necessary, then the school is not merely entitled but obliged to, in my view," she said.

"That's clearly stated, Filomena," said Kelly. "But in our last class, you said that you favored the principle of in loco parentis. Do we have a contradiction here?"

"So what?" said Miguel. "I wouldn't go to pieces over it. Teach basic values and get on with it. As I've said all along, stick with the basics, and you won't go far wrong. It's when we complicate things that we go astray."

"I don't see any contradiction," said Jean, seeming to agree with Miguel. "I mean, aren't these the values the parents should be teaching? Isn't that the point of in loco parentis?"

"Jean, let's say the parents believe that it's OK for their child to strike other kids in class or on the street, but the school teaches that you shouldn't strike others. Is the school not violating the principle of in loco parentis in that case?" asked Kelly, looking at Jean and then Filomena.

Changing the subject without answering the question, from the back of the room, and keeping an eye on Anette for possible retaliation, Levi said, "I agree with Dewey here. What I mean is, in the recommended reading, *My Pedagogy Creed*, Dewey said…"

"That's *My Pedagogic Creed*," said Kelly.

"Yeah, *My Pedagogic Creed*, the one you put on our reading list, he says the school should build upon the values of the home. That's like saying in loco parentis in another way. I agree with him. What other values are going to work for a kid?"

Kelly countered, "So, let me ask you, Levi, what if the home does not teach values that the school or society deems necessary, such as treating others with respect. Should the school do nothing? Or should it take the values of a home that preaches hitting first and teach such children to be violent because the home holds that value?" Kelly added, "Miguel, I guess that's a question for you too."

"No! That's outrageous!" said Christine, beginning to figure out where she stood on the unconditional acceptance of in loco parentis.

"Why?" asked Kelly.

"I just feel it is."

"Nothing more than a feeling? Is that sufficient?"

"Well, I guess... I mean, while I believe that parents have the primary right in the rearing of their children, parents also have a responsibility to the society. The society, in turn, has rights, including the right to rear children of wayward, misguided, or downright evil parents. We often forget that any society will fall apart without certain requirements and constraints being placed upon individuals, and the same is true for the family. So, no—I do not believe in the unqualified acceptance of in loco parentis."

"Next you'll be telling us that you think the public schools should have the right to teach religion," Anette declared. "Jeez!"

"As a matter of fact, you're right," began Christine. "And I believe there's strong evidence on my side, as well as good sense."

"That's an interesting point you've raised there, Christine, and it's one I'd like to explore," said Kelly, collecting his lecture notes. "But it will have to wait for another day. As you know, it's also debated in the reading. By the way, if any of you have the time, you might follow up on the pieces by Butts and Cord, which are referred to in the article and are available in the library and online for our class."

"These are tricky questions, Prof," said Miguel to Kelly as they were leaving the classroom. "I mean to say this class is no pushover. I feel like Plato's prisoner making his way out of the cave. It's tough going. You might need someone to drag you out."

"I think you're out now, Miguel," said Kelly laughing. "But sure enough, it's not supposed to be a cakewalk."

***

It was the item on the agenda for the special Metro board meeting dealing with Sainsbury's Committee on General Education and the Major that prompted Conners to visit Beame that morning. After instructing Sainsbury to suspend her committee, Conners wanted to hear what Beame had learned about Sainsbury and the work of the committee from the students on the committee.

"As you know, Jim, I have called Sainsbury to appear before a special meeting of the Metro board on October 16 to justify the existence of her committee. Now that it's getting close to the meeting date, I'm wondering if I should invite the students on the committee," he asked when they got together in the president's office. "I don't want her spouting off about how favorably they view her if none of them are there to check her."

"Of course that's up to you as chair, Butch, but I can tell you right now that it would be hard for them to overstate their positive opinion of her and of the committee. They speak glowingly of her to me, and they're upset that the committee has been suspended. Besides, I'm not sure if the board members are quite ready to have them in attendance. My guess is that they would not find it appropriate to have students involved in reporting on the work of the committee in her presence."

"We could ask her to step outside," argued Conners.

"Again, I'm not sure how that would be received either, Butch," said Beame as he asked himself how the heck did this numbskull get appointed chair of the Metro board?

Changing the subject, Conners asked, "Is that an open bottle of JB that I see on the cupboard over there, Jim? I hope you're not saving it for a special occasion."

"It sure is, Butch. Is it time for a drop?" Beame asked, not realizing the bottle was sitting there but more than happy to rely on it as a source of distraction.

As they imbibed and came to know each other a little better, Beame began to think that Conners's career in finance must have appealed to the governor even more than his political leanings. That's the only explanation for how he landed this gig, he thought. He had plenty of brashness even if he was a little slow on the uptake—yet on this day, nothing to sell that Beame considered worth buying.

Having been softened up with a few JBs, Conners was coaxed into lifting the suspension on COGEM, thinking it would look good before the Metro board meeting. Happy to get at least that much accomplished, and following some further small chat, Beame was not reluctant to see Conners on his way, along with what remained in the bottle.

***

"Well, Christine, did you think any more about the place of values and religion in the public schools?" asked Kelly to kick off the next day's class.

"I certainly did, and I read Butts and Cord. I agree with Cord, and I am now more convinced than ever that religion should be taught in some form in schools."

"Can't do it," Anette ruled, stepping into the role of class lawyer. "Against the Constitution."

"Not according to Cord," Christine protested.

"What would he know about it? It's a legal question, not an education one," Anette replied.

"Cord's a political scientist," said Christine. "He's a lot more convincing than Butts to me. As I understood his argument, it's all right as long as the government is not supporting an established church as is the case in England."

"Sorry, can't buy that," replied Anette.

"You don't have to buy it, just read it. Then make up your mind," said Christine confidently.

"Sorry, but I've more important things going on. As you know, my husband's a lawyer. I'll take that expertise over political science any day, thank you. He said he's never heard of Cord or Butts, and not to waste my time on them."

"But Cord's argument is that the lawyers are largely wrong on this one. Maybe that's why he's never heard of them."

"You mean to say that a political scientist knows more about the law than a lawyer? Ha! You know, you're good fun."

"Lawyers are good fun, too. They make money out of it. Cord just studies it, I guess," Mark chipped in, leading to a protracted debate on the relative merits of the legal profession and the teaching profession.

Kelly hoped to change the course of the discussion, so he was grateful when Filomena raised her hand. He was just as keen to admire her posture, even her elbow, as she held her hand in the air.

"I can't agree that whether we teach religion is merely a legal question. It's a more important educational one than a legal one, in my view. If we could settle that issue first, the legalities would probably take care of themselves," began Filomena.

"For a fee," interjected Christine, with a glance toward Kelly.

"There are two arguments that I see in favor of religion in all schools, even public schools," Filomena continued, attracting the interest of the class. "First, religion is a phenomenon of culture. It dictates the course of history; it shapes our lives, our morals, our customs. How on earth can one claim to be educated and know nothing of religion? My Lord, it's like claiming to be educated while knowing nothing of politics or science, which also shape our lives. We consider it politically correct to respect diversity and all cultures, but in the next breath, we deny it by pretending to understand our multicultural society without ever understanding religion."

"That sounds great on paper, Filomena, but how are you going to do it? Where's the space in the curriculum?" asked Serena.

Once again, time was up, and once again, a lively discussion had to be cut short. Kelly feared it might well have lost its momentum by the time the class met again.

***

As Filomena was leaving class, Kelly asked if he could speak to her for a minute. He told her that he had been in touch with President Beame and would be meeting with him soon to chat about Sainsbury's committee. But Kelly would like to get her side of things over lunch someday before that.

"I'm happy to hear that you've spoken to the president, Dr. Kelly," she said, adding that she'd love to go to lunch, preferably on a Tuesday or Thursday.

"Should we say Tuesday, then? Right after class?"

"Sounds great. Thank you very much for offering."

"It's my pleasure."

"Not exactly a date," Filomena thought, but she knew that wasn't going to happen as long as she was in his class. Enjoy the moment, she said to herself as she walked and made small talk with him on the way back to his office and then went her own way. He was easy to be with.

She too, Kelly thought, and he wondered if the feeling was mutual. If so, it would be a first for him. A first relationship, and the last book? Maybe it's time, he mused as he picked up the mail and headed for his computer. Naw. You've got to stop thinking this way, he thought. She was a married woman with kids. Right?

Yet, it dawned on him, he was 32, just about six times the number of books he'd written. And his first date as an adult was in the faculty dining room!

CHAPTER 7

"Order, order," announced Conners to open the meeting of the board of governors. "We've got some new business to attend to, which there's no need for if you ask me." As everyone knew, this was a special meeting of the board, and the only item on the agenda was to decide whether to abolish COGEM.

"As you know," Conners continued, "we've got this new woman who wants to change the way the Metro does gen ed. It's been working well for the last 30 years, but obviously, the good ole days aren't good enough for her. Well, the way we do things now is good enough for me, as they were for the Yale Report of 1812. And they're good enough for the esteemed faculty members who have been around here for 30 years or more. So, Dr. Sainsbury, have at it."

"I beg your pardon, sir."

"Get on with it, ma'am. Say your piece."

"Well, sir, I've already said my piece, if that's what you want to call it, in my submission to the board last week. I trust everyone has read it."

At this point, Beame intervened to say that, as was the usual practice, he'd like to introduce Dr. Sainsbury to the board, as it was the first time she appeared before it.

"Jim, this is a special meeting, so special circumstances, eh. Let's just get on with it," Conners responded gruffly, indicating that he saw no need to waste time before getting to what he already considered a settled question.

Seated near the front of the room and catching everyone off guard by rising to her feet, Sainsbury made it clear she was not pleased by Conners's tomfoolery. Turning sideways to address the members at large while facing slightly away from Conners, she said in a loud, confident voice and to the outward amusement of no one, "I have not read the Yale Report of 1812, but if Mr. Conners wants to claim the Yale Report of 1828 was written by Beethoven, maybe we can have it set to music once I've summarized my submission for you."

Then, "For my part," Sainsbury continued to an audience stunned by her fearlessness, "I consider Newman's presentation in *The Idea of a University* a clearer and more thorough articulation of the idea of a liberal education than that found in the report by the faculty of Yale College. Yet it too has lost some urgency, or should I say cogency, over the years. If ever the university produced a gentleman, as Newman held that it did," she continued, looking dismissively for a moment toward the chair, "it needs to widen its scope in our day. So, I trust you will all agree that it is proper to have gentle*women* as well as gentle*men* serving on COGEM, that is, the committee I have established to look into the future of general education and the major at the Metro. Why, in our small subcommittee that is looking into Newman's idea, even if— to quote from the good old days of the Reagan administration—it's not a group composed of 'a black, a woman, a cripple and a Jew,' most of the members are female: one professor and two students. At the same time, no one can say we don't also have a living representative of days gone by, as I am sure he has already conveyed to you in some fashion."

Edwards, the representative of days gone by in question and one of the faculty representatives on the Metro board, had heard enough, being painfully aware of what was to come. Having learned not to challenge Sainsbury in public, however, he decided to say nothing. Maybe one of his buddies on the board would put his neck on the chopping block instead.

There were no such volunteers at the ready, so Sainsbury pushed ahead into some of the finer points of her position unimpeded. "Several members of the faculty have quietly shared some of their concerns with me about the long-standing curriculum practice at the university, concerns that I do not intend to ignore. Although I have not yet fully articulated my views for anyone, since my views are undergoing modifications as I engage with members of the committee, I do wish to make it clear that it is time for a shakeup."

With this announcement, Edwards had to be restrained by his friend and fellow board member, Vic Torino.

To a mixture of dread and delight among the members, Sainsbury continued, "Whatever else such a shakeup brings about here at the Metro, it could have significant financial benefits for the university and for our undergraduates." Before sitting down, having already used up the ten minutes allotted to make her oral presentation, Sainsbury finished with a rhetorical question for effect: "Now tell me, gentlemen, what board of governors could shy away from such a prospect?"

Unaccustomed to such straight talk, the members were rendered speechless. So, Beame cautiously took to the floor. "Thank you for your presentation, Dr. Sainsbury." Taking charge of the proceedings, Beame proposed that the board establish its own subcommittee to initiate further dialogue with the vice president. No one, including the chair, had the temerity to object, and a subcommittee comprising Edwards, his sidekick Torino, Beame himself, and several other members of the board was established.

Before drawing the board meeting to an unexpectedly sudden and, from Conners's point of view, inconclusive close, and since he had previously agreed with Beame's earlier request that Sainsbury could return to holding meetings of COGEM, Conners ordered her to submit a written report to the board following each future meeting of her committee. Edwards thought this to be something of a win for his side.

**

"Here I am again, folks, Arnie Smatter from Radio YOY. Yes, this is me, Arnie, and this is the best of the news. How good to have you all with me on this wonderful morning. My special guest today, you will be glad to learn, is Butch Conners, chair of the board of governors of Metropolitan Atlantic University, universally loved and known by all as the Metro. Good morning, Chair Conners, and welcome to the show. Tell me, Butch, is the Metro still strong? Before you give us the scoop, first let's have a word from our sponsors."

> *McARONI brand cheese*
> *La la lalala la*
> *May I have some more, please?*
> *La la lalala la*

Many thank yous to you
Aaaaaand... to McARONI brand cheese!

"OK, Butch, it's all yours."

"Thanks, Arnie. It's good to be here, and I'm happy to say, the Metro is as strong as…"

"I hear its traditional values around gen ed are being disrupted. What's the purpose for this disruption, and is the vice president right to say such talk is nonsense? That's what she told me on the air back in August. Is this talk nothing more than a rumor?" asked Smatter with a frown undiscernible by the radio listeners.

"Before I answer your question, let me tell you, Arnie, you've got a real nice setup here," said Conners. "What did Sainsbury think of it when you had her on?"

"Unfortunately, she didn't see it. Her interview was conducted from my mobile broadcasting studio."

"I haven't seen that yet. You've got to show it to me someday."

"I'll be happy to do that, Butch."

"Now, getting back to your question, Arnie, some people see things as they are and try to change them. I see things as they are and say, 'Why change them if they're working?' But that's just me."

"But is the Metro still going strong?" pushed Smatter.

"It was not strong when I was appointed, Arnie, but I'm already leading things in the right direction. We'll be strong again soon. Just look at what we've done since I came in. Look at what we've accomplished in the NCAA these past few weeks. We competed beautifully in track and field, we made it to the Sweet Sixteen in the local basketball tournament, and so on. Watch this space, Arnie," said Conners.

"Not to mention ice hockey. This is just beautiful," added Smatter.

"Thanks, Arnie. And, yes, it is beautiful. Beautiful as the day is long."

"Which reminds me," said Smatter, "do you put in long days?"

"I've come here to serve, not to pass the time. I'll serve the great students and faculty of the Metro by leaving things as they are. Or demanding that they stay where they are. I'm that kind of a leader."

"That's what the big boys do, Butch. Make their demands. And now, another quick word from our sponsor."

> *There once was a cyclist named Kaiser,*
> *Who smiled as he rode on a tiger.*
> *He came back from the ride*
> *With red marks on his hide,*
> *Singing 'COMYF's the bike for a rider!'*

Switching focus, Smatter went on, "So now that you've settled into your new office, Butch—with a lovely leather chair, I bet—what are your plans for the Metro?"

"My plan is simple: no change for the Metro. The Metro is the Metro, Arnie. Watch this space," said Conners.

"Yeah, I keep watching. So, with no change, what improvements should I be watching out for?"

"Just watch for my leadership when it comes to the VP. She's a woman, you know."

"I noticed that when I spoke with her, although I must admit that I have not laid eyes on her yet."

"Well, Arnie, it was good to talk to you. I've got to be off now. I've got an important meeting with President Beame," said Conners to Smatter's surprise. "Actually, all of my meetings are important," he added. With the conversation coming to an abrupt end, Smatter was left with no option but to play some music as his guest got ready to depart.

On his way out, Conners whispered, "I'm going to see Beame to talk about the woman. We need a team player, Arnie." He grabbed a can of Coke for himself, leaving Smatter to look on empty-handed.

***

Having left Smatter's talk show earlier than expected, Conners arrived at the president's office ahead of schedule, only to catch a glimpse of a satisfied-looking Sainsbury as she exited. He was greeted by the receptionist, faking, "Oh, Mr. Conners, how good to see you."

Standing up and scribbling on her notepad, the receptionist added, "President Beame is on the phone right now. He's not expecting you until 12:15, but I'll let his secretary know you're here. Please, have a seat, sir."

Leaving Conners in the waiting area, she went in to slip her scribbled note to the president's secretary. It read, "He's here already. I think he bumped into the VP as he arrived. Buzz me to show him in or just have the president come out when he's ready."

Beame was in no hurry to greet Conners, leaving him to chat with the receptionist while the secretary hurriedly tried to remove a tray of biscuits, coffee cups, and papers dealing with the plans that Beame had discussed while meeting with Sainsbury. Eventually, Beame welcomed Conners and invited him to come in for a JB. Aware that a half-bottle did not last very long with Conners, the secretary contacted the catering staff to have them speed up lunch service to the president's dining room.

"Well, Butch, I've got some good news on the football stadium," began Beame, hoping to get started with an agreeable topic. "The new seating will be up and ready in late spring or early summer, so we should be in good shape for next fall."

Hoping that all traces of the models for a reformed general education program that he examined with Sainsbury had been removed, Beame laid out the seating plans for the stadium on his desk to show to Conners. He then poured Conners a hefty glass of JB and himself a more modest one.

"But Jim, this means the VIP box can't be approached from the front. You know that the fans expect to see the chair and his guests as they enter and leave. That will need to be changed."

"That's going to cost, Butch," said Beame, "and the project is already running over budget because of the other alterations you sought."

"Can't we just jack up the price of tickets? No need for penny-pinching here. I mean, our stadium is meant to showcase us—the Metro—at its finest."

"OK, I'll see what I can do," said Beame before changing the subject. "But that's not why you're here today. You said you wanted to follow up on Vice President Sainsbury. I just had a good meeting with her, and I think we can sort out the little disagreement between you two."

"This is no little disagreement," Conners emphasized, as he emptied his glass of JB. "Fill me up," he continued, pointing to his favorite bourbon as the meal service arrived.

After Beame and Conners were seated at the dining table, Conners pressed on. "I don't know why you ever agreed to that woman in the first place, Jim. If I had been around here then," he added, having swallowed a second glassful in one go, "she wouldn't have even been brought to interview."

"But you've hardly met her, Butch."

"I know her type," Conners insisted, pouring himself another hefty JB. "She's just one of those left-wing academics."

"This is an academic institution, Butch. We do more than play football here."

"A liberal left-winger. That's what you have, Jim. Do we really need that type around the Metro? Anyway, that's a guy's job she's got herself into."

"She came here from the Midwest. Hardly a hotbed for left-wing liberals."

"She was infected in grad school, I bet. These types—and I include her husband in this, a goddamn know-it-all—need to spend some time in the corporate world. Get some real-world experience."

"So that's what happened to Joe Edwards in mathematics," said Beame with a laugh. "He came here from one of the big automakers, if I remember correctly."

Conners was not pleased. "Forget Edwards. Being in the corporate world beats the shit out of her kind. Speaking of which, don't you think you could get a key for the men's toilet in the reception area outside? You know this is the second time I've brought this up."

Laughing again, Beame replied, "For crying out loud, forget about that toilet. To paraphrase what a Kerryman said to me in a bar in

Dublin one day, 'In all the years it's been without a key, no one's gone in there to steal any shit out of it.'"

With Conners missing the point, Beame continued, "Anyway, what do you really want to talk about, Butch?"

"Well, I came to talk about Sainsbury, but it looks like you don't want to talk about that, eh?"

"Come on, Butch, I've got a university to run here," said Beame, showing some annoyance.

"And I'm here to see that you run it right, remember?" said Conners, maintaining his habitual state of agitation.

"OK. So, what do you want? Tell me plainly."

"I want her out."

"I can't do that."

"Yes, you can. She serves at your pleasure," demanded Conners.

"And she *is* serving at my pleasure."

"But not at mine."

"Then, that's your problem. Why don't *you* fire her?" replied Beame, shoving his lunch plate aside.

"It's not in my power, and you know it. But maybe I can recommend it to the board. Let's find out," he said, standing up and storming out, a little wobbly on his feet.

***

"Good to see you, Pat," said Beame when Kelly came to see him after office hours the next day, as had been arranged.

"Hi, Jim. Are you OK?" asked Kelly with Beame looking a little stressed.

"I'm fine, thanks. I wish I could say the same for Conners. You know, things have become even more complicated since we spoke last week," said Beame, slipping off his shoes and sitting back on an office couch. "Things could get rough when I was dean of the School of Professional Studies, and even as chair of your department, but the craziness in this office is totally unreal. Originally, I was planning to see if I could coax you to join COGEM, Valerie Sainsbury's gen ed committee. Aside from your expertise in curriculum matters, I thought your interpersonal style could be helpful. But it's gone way beyond that now, even though I was able to convince Conners to rescind his suspension of the committee."

"Good," said Kelly.

"Yes, that's the good news. But, in confidence, let me tell you, Conners wants me to fire her."

"Wow," Kelly exclaimed, "she's just 12 weeks on the job, and Conners even fewer. That sounds desperate."

"When I refused, he stormed out of the office, saying he'd see if he could get the board to do it."

"Why is he so uptight about the VP?"

"It's hard to know for sure, but a few things come to mind," said Beame. "Conners just doesn't like Valerie. She's a left-winger, he complains, although he's scarcely met her. Her husband is put in the same category. What really irritates him, however, is the fact that she wants to reconsider the Metro's gen ed requirements. And it doesn't help that she's a woman. I happen to agree with Valerie that the gen ed program probably needs alteration, but Edwards is pushing Conners the other way. It's no coincidence that Edwards and one of his buddies came to see me about it last month. You see, Edwards and Conners go way back, all the way back to high school. It was after Edwards and his sidekick Torino came to see me that Conners asked for Valerie to come before the board to justify her darned committee. She appeared as instructed and dismissed his objections to COGEM in her no-holds-barred style, to the astonishment of the board."

"Gee, that's wild. But how can I help?"

"Well, this time last week, I was going to ask you to join Valerie's committee, but things have changed and the situation is volatile," said Beame, caught for answers yet realizing that this was not Kelly's domain. Mostly, he was just looking for support from a friend for whom he was once a mentor when a very young Kelly first joined the faculty and since then had rapidly grown into a well-regarded scholar in his field.

"OK, let's go back a week. If I had joined the committee back then, what could I have done?"

"Good point, Pat. Let me think. I would have asked if you could bridge the distance in the thinking between Valerie and Edwards while voicing your own thoughts and ensuring that the student input got a full and respectful hearing."

"Oh, is that all? Now that my manuscript has gone to press, and since I want to take a break anyway, I'm happy to do that much for sure," said Kelly.

"Thank you, but I don't know if that's enough at this point. I have no idea how Conners is going to present his notion about having Valerie fired to the board, or how they are going to respond. And I don't know what the legalities are. I've asked our attorney to check it out for me, although Conners is probably doing the same."

"Boy, that is tricky," Kelly acknowledged. "But look, I'll do anything I can to help out. Sort of a role reversal, if you like."

"Thanks, Pat. Maybe for now, the best thing to do is have a chat with Valerie to see if she'd still like to have you on her committee, and we'll see where to go from there."

"Happy to."

"Many thanks, old friend. Now let's have a quick one before we head off. And by the way, not a word of this stuff to the young lady from Swasser, you lucky boy," said Beame, handing a cold beer to Kelly and fetching another for himself.

CHAPTER 8

Back in class following a midterm exam the week before, it took Kelly a while to return the answer papers to the students. In doing so, he made some general comments on the answers he received and fielded questions. Next, he explained that the final exam would also be an essay, just as the midterm had been, and he urged students to pay more attention to the discussion of issues raised in the exam questions and less to a recitation of the facts surrounding them. "I've made comments to this effect on many of your exam papers. If you wish to come and see me to discuss further, just let me know. Critical consideration of issues, not mere recitation of facts, is what enables us to develop a critical consciousness or, as people used to put it, to sharpen the mind. This is what we need if we are to be critically aware when listening to cable TV news, the speeches of politicians running for election, and policy debates in education, to give just a few examples. And this is partly what I try to have you develop in our class discussions, skills of critical analysis. Now, changing the subject, let me remind you that I will be attending a conference out of state, so our next class session will be canceled."

With administrative matters dealt with, and almost a quarter of the way through the class period, Kelly began to reconnect with the previous class discussion. "Before the midterm test last week, we had begun to discuss the challenge of making space in the curriculum for subjects currently excluded, and whether these should supplement or even displace existing subjects."

Following a pause by Kelly to see if anyone had anything to say, Filomena raised her hand. "I agree that deciding to introduce subjects such as religion raises tough questions, but these decisions also apply to the teaching of any subject, including history, math, and science. But nevertheless, we try. We try to teach them all, and we try to fit them in," she said, as she had attempted to explain before the end of the last class. "Why not try to include religion also? To say it's difficult or that there's not enough time is an excuse, not a reason."

"But there's proof of science. I mean objective proof," answered Jean. "There are just too many religions, no proof, and huge disagreements. It's too contentious a subject."

"I'm sorry, but I see it differently, Jean. Science is also replete with disagreements," countered Filomena. "This is not to mention philosophy, politics, economics, and literary criticism. And what about art? Often there is little or no agreement in some of these areas, and yet we teach them all the time. And how different is the proof in science, anyway? According to Einstein, even science is built upon assumptions. So, what's the difference between these other subjects and religion? If you want my opinion, maybe it's just prejudice!"

If EDUC 401 had ever gone silent, it was now. Even the lawnmowers that had been humming outside the large window joined in the hush. Soon it would be time for the faculty dining room, Filomena remembered. Kelly did too. But they were not there yet. There was still a whole 20 minutes to go.

Finally, Miguel piped up. "Whose religion are you going to teach? Yours or mine?"

"Yours *and* mine. We don't have to see this in divisive terms," Filomena replied.

"You know," added Christine, "if we taught a little religion, I'm sure we'd see it in less divisive terms anyway."

As Filomena was about to continue, Serena said, "Even with two religions, I don't see how that's going to work in a public school, which is supposed to be a common school for all. But with one or two hundred religions or more, how are you going to fit them all in? And what about a parent who objects to having a different religion taught to her child?"

"Religious education is compulsory in other countries. They do it in England," said Filomena.

"England's a bad example," replied Serena. "They have an official state church there, the Church of England, and the Queen's the head."

"Actually, I think England is an excellent example of what can be done, even if it has some flaws," Filomena countered. "By law, in England, religious education must be provided in all state-funded schools, although every child is not compelled to take it. And a variety of religions must be taught, not just Anglicanism, which is pretty much the same as Episcopalianism here. If that's done in England, where you do have an established church, the Anglican church, it should be easier to do it in the U.S. where this is not so.

"Personally, I tend to agree with Newman, and I believe religion can be taught in two different ways. First of all, a comparative study of religion or the history of religion should be a requirement for all students. There, the basic ideas of different religions would be taught in much the same way as different philosophies might be taught in a philosophy course, or different economic or political theories in economics and politics. Then there is the doctrinal teaching of religion. One teachers' union in England—and I agree with this—went so far as to recommend that parents should be able to have religious ministers teach the religion of choice to their children in state schools."

"You'd be sued every day of the week if you tried that in this country," said Serena, wondering if Filomena was serious.

"I realize that, Serena, and that's part of the problem. There is one dominant interpretation of the matter out there, and no one's willing to challenge it, although President Clinton did ask the U. S. Department of Education to explain the legalities and provide new guidelines. I agree with Christine, although I'm not a lawyer. I think Cord is right; there is no adequate constitutional basis for what, in practice, amounts to a ban on teaching religion in some form in our public schools. It's a cop-out, and it just doesn't make sense."

"Are you insinuating that the Constitution is bunk and that the framers were incompetents?" asked Anette, appalled yet again. "In my view, the U.S. Constitution is one of the greatest documents of humankind, and the framers are among the most brilliant men who ever lived, even if they all were men. I don't think I'm alone in believing that."

"I agree," said Jean.

"And I," added Mark and some others.

Filomena sat back to think.

The class went silent again, so Kelly said, "Well, Filomena? Are you throwing in the towel? Would you like some more time, or do you want to come back to it later?"

Anette shook her head. "Time isn't her problem. It's her wacky idea. Can we move on?"

"Let me try putting it this way, Dr. Kelly, if I may," said Filomena pensively.

"Off you go."

"Anette just said that the framers of the Constitution were brilliant people, and that the Constitution is a wise document. I agree with all of that."

"Then what's your beef?" asked Anette impatiently.

"Those statements change nothing about what I've argued about the place of religion in the school. Look at it this way: From the arrival of the Pilgrims, religion played a major role in the lives of our people, and surely before that too. One of the first things the Pilgrims did when they settled in New England was to build schools and require attendance. One of the main purposes of these schools was to teach religion. Ever since, religion has had a special place in our country. There was and always has been respect for religion and for the freedom to practice it. Now, we are told that to include it in schools today is illegal and against the Constitution. To me, that's gibberish and completely at odds with our history and with common sense. If the framers of the Constitution were so brilliant, does it not strike anyone as odd that they would have been so mistaken about religion as to accept it? It's because these were such brilliant men, and the Constitution such a singularly fine document, that to construe it as striking down a central aspect of traditional American culture is outrageous yet believable. Believable but wrong."

"What do you mean," inquired Anette aggressively, "outrageous yet believable? That's some real hogwash."

"Just like the doctrine and practice of slavery or the encagement of children and their separation from parents," replied Filomena. "Outrageous, believable, wrong, and yes, unjust and cruel, too. No need to be surprised here," she said in conclusion.

Christine was mesmerized and began to applaud but switched to a thumbs up when no one joined in. "That was marvelous, Filomena," she said. "Can I ask her a question, Professor?"

Looking at his watch, he said, "A quick one, but first, let me remind everyone to read the chapter on the forms of knowledge by

Paul Hirst for the next day; it's next on the reading list and is now available online like the others."

Kelly nodded to Christine, who said, "I know you've read Cardinal Newman on this subject. What does he have to say about the place of religion in education?"

"He believed it ought to be included in a university. That's why…" Filomena began.

"I'll have to ask you to keep this brief, Filomena," Kelly broke in, seeing that she was already on a roll. "People are getting hungry. It's almost 12:30, and I'd rather they didn't have you for lunch."

"Me too," she laughed.

"Do you want to finish what you started?"

"No, it's all right. I'll be seeing Christine later this afternoon," she said, becoming a little excited. "I'm looking forward to lunch myself today," she added with a shy smile.

***

Following that very lunch and a discourse between Kelly and Filomena on the challenges of single parenting, the trials and attractions of academic life, the belief that hope springs eternal in the human breast (especially of shapelier-than-thou 24-year-olds), the warmth of companionship, and a cursory rundown on the comings and goings of the Sainsbury committee, Kelly felt upbeat and full of new but inexpressible optimism. Although he had learned little over lunch about COGEM, he was glad that Sainsbury had agreed to appoint him to it. He would need to fill the gap in his understanding of its deliberations when he met with Sainsbury in a day or two to be actually briefed on developments to date.

***

Given the growing intrigue surrounding the activities of COGEM, Sainsbury and Kelly met off-campus for lunch to discuss matters. They were not well-known to each other, having only met in mainly formal situations since Sainsbury arrived on campus over the summer. So, their small talk centered on their professional interests as they began to become acquainted with each other.

"I remember seeing on your CV that your scholarly interests lie in Shakespeare," began Kelly after they placed their lunch orders.

"That's true," Sainsbury replied. "As a young professor, I was especially interested in his plays, and many of my early publications centered on his use of space. But at Murryfield U, where I taught at the time, scholarship counted for little. It was a madhouse, reeking of politics and scandal, and I had to learn quickly how to look after myself. The chair of my department advised me to stay out of academic politics, but I couldn't resist. So, I looked around for an administrative post and, to my surprise and with a little help from space in Shakespeare, I was appointed chair of the English department at Michigan. That pretty much put an end to my research career, but I have no regrets. And that's where I met my husband, Jack."

"Sounds like you've come to the right place then," said Kelly with a chuckle.

"And enjoying it, believe it or not!" Changing the subject, Sainsbury said, "Unfortunately, while my background is helpful in campus politics, it doesn't throw much light on curriculum issues in higher ed other than the bits and pieces I've picked up along the way. So, when Jim told me your research revolves around curriculum issues in general education and the major, I was delighted to invite you to join us. I'm glad you have agreed."

"Yes, but I haven't been much of a committeeman in recent years," said Kelly, before adding that he was looking forward to joining this particular committee and facing the challenges it offered, especially because it coincided with his research interests. He also added that his thinking about general education was influenced as much by how the topic was treated at the level of schooling as in higher education.

"Please remember," interrupted Sainsbury, "the real challenges in my committee will likely be more political than philosophical. For some members, sadly, there may be reading challenges too. This is not to say I have an adequate grasp of the issues myself, and to be truthful, I recognize that my background gives me a liberal arts bias to conceptualizing issues in general education. One of the student members on the committee, Marilyn, and at least one faculty member, Arlene Jackson, a young professor from political science, seem to have a different perspective. Your biggest fan, Filomena, who is such a charmer, is very much of my own view, and I don't think she and I are alone in that. That dolt, Edwards, seems to think he shares this position, but Filomena has grave doubts about that. I'm sure she's right."

"Yeah, I know Filomena; she can be pretty forceful and confident in her own way," said Kelly, beginning to wonder if Filomena had been signaling her views about him to everyone on campus and social media.

"Turning back to the politics of all this," said Sainsbury, "I understand that Jim has filled you in a little on the background between Conners and myself, to say nothing of Edwards. As you might also know, I can be pretty blunt without meaning to offend, and it seems the view of me as being heavy-handed and even strident is gaining traction and causing some annoyance."

"Without knowing all the details," said Kelly, "my guess is that you're probably right. I know Edwards can be a bit of a throwback and a spoilsport—more like a character out of Tom Sharpe than Shakespeare—and that can be a nuisance if you want to move in a different direction from him. I also believe the version of general education that he holds on to is rigid and diehard. It is undoubtedly offensive to people like Filomena, who are less inflexible in their views. While academic politics readily invade this realm, I think differences of viewpoint can generally be handled reasonably by reasonable people, even if Edwards is on the outer fringe of that. As for Conners, from what I hear from Jim, he's a completely different kettle of fish. It sounds like he exudes self-promotion and politics with a capital 'P.' Have you any sense of how you might handle that side of things? I mean Conners and the board."

Sainsbury smiled at his question. "I'm glad you asked. Jim and I had a good conversation regarding that about a week ago, in which Jim indicated that he would support me on keeping COGEM alive. But following our meeting, he and Conners had some hard words, I understand, so I'm not sure where that leaves things. Jim tells me that even though he was your mentor and is many years your senior, he welcomes your levelheaded perspective on tricky issues. So, what do *you* think I should do?"

"You know that Jim and I are good friends, I see. Then let me ask: Even though you have only a short-term working relationship with Jim so far, what kind of rapport do you two have? Do you share common views on a range of matters? Do you find him generally supportive and collegial?"

"I can answer yes to that, Pat. That was my assessment of Dr. Beame when I decided to come here. So, yes, I think we get along very well together and will have a productive working relationship."

"To answer your questions, then, I think you should be guided by Jim. He's perceptive, supportive, and he has his feet on the ground. I have benefitted greatly from his advice to over the years."

"Thank you for that. And, by the way, I also look forward to working with you and to your attendance at the meeting of COGEM on Friday. I hope you don't mind if I allow you plenty of talking time."

CHAPTER 9

Realizing that the next meeting of COGEM was only days away and that he had not yet called a meeting of the Newman subcommittee, Edwards thought it best to have at least a perfunctory meeting, rather than have nothing to report. So, he called around to set up the meeting. To his good fortune, all members were able to get together the next day.

"Thank you all for coming on such short notice," Edwards began as they gathered after lunch in the mathematics meeting room.

"Can you turn down the air conditioning a little, Dr. Edwards? It's freakin' cold in here," asked Marilyn.

He obliged, then looked to Filomena and asked her to say a few words about Newman. "It appears you know something about him," he said.

"As it happens," began Filomena, "I've just come from a class where we were discussing his ideas on religion in education."

"You can skip that part," said Edwards. "I think the part that's relevant here is his view on teaching. That's where we were in the discussion when Dr. Sainsbury ordered us to form this subcommittee."

"OK, I can begin there if you like," Filomena responded, "although it's best to see his work in its entirety. As I recall, the point that came up in COGEM arose from your comment, Dr. Edwards, regarding dispensing with the professoriate."

"That's true. I can't imagine Newman was foolish enough to suggest that," said Edwards, sitting back in his chair, confident in his view.

"I don't think anyone would," said Marilyn. "Professors aren't that dopey, though some are pretty clumsy, to be sure."

"I beg your pardon? Marilyn, is it?" replied Edwards, becoming annoyed.

"Well, what I mean is, I have a professor who walks into the door every so often. That's clumsy, if you ask me," Marilyn said.

"I've never seen that," said Edwards, turning to Jackson to ask if she ever observed such a thing in her time at the Metro.

"Let's not get sidetracked, Dr. Edwards," said Jackson, who asked Filomena to continue.

"To be honest," said Filomena continuing where she left off, "I don't think Newman ever imagined fully dispensing with the professoriate. He believed that professors have a unique and essential role to play in the university, but he did see their role being complemented by tutors and even by members of the clergy. Newman himself was an Anglican minister before converting to Catholicism, and students used to flock to his sermons, some of which were later published in a variety of forms, including in his *Oxford University Sermons*."

"All right, Filomena," said Edwards, growing impatient and anxious to have his say. "What exactly did he convey about professors and teaching?"

"As I'm sure you will appreciate, Dr. Edwards," said Filomena, who was not at all convinced of that, "writers such as Newman can be rather nuanced in how they express themselves. But Newman did write clearly that in certain circumstances, students may learn as much from engaging in a small group discussion among themselves—maybe even in settings such as The Pizza Pan—as from professors."

"Get away!" interjected Marilyn. "Newman's my man!"

"I'm sorry," announced Edwards, "but I've looked at *The Idea of a University* by Newman that Sainsbury referred to, and I didn't see any mention of The Pizza Pan."

"Well, it's there, all right, Dr. Edwards. Not The Pizza Pan, of course, but the piece about the educational value of students discussing matters among themselves without professors present. You must have missed it," said Filomena without batting an eye.

"Goddammit. Can you prove it by showing it to me?" Edwards responded impatiently.

"I don't have a copy of the book with me here. I'm speaking from memory. If you have your copy with you, I'll be happy to show you where he says it."

"Look, we need to get a move on. Sainsbury will be expecting a report from us. So, what do we want to say?" asked Edwards, becoming frustrated.

"I can check it when I get home," Filomena replied.

"That's not much good to me now, is it? Why didn't you bring the damn book with you?" Edwards retorted, now visibly annoyed.

"Why didn't you bring your own copy?" asked Marilyn, not easing the situation.

"Why don't we just report back what Filomena said?" suggested Jackson, looking once again as if she were the one in charge. "If she can find an exact quote when she gets home, that would be helpful, and she can report it at the full committee meeting. I really don't think we need to drag it out beyond that."

"Yes, I'd be happy to do that," said Filomena.

"OK, then. We're done," said Edwards abruptly, turning on the air conditioning again and departing angrily.

"That's a strange way to end a meeting," said Marilyn to Filomena as they left the room. "Is that how Kelly does it in your class?"

"Not quite," she replied. "It will be interesting to see how things go when Professor Kelly joins the full committee."

"What did you think of that, Dr. Jackson?" Marilyn asked, turning to Jackson as she came up behind them.

"I don't know Dr. Edwards at all, other than by reputation," said Jackson, "but he is living up to it, that's for sure. Anyway, he's not the one in charge of the full committee," she added, unaware of his links to Conners or the fact that Sainsbury had been called before the Metro board.

***

In the next meeting of EDUC 401, Christine asked if Filomena could share what she had told her after the last class with the others.

"Sure," said Kelly, even if he wished she had not asked. "If Filomena is agreeable, let's do that quickly and then we can move forward."

The class was less than absorbed as Filomena explained that Newman believed religion could be treated in two different ways in the university. It could and should be dealt with, much as Filomena had earlier stated as her own opinion, in the form of theological or divinity studies as an academic discipline, as well as a form of religious belief and practice in the daily lives of students, where prayer and religious observance, such as attending church, would be included.

"Listen," said Miguel, "the public schools I know don't have a church, and I don't believe it's even realistic to talk of teaching theology in school. Is this really relevant, Professor?"

"That's a fair point, Miguel," said Kelly. "Yet some schools don't have much in the way of science labs, either. Does that mean we should skip science classes too?"

Then someone brought up the matter of sports facilities; they seemed to be quite extensive in many high schools, but less so in others.

"We had great facilities in my high school," said Jean. "That's what encouraged me to become a phys ed teacher."

"You must have gone to a suburban high school, Jean," said Mark.

"Every high school I've ever been to has first-class sports facilities," said Anette.

"That's not the case in some inner-city schools, and definitely not in the inner-city school where I did some of my student teaching. You should go and check it out for yourself," said Mark.

"You won't find me teaching in an inner-city school," said Anette haughtily.

"Did any of you see that video where this guy compared the facilities in an inner-city Chicago school to one a few miles away in the suburbs?" asked Serena. "It was like night and day. One of my profs showed us the video in class last semester. It blew my mind. I wouldn't have believed it if I hadn't seen it myself. The video did a great job."

"Which reminds me," said Miguel, "in one of my other classes last year, our prof was discussing the role of testing in schools, and he said that a huge factor that differentiates between test scores among students is where they live. He was quite funny, and I agree with him on this point. According to him, there is too much testing in schools, and much of the time, all it does is rank students. It doesn't evaluate how well they have really learned. I don't know what you think about that, Professor Kelly." He let the pause linger, wondering if Kelly wanted to add anything.

"Keep going," said Kelly. "I think I know where you're headed."

"OK. Well, the second thing the prof said is that there is a writer out there who claims we could scrap testing if we are only interested in ranking students; his method is easier and less stress for the kids. The alternative, he said, is to simply drive around their neighborhoods to see the size of the houses the kids live in. The larger the house, the higher the kids get ranked in their test scores."

Kelly thanked Miguel and Serena for their comments. Then he said, "Let me add that those students in Miguel's example did not get higher scores because the teachers went to measure the size of their houses to assign grades accordingly. If I remember correctly, the writer in question wanted to convey that the economic standing of students' families, as indicated by the approximate size of their homes, has a substantial bearing on how well they will do in testing. It doesn't convey anything of consequence about the quality of their learning, which is surely a key consideration in considering test performance."

Following a question and answer session on the impact of socioeconomic factors on learning, Kelly looked at his watch and said, "I don't quite remember how we got on to all of this, but however we did, we are out of time again."

***

After convening the next meeting of COGEM on the following Friday, Sainsbury introduced Professor Kelly to the group, explaining that she had invited him to join the committee because of his scholarly expertise in the matters the committee dealt with. She also informed the members that she had been called before the board to defend the activities of the committee.

"Madam Chair," demanded Edwards, "I was not aware that Mr. Conners gave you the go-ahead to inform members of this non-standing committee that you were called before the board to explain the activities of the committee."

"Too bad, Dr. Edwards," Sainsbury responded defiantly. "It's a little late to bring that to my attention now, is it not? Or do you wish to have the members banish what I said from their memories as if they were members of a jury? Besides, who are you to tell me what I may or may not convey to the members of this committee?"

Changing the subject when no one seemed to be troubled by Sainsbury's revelation, Edwards went on. "And I don't approve of Dr. Kelly joining this committee. We did not vote on that, madam."

"We didn't vote on you becoming a member either, Dr. Edwards," Sainsbury responded, her patience wearing thin. "Each member of this committee, yourself included, was invited here by me. This is my committee, not yours. So be careful; you're tempting me to drop you."

Whatever else, Edwards did not want to be dropped, nor did Conners want him out. Knowing he was beat, Edward shut his mouth. Once silence returned to the meeting and the minutes were agreed to, Sainsbury moved on to the next item on the agenda, which was the report from the Newman subcommittee.

"As chair of the subcommittee, it's your turn to talk, Dr. Edwards," said Sainsbury, looking toward him.

"We met and decided that what Filomena presented to the subcommittee could constitute our report to this committee. So, I'll ask her to speak," said a dour-looking Edwards.

"Thank you, Dr. Edwards," said Sainsbury, and she turned to Filomena.

"This is what I reported to the subcommittee," said Filomena, standing up. "Even though writers such as Newman can be rather guarded in how they express themselves, Newman did write that in certain circumstances, students may learn as much from engaging in a small group discussion among themselves—maybe even in settings such as The Pizza Pan—as from professors. In the time since our subcommittee meeting, I have had an opportunity to locate exactly where it was that Newman expressed this, and precisely what he said. I will read it to you all right now. It appears in what is called Discourse

VI—much the same as a Chapter 6—of *The Idea of a University*. Actually, his point comes up twice there, but I'll just read one of the passages. It goes as follows:

> When a multitude of young men, keen, open-hearted, sympathetic, and observant, as young men are, come together and freely mix with each other, they are sure to learn one from another, even if there be no one to teach them; the conversation of all is a series of lectures to each, and they gain for themselves new ideas and views, fresh matter of thought, and distinct principles for judging and acting, day by day.

"In the other passage that I did not quote, Newman actually mentions professors, but that passage is a long and complex one, and it conveys essentially the same point of view. So that's our report, I guess. Oh! I should add that what I have reported here refers only to some of what Newman had to say regarding teaching. He also had a sophisticated epistemological and theological point of view that supported his more comprehensive position on liberal education, as I'm sure Dr. Kelly could explain better than I can."

"Thank you, Filomena," said Sainsbury. "Do we have a motion to accept the report?"

Once this was agreed to, Sainsbury turned to Kelly. "Well, Dr. Kelly, it looks like Filomena has invited you to speak, and I am not going to rule it out of order."

"Thank you, Dr. Sainsbury," said Kelly, not expecting to be called upon so early in the proceedings. "Yes, I would like to say a few words," he added, severely underestimating how many words there would be. "Let me begin by providing some context. Much has been debated over the centuries regarding the 'proper' form of a liberal or general education, and I'm sure you do not want a full account of that debate here. So let me instead begin by saying that I view liberal education and general education—or as it is often labeled in shorthand around here, gen ed—as essentially the same thing, that is, a form of education intended to enable us to attain our full development as human beings."

Looking around as if inviting questions, and on seeing an agreeable nodding of heads and nobody wanting to speak, Kelly continued. "The beginnings of this idea are usually located in ancient and medieval times, but delving too deeply into that runs the risk of engaging in a debate regarding the meaning of words rather than what is of primary interest to us today. Yes, Plato, Aristotle, Cicero, and the emergence of the medieval university all contributed to the evolving debate. So, I suppose I should say just a little about that."

Following some elaboration on these contributions, Kelly changed direction, saying, "More contemporary contributions to the debate, while not without their own impenetrable elements, provide greater guidance to us as we search for a way forward in our time. And this I take to be our essential task in this committee. That said, I should add that the contemporary debate also reveals considerable disagreement about the preferred form that general education might take, and it is quite contentious at times."

As most of those in attendance followed along with interest in what Kelly had to say, Edwards was feeling uneasy about it all and raised his hand to say something. Not wishing to generate a protest, Sainsbury ceded the floor.

"Thanks for coming, Dr. Kelly, but I understood you intended to deliver just a few words. That is what you promised, remember?" said Edwards, having risen to his feet. "Besides, I don't think we needed that history lesson. Some of us here have been doing this gen ed thing for quite a while, and I think we've gotten the hang of it pretty well."

"Excuse me, Dr. Edwards," said Sainsbury as Edwards was ramping up. "I've asked Dr. Kelly to join us because he has an expertise in this area that may be of help to us. If you prefer not to listen, I recommend you read any of his books on the topic. That way, you could have your beer and hear him too."

Following a chuckle, Marilyn thought she should get a word in. "Dr. Edwards, I come here from surveillance services, and I've never heard any of this before. If I'm going to be advising this committee, which includes you, on how we ought to proceed, I'd sure like to hear more from Dr. Kelly and ask questions when I have the opportunity. I think our gen ed program stinks to high heaven, if you want to know the truth of it. And I have to pay for it while being bored by much of it. Geometry doesn't do much for me, ya know."

"OK, Marilyn, thank you," said Sainsbury.

But Marilyn persisted. "Even friends of mine who've taken your course in arithmetic tell me…"

"Excuse me, miss, that's 'Arithmetic Around the World.' It's a unique course for gen ed purposes," growled Edwards.

"Yes, that's it… Well, my friends hate it. Arithmetic Around the World seems exactly like it was in their elementary schools up the street. Many kids at the Metro don't feel the need for trig or any of that stuff."

"Thank you, Marilyn," said Sainsbury, trying once again to steer Marilyn toward safety. She asked Kelly to continue.

"I'm happy to," said Kelly, "but maybe I could ask Dr. Edwards what he considers to be the way forward, given what Marilyn has just said and what many scholars who write on this subject today have to say about where we are in our thinking on general education. For, as I said, what I think we are looking for here is a way forward."

"I don't agree with that at all," insisted Edwards. "We already know the way forward, and we enforce it every day around here."

"If I may," asked Kelly, "did you say 'enforce it?' Why would we do that?"

"Because kids don't want it, for the most part, as the kid just blurted out," responded Edwards. "Are you living in cloud-cuckoo-land, young man?"

"You're the one in cloud-cuckoo-land, Dr. Edwards, if ya don't mind me sayin'," Marilyn interjected.

"Could you conceal your ignorance, miss, and let me talk," shouted Edwards at her, flaring up.

"You talking to a mirror, sir?" asked Marilyn.

This is spiraling out of control, Sainsbury thought. Unsure of how to manage the proceedings, she was relieved that Jackson wished to speak. "Please go ahead, Dr. Jackson."

"Dr. Kelly, I'm especially interested to hear that there is an ongoing debate regarding the shape and future of general education,"

Jackson began. "While I have concerns about our approach at the Metro and other institutions I know of, this is not the impression I gain from reading mission statements of colleges and universities, and even some articles in a journal put out by one of the university associations. They tend to speak in glowing terms of what is referred to as the 'respected traditions of the liberal arts,' and decry efforts to modify or even question these traditions. They don't appear to connect these traditions to the points expressed by Marilyn just now. I share some of Marilyn's concern, while accepting that there are limits to specialization. It's fair to say that many of the faculty at the Metro express reservations regarding our approach to general education."

"Thank you, Dr. Jackson, for saying that better than I could," said Marilyn. "But I'd also like to hear from Dr. Kelly on how he would solve the problem of general education."

"Before Dr. Kelly responds," interjected Sainsbury, "I shall ask him to be brief, as we are almost out of time, although I hope we can hear much more from him in the future."

"Believe me, I would like to answer your question, Marilyn, as I have fairly strong views on the matter. But as anyone in my classes will tell you, I do not consider myself to be an oracle on general education. Besides, I do not wish to preempt the deliberations of the committee before we can hash out our questions more fully. As we approach the end of our deliberations at a later point, I will leave no doubt in your mind as to where I stand on all of this. I hope that will suffice for now."

This was welcome news for Filomena, who often wondered while listening to him in class if Kelly had any convictions at all about such essential matters beyond process and pedagogy.

When Kelly had spoken, Edwards could not restrain himself, even if time were running out. This lack of restraint was not toward Kelly, to whom he paid almost no attention, but toward Sainsbury, who had not invited any discussion of the subcommittee report before asking Kelly to speak, toward Marilyn for her outspoken comments, and toward Filomena for what she had reported and by all of which he was still consumed.

Sainsbury allowed him to speak.

"Dr. Sainsbury, I would have expected an opportunity to discuss the report from the subcommittee and its implications for the work of the committee before having to listen to Dr. Kelly ramble on. Because of that omission, let me now respond, if I may." Turning to Filomena and raising his hand to accentuate his point, he said, "The least you could have done, Miss Ponytail Smarty-pants, was to quote Newman's words at the subcommittee meeting and not wait until now. And then you made the addendum that Newman had more to say, but you revealed none of that at our subcommittee meeting. What kind of a fu… futile crapshoot of a process is this anyway?" His face growing more and more purple as he spoke, Edwards then turned his wrath to Marilyn. Pointing an accusatory finger at her, he shouted, "As for you, you're an effing waste of space." Not finished, he invited his colleague, Dr. Torino, to lend his support. "Come on, Vic, give 'em some crap!"

"May I speak?" asked Marilyn. "I did not expect to witness this kind of crude behavior in this committee, sir," she said. "Anyway, you could have checked Newman properly for yourself. Besides, in the subcommittee, you did not permit Filomena to elaborate beyond what she reported here. You actually cut her short twice."

"Thank you, Marilyn. That's enough," said Sainsbury as Torino prepared to speak.

"Madam Vice President," began Torino, caught off balance and searching for words. "We need proper order here. This is no way to treat anyone in this institution. I have been on the faculty here for over 34 years and have a lot of institutional memory that goes with it. When I first came here, our gen ed program was in shambles. It was Dr. Edwards and me that fixed that. So, let's show some respect where respect is due."

"Thank you, Professor Torino," said Sainsbury. "I'm all for giving respect where respect is due. So, before we finish up for today, I'll remind Dr. Edwards to show and to model some in the future. Let's reconvene a month from today. This seems to be a reasonable hour for most people, and I'll notify you of a specific date next week. Let me also remind you that following a directive from the chair of the board of governors, I shall be reporting to them as regards our proceedings here today. I'll be glad to let you all have a copy of my report."

As they left the meeting, Marilyn asked Filomena what an oracle was. "I thought that was some kind of high-tech company in California," she added.

"Well, there is that, for sure, but the ancient Greeks believed they had reliable sources of wisdom known as oracles. That's what Professor Kelly was referring to. One of the most famous oracles was at a sacred site at Delphi, where 'voices' from a sort of underground passage revealed the 'truth' to the chosen one or oracle. So when Dr. Kelly said he is not an oracle, he meant that he does not claim to know the whole truth about general education. By the way, the holy site at Delphi, which is also associated with the Greek God Apollo, is located close to an ancient athletic facility on the slope of Mount Parnassus, some 100 miles from Athens."

"Cool," said Marilyn. "I must remember that about Delphi."

"Better still, why don't we go visit it sometime?" suggested Filomena. "That reminds me: I won't be able to attend the get-together at The Pizza Pan this evening, but I hope you can."

"Yes, I plan to be there," said Marilyn. "Maybe I'll have a chat with Newman if he shows up!"

***

Over lunch in her office on Monday, Sainsbury met with Lukas to review his draft of the minutes of Friday's meeting of COGEM, which included a summary of Kelly's presentation and the discussion that surrounded it. Given the sensitivity of the matters it dealt with, Sainsbury took particular care in writing up the report that was due to the board of governors. She thought it best to have it hand-delivered to Conners on Tuesday morning, and she set a release time of 9 a.m. for sending electronic copies to members of the committee and the Metro board. The report to the board read as follows:

Chair Conners,
As instructed, I am submitting this as my report to the board on the meeting of the Committee on General Education and the Major (COGEM) that was held on Friday last, October 25 of this year.

Following my introduction of Dr. Kelly to the committee, the chair of the Newman subcommittee, Dr. Joseph Edwards, kindly arranged for one of the student members to present the subcommittee report. The report was accepted, and following this, Dr. Kelly was invited to speak to the full committee. Following some discussion of his remarks, the wish was expressed that Dr. Kelly could make a further presentation at a future date. There followed a short but heated exchange between Dr. Edwards and members of the committee that I think is best presented here as it will appear in the minutes of the meeting. Here it is, with Edwards's words as recorded on the tape:

> Turning to Filomena and raising his hand to accentuate his point, he said, 'The least you could have done, Miss Ponytail Smarty-pants, was to quote Newman's words at the subcommittee meeting and not wait until now. And then you made the addendum that Newman had more to say, but you revealed none of that at our subcommittee meeting. What kind of a fu... futile crapshoot of a process is this anyway?' Edwards face grew more and more purple as he spoke. Then pointing an accusatory finger at Marilyn, he shouted, 'As for you, you're an effing waste of space.' Not yet finished, he invited his colleague, Dr. Torino, to lend his support. 'Come on, Vic, give 'em some crap!'

In conclusion, I ask that you please advise on how the board proposes to address the attitude and vulgarities expressed by Dr. Edwards, and, in particular, if you consider such behavior merits censure or dismissal.

Signed,
Valerie Sainsbury
Vice President for Academic Affairs

CHAPTER 10

Sufficiently perturbed by the events at COGEM on Friday, over the weekend, Edwards persuaded Smatter to have him back on his chat show to vent his feelings. The soonest this could be arranged was Tuesday's early-morning edition. Not giving Sainsbury's forthcoming report to the Metro board much thought, Edwards nonetheless gave its contents an almost verbatim public airing on Radio YOY that morning.

"The students on Sainsbury's committee are punks, Arnie," Edwards declared for listeners while he was not yet fully sober following a late night of drowning his sorrows.

"I see," said Smatter, not knowing what to expect from Edwards.

"One of them, Marilyn, is an ignoramus from the business school, which ought to be shut down anyway. The other, Saint Filomena, thinks she's a Newman scholar; I think she's a Swasser College smart-ass. Unfortunately, these kinds are all too common at the Metro these days. I put it down to our socialist and left-leaning faculty."

Once done with his radio interview, and while students and faculty were still arriving on campus for a regular day's work, Edwards was on the phone to Conners, counseling him against entering the special election and challenging Singleton. A few minutes before 9 a.m., with Conners complaining to Edwards that he was unable to decide if he wanted Mobilo or Singleton to come out on top in the election, Conners's secretary arrived with an envelope from Sainsbury marked, "Urgent, Private, and Confidential."

"What's she up to now?" Conners mumbled, setting down the phone as he opened the envelope.

He quickly got the gist of Sainsbury's report. His hair standing on end at what he read, he picked up the phone and yelled, "Joe, what the fuck is this?" Rather than merely telling Edwards that the report painted a damning picture of him, he thought it best to describe what he looked like: "Joe, you've got shit all over you—face, ass, everywhere! Have you seen this goddamn piece of garbage from the control freak, the report on Friday's meeting of her goddamn committee?"

"No, I haven't," Edwards told Conners more or less truthfully, as it had only just popped up on his cell phone at that very moment. "I guess I'll receive a copy when the committee members get it."

"You mean every frigging member and the student punks too?" asked Conners, beginning to wonder if he should throw his hat in the ring for the seat in the Fourth District after all, even at this late stage.

"That's right. Everyone," said Edwards, adding that he had left the Radio YOY studio and was in traffic. "I'm headed to see you right away."

By 10 a.m., and before Edwards arrived on campus, Marilyn, who had been told of the radio interview and had seen her own copy of the email, had already rounded up a group of friends to brandish makeshift placards in the parking lot outside mathematics.

"Dr. Edwards is toast," was the first sign he saw when he arrived. Edwards stepped from his car and charged like a train toward Conners's office next door in the administration building. He pushed his way through a small group of protesters, even as they and a bunch of curious onlookers were already growing in size.

"Conners, she's got to go. Our control freak, I mean. She's got to go," Edwards shouted as he barged into Conners's office. She was right there in front of him to hear it for herself, along with the secretary.

"Shut the hell up, Joe, and scoot. Jim will be joining us shortly. I'll let you know how it goes," Conners said.

"I'm not going anywhere, Butch," Edwards protested.

"Oh, yes you are, Joe. Now get while the getting's good," demanded Conners.

Knowing Conners from their schooldays, and realizing who he was dealing with, Edwards reluctantly decided it was best to leave before the campus police got there.

As it transpired, Beame could not make it to any meeting before the afternoon, so shortly afterward, Sainsbury also left, returning to her office and planning to come back later. Since the hideaway he had ordered to be built for himself was not yet ready, Conners went to speak to the press.

**

When students turned up for Kelly's class at 11 am that morning, pushing their way through the expanding and noisy gathering of placard bearers pouring into the green that ran alongside the education building, they were not sure what to expect from him. This was now a genuine protest. Would class be business as usual, or would there be a change of focus? Of those who had placed bets, about half said there would be no change. As it turned out, the reality was a combination of both, so no money changed hands.

"I'm sure many of you have seen the posters and protesters on campus today," Kelly began. "I've seen them myself, but only through the windows. I'll come back to these events later, but first, please discuss the reading assigned for today in your small groups. We'll spend about 15 minutes on that."

When the 15 minutes were up and Kelly had drawn up in his head a revised class plan built around the protest rather than the assigned reading, he began, "Does anyone wish to raise issues with the reading?" Nobody did. Keen to see what his next move would be, all stayed quiet. "OK. Then I'd like you all to write down your answer to this question." Following a pause, while they got ready, he continued, "If you were invited to add a placard to those outside, what would it say?"

Catching people off guard, and as everyone gawked out the windows, no one was ready to answer when he asked what people had written down.

Miguel was the one to break the silence. "I'd write, 'Go for it,'" he said with a grin of satisfaction.

"Go for what?" asked Anette, showing her displeasure.

"That's for you to fill in," Miguel replied to her further dismay.

This led to a lively bout of discussion, so Mark put the focus back on Miguel. "Does that mean you take no position? Isn't that kind of a cop-out?"

"Oh, I've taken a position, for sure. Right, Professor?" he asked, trying impatiently to figure out where Kelly stood.

"I didn't expect you would be aiming for an A in this class," Kelly replied, recalling Miguel's general tone of resistance earlier in the semester. "If I give you an answer, will you explain your placard slogan? I will need that if I am to evaluate your effort."

"It's a deal," said Miguel creating a sense of anticipation.

As people began to wonder what pedagogical form this engagement would take, Kelly asked for silence and then, having created as much interest in what his own answer would be as in Miguel's explanation, he said simply, "Yes."

"Ah, come on, Prof. Just one word? You can't do this to us," exclaimed Jean, laughing. "We paid to get into all our classes, thinking we'd have some new information to show for it. So far, this is the only class where I've written nothing in my notepad yet."

"So, that's one fewer notepad that you'll need to buy for next semester," said Kelly laughing along with the rest of the class. "Maybe Miguel will give you something to write down," said Kelly, prompting Miguel to deliver on his end of the deal.

"OK, then. Here's my explanation, Professor, and I'm betting you will agree." He explained that "Go for it" is meant to show respect for those feeling hard done by. It invites participants and onlookers alike to fill in the blank space denoted by the 'it' in his ideal placard. It reflects both a democratic sensitivity to a variety of viewpoints by singling out no one for blame. And, dare he use jargon, it exhibits a pedagogical sensitivity because it is supportive in tone and inclusive of all. He also suggested, "It shows I have already earned my A in this class!"

"Bravo!" said Jean. "I agree with that. Do I also get an A?"

"Miguel's placard would be fine, I guess," said Serena, "but mine is better. It comes in at an A+ level because it is specific about Professor Edwards's objectionable language. Here it is: 'Edwards = F-words.'"

"I prefer that too," said Christine, "partly because it's more like mine, which also picks out the most objectionable word that many of the placards are attributing to Dr. Edwards. Here's mine: 'No More F-Wards.'"

"Good work! Some attractive and creative efforts here," said Kelly as he walked around the room, looking at the students' contributions. Switching focus, he said, "Before we go any further, and I should have acknowledged this from the beginning, we have among us one whose name appears on some of those placards outside. Filomena, would you like to say anything?"

"I'd love to. I only observed what is going on outside as I was heading to class, and I didn't want to hog the show," she began. "First thing, I have to say that attending the Metro is a wonderful educational experience, even if there is room for institutional improvement."

"Go, Metro!" said someone, interrupting.

Filomena continued. "This is a participatory education as well as an intellectual one. By which I mean that I am learning by seeing good pedagogy and a democratic attitude in action, in which I myself am a participant. Here, we are being asked to consider what is going on outside our classroom window. This is civics education as well as teacher education. Miguel is exhibiting heightened intellectual awareness of a complex idea and is explaining it to us. I am also lucky enough, at least up to a point, to be a member of COGEM. And by the way, although I like Miguel's suggestion, I am leaning toward those signs that reject the F-word."

"Thanks, Filomena," said Kelly, thinking she had gone as far as she wished in addressing some of the questions on the list she had prepared for her inquisition of Johnson in the student teaching office at the beginning of the semester.

"Can I say something else, Professor?" she asked.

"Of course. Please do," said Kelly, leaning back against the windowsill near the front of the room.

"I'd like to talk about what actually took place in the last meeting of COGEM because it provides context for the protest outside.," she went on, asking Kelly if it was ok to touch on that.

Kelly nodded his assent, believing that she would respect the necessary confidences.

"You see, Marilyn and I also served on a subcommittee of the full committee, and we were reporting back to the full group on what the subcommittee had decided. By the way, Marilyn is in the surveillance services program, and she is the one who got the placards up and running this morning. She texted me on my way to campus to ask if I wanted to join her, but I didn't want to miss this class. Anyway, as we were reporting back to COGEM, Dr. Edwards from mathematics, who is also on both committees, became angry at the COGEM meeting on Friday afternoon and used foul and undignified language in addressing Marilyn and me. I believe he did the same on the radio this morning. Also this morning, in the report Dr. Sainsbury is obliged to send to Mr. Conners as chair of the Metro board, she described Edwards's behavior at the committee. I have already seen the report and I'm sure you will be able to read it in *The Metro Memo* before long, as I cannot imagine the student newspaper not getting hold of it. When Marilyn received the report this morning and around the same time was told by friends of Edwards's performance on Radio YOY, she 'put her business skills to work,' as she described it to me. Hence, the placards and the protest. She's a real up-front person. So is Dr. Sainsbury, the VP."

"If I may," said Christine who wanted to comment, "I'd like to bring the issue of today's protest back to what we talk about in this class. Discussing the protest in class today is a really good example of seizing on a teachable moment, and it even makes me feel good. It brings home the importance of the question we talked about a few weeks ago when we considered whether the school should delve into the moral and civic domains, and if society needs its members to have certain shared values taught in school."

"You all know what I think about that," said Filomena, speaking up again. "I agree entirely with Christine. This protest, and especially our discussion of it, brings the issue right up in front of us again."

Serena added, "I read recently that there is a body of scholarship that examines bullying by faculty in higher education. To me, the behavior of Dr. Edwards looks like the bullying of students in the Metro, and the Metro is better than that. It also makes me think of bullying by politicians who abuse their pulpits, and the terrible example that sets for the rest of us."

"Thank you, Filomena, Christine, and Serena. That's very nicely said by all of you. Let me also say to Miguel, I think your explanation was also well stated," said Kelly, looking at his watch and indicating that class was over.

"That was a really great class, Professor Kelly," Jean said as several students approached him to express the same sentiment. While Filomena had felt his personal touch before, Miguel was beaming when Kelly shook his hand as they left the classroom together.

***

"Who the hell told you to send out that damn report to those kids on your committee, Sainsbury?" Conners charged when he met with Beame and the vice president in his office that afternoon.

"The Standing Rules for Committee Procedure at the Metro told me, sir. You should read them," said Sainsbury assertively and not ready to take any guff from the likes of Conners.

Further enraged following his earlier meeting with members of the press, and disregarding what she said, Conners raised his voice in frustration. "This goddamn phone has not stopped ringing all morning." Seemingly more irritated now by Sainsbury than anyone else, he lashed out. "Who on earth do you think you are anyway? There are reporters, photographers, and cameramen running around campus to spread the news far and wide. What am I supposed to say when they shove a microphone in my face?"

"I hope you'll do better than your pal Singleton did on Radio YOY when he faced Superintendent Price a few weeks back," she said, brushing off the implied accusation.

"You realize that your damn committee is the cause of all this? And that kid, Marilyn, is a troublemaker who needs to be dealt with," he responded, insinuating she should never have been invited to serve on the committee, which should not even exist in the first place.

"She's more like a whistleblower, I'd say," Sainsbury replied. "As for your misplaced accusations, sir, let's be clear that neither Marilyn nor I am the wrongdoer here."

"Butch, let's ease up here," said President Beame, attempting to lower the temperature. "I'll call Joe Edwards into my office and have a word with him."

"And what about the brat, Marilyn?" inquired Conners.

"You can call her in if you want to, Butch, but she's off-limits as far as I'm concerned," said Beame. "Free speech is not a crime in my book. Maybe I'll ask Valerie to have a quiet word with her, but that's about it." Then looking toward Sainsbury, he asked, "How does that sound to you, Valerie?"

"I'm OK with that."

"I hope you two know what you're doing here," said Conners, finally beginning to feel he was out of his depth and not wishing to make a bad situation worse. He could see that Beame was trying to ease the tension before any more damage was done, and so for now, he called it quits. As they broke up, Conners said he would also be in touch with Edwards.

Yet, Conners was not entirely done with the matter. Looking to make the best of his situation, he thought that maybe he could get payback by moving forward with his case for the dismissal of Sainsbury. After all, she was not ingratiating herself to him. So, perhaps now is a good time to make my move, he thought.

***

Dick Blair was not impressed by the goings-on at the Metro as relayed by hysterical media reports throughout the day. Yet perhaps they did have an upside for the Midleton school board and its improvement plan.

With Singleton trying desperately to dig himself out of the hole he created for himself on Radio YOY, looking like less of a shoo-in to win the fast-approaching election than before, and with Conners in a less clearly defined hole of his own, Blair began to think that maybe the school board could capitalize on the misfortune of the two men and bring the improvement plan forward for approval at the board meeting in November. As it happened, Price and her staff had already carefully reexamined the improvement plan. In the course of a phone call from Blair, she was persuaded to bring the plan to the November board meeting while Conners and Singleton, its two main adversaries, were distracted by other matters.

***

The regular November meeting of the school board was to take place on November 18, the evening before the special election. Although Price agreed with Blair to bring the improvement plan forward for approval, she thought the part of the plan dealing with the curriculum needed further attention. She was disappointed that the board members showed no interest in considering the curriculum side of things when developing the plan. She was also troubled that many of the textbooks in use in the district were out of date. Johnson was not of much help in any of this, even as Price had expressed concerns about these matters being pushed aside.

When Blair met the next day with Price, Burnett, and Johnson to expedite the submission of the plan to the board, Price again expressed her view that aspects of the plan dealing with the curriculum were lacking.

"Terry, is there anyone at the Metro in the Department of Curriculum and Teaching who could help us out here?"

"Gee, I'm sure there is," Johnson responded, not really knowing one way or the other, but he did agree to make inquiries.

"That would be helpful," said Price. Even if the board could get the other parts of the plan finalized for submission at the November meeting, while Singleton was otherwise engaged and Conners otherwise enraged, that would be a real step forward. We could submit the curriculum part later as an addendum, she thought, revealing her own shortcomings when it came to curriculum planning.

***

Wasting no time, Johnson sent an email to Filomena asking if she could drop in to see him when she was on campus, and she did so after class the next day.

"It's good to see you, Filomena," said Johnson. Before she could sit down on the visitor's chair, he asked if they could talk over lunch. That's a bonus and a good omen, Filomena thought, and they headed for the faculty dining room.

As they walked over, Johnson explained that he was a member of the Midleton school board, which was in the process of drawing up its school improvement plan for submission to Washington. Once they were seated, Johnson elaborated.

"One of the odd things about our planning process is that we gave priority to things like budgets, salaries, teacher recruitment, enrollment projections, building construction and maintenance, and the like. But somehow, we thought the curriculum side of things, such as the subjects on the curriculum, didn't need much attention, that they were good to go. But Margaret, she's our superintendent, is uneasy with that, and she wondered if there were someone who might take a look at that part of the plan."

"My, that is a crucial part of any school plan, I would have thought," said Filomena.

"Yes, I thought you would. So, I thought I'd ask you," he continued before pausing.

"Ask me what?"

"Oh, ask you to lunch," he said, unsure of how to get to the point. "That is… Well, let me put it this way: We would like someone to contribute to our work on the curriculum plan. When you and I have chatted in the past, and as you do at COGEM, it's clear that you are interested in curriculum matters."

"Very interested, but I'm only a student."

"Well, you are a graduate student, and if it would help, I could see if we can offer you a graduate assistantship if you're willing to help us out on this. We do have one available."

"That's very kind of you, Dr. Johnson. Do you mind if I think about it for a day or two? An assistantship would be a great help, but I also have little Rachel to think about, as you know."

"Sure, I can wait for a day or two. I'd be surprised if it were much of a burden on you. I would not have approached you if I thought it would be."

***

Following lunch, Filomena's next stop was Kelly's office. This could not wait until class next week.

"Do you have a minute to spare, Dr. Kelly?" asked Filomena when she arrived at his office and saw him looking out the window.

"Of course," he said, turning toward her. "Everything OK?"

"Everything's fine, thank you," she replied. "I've come for a little advice on something that has just popped up. Dr. Johnson asked me if I could drop in today to see him about developments in the Midleton school district. He even brought me to lunch. Anyway, he explained that the school board needs someone to look at the curriculum side of the school improvement plan they are developing. It's for the feds, I think."

"Yes, that would make sense," said Kelly.

"When he asked in a roundabout way if I could help them out, I said I was only a student. But he did not think that would be a problem, and he even indicated that he might be able to offer me a graduate assistantship if I was willing to help. But to be frank, I feel out of my depth on this. I did not want to recommend that he talk to you about it without speaking to you in advance, but you were the first person that came to my mind for the job."

"OK, Filomena," said Kelly, slowing her down in her excitement. "This is not EDUC 401, and there's no need for me to probe around the edges here. So, do you want my opinion?"

"Yes, please!"

"Take it! This isn't a big deal, Filomena. You know as much about curriculum issues as anybody on the school board, including maybe the superintendent. I'm not surprised he asked you; you're a great fit for the job."

"Gosh, that's awfully nice of you to say," she said, not believing her good fortune. "Would you be willing to talk with me about it once in a while if I have any questions?"

"Not just once in a while, Filomena. Anytime! I mean it. I'd love to spend more time with you… You know, looking over any papers that you need to read or write, that sort of thing," Kelly equivocated, having revealed more than he meant to. "I've done the same for other school districts across the country."

"Maybe I should go right back downstairs to tell Dr. Johnson that I accept," Filomena said, doubly excited on hearing he wanted to spend more time with her.

"Not a bad idea," said Kelly. "And if you need anyone to write a quick reference or if someone asks to speak to one of your professors, go right ahead and give my name," said Kelly, who was only too happy to help. "All the best, and please let me know how it goes."

"I certainly will. Thank you!"

CHAPTER 11

It took Conners a few days to tell Edwards that he was letting Beame handle the matter of his behavior at COGEM, and that Beame would likely be calling him in. He also informed him that he was still planning to bring up the question of Sainsbury's dismissal to the board, and that for that reason, Edwards should keep his cool or risk putting the dismissal offensive in jeopardy. Other than cursing and fuming on the phone, in part because of Conners's delay in getting back to him, Edwards promised to oblige and would simply go on about his business more or less as before.

**

"Tell me your side of the story, Joe," said Beame to Edwards, who reeked of beer and tobacco when he came in to see him the next morning.

"There are two sides to every story, as you know, so I'm glad you asked," Edwards began. "Why is it always the flipping women who cause trouble, can you tell me? Sainsbury can't do her job as well as I could have, and you are partly to blame for that. If Butch were here then, she wouldn't be here now, you can be sure of that."

"But he wasn't, and she is. Let's get real, Joe. You've got to let go of all that now; it's water under the bridge. And you haven't answered my question about your side of the story. Did you speak disrespectfully and use foul language toward the students at the meeting? Is Valerie's report reliable?" asked Beame unambiguously.

"Hell, Jim, didn't I tell you she's full of it? What else can I say? As for this Filomena dolly who claims to be a grad student—believe me, she is a smart-ass who should be sent back to finishing school. Another dumbass is that little tart from the business school. Just another reason to get rid of that school at the Metro. All they do is take up space on our form courses and area studies worksheet."

Then, following a pause and a bout of coughing, he said, "You know the Metro started out as a teachers college and gained respectability only when we added arts and sciences. It's time to get back to that, Jim. Cut out the frills: women's studies, social justice concentrations, phys ed. Now we have Sainsbury's darned committee hurtling us in the opposite direction."

Not getting an answer from Edwards, Beame decided he was not getting an answer, so he changed tack and decided to save some time on his schedule. "Like it or not, Joe, you've landed yourself in a right pickle. I'm not going to take disciplinary action this time. But be forewarned: Just be sure you don't set about business as usual. And stay away from Smatter and that sorry excuse for a talk show he runs on Radio YOY. It's almost as bad as TVViews," said Beame, getting to his feet, shaking hands with Edwards, and showing him out.

***

"I saw you on TV a few nights ago, Marilyn," said Sainsbury, hoping to convey a serious tone when Marilyn arrived to meet with her in her office that afternoon.

"Gee, thanks, ma'am. I saw it myself too," said Marilyn. "What did you think? By the way, thanks for having me on this committee. I thought I'd hate it, but it's fun except for Dr. Edwards."

"Why do you like being on the committee, Marilyn, and what's the problem with Dr. Edwards?" asked Sainsbury, as they were seated and she already being swayed off course.

"Well, it's like this, Dr. Sainsbury. I love the opportunity to give my input and mix it up with folks on the committee. As for Dr. Edwards, he's no ad for gen ed, that's for sure. If I were you, I wouldn't have him out front trying to sell it, ma'am. Another problem, as I mentioned before, is that I came here to get into surveillance services, and I have all this gen ed stuff thrown at me. And then some professors that don't impress me try to tell me it's good for me. But I say that if I don't like it, it's not good for me. I don't care for the attitude around it. You see, some professors hint that we ought not to be watching TVViews. I don't need to be told that TVViews is garbage; even a redneck like me can see that. It's the same with gen ed."

"What do you mean, Marilyn? Could you expand on that point?" asked Sainsbury as if conducting a class in literary criticism. "I'm intrigued."

"Sure, ma'am. You see, some surprising people watch TVViews. I've heard of doctors watching it, and lots of politicians live by it. The worst part is that they believe it, and people go out and vote that way. It's kind of a snow job, if you see what I mean. The people are brainwashed," said Marilyn sternly.

"Thanks, Marilyn. But how does that make it like gen ed, I mean general education?"

"Well, if you read any of the college mission statements out there, and I'm sure you do, they also do the same sort of thing. I've been reading a bunch of them for COGEM. Their mission, they say, is to provide an excellent general education that will enable their students to become well-developed, responsible, and civic-minded members of a wholesome, democratic society. Many of these colleges charge people through the nose for it. So, we're all supposed to believe that the 'liberal arts are good for you,' either because it's printed in a glossy brochure or because professors in arts and sciences have been saying so for years. I don't believe these glossy brochures any more than I believe TVViews. As Dr. Edwards reminds us in the committee most days, he attended one of those elite liberal arts colleges, as he puts it. Now, do you think he's a well-developed human being and citizen? He might have a well-developed beer belly, and that's about it," Marilyn concluded with a giggle.

Sainsbury giggled too but tried not to. "Well, Marilyn, you are a charmer," Sainsbury admitted to her own surprise, though she still hoped to move the chat to where it was supposed to be going.

"I'll tell you who's a charmer," said Marilyn before Sainsbury could finish, "it's that kid from Swasser, Filomena, who, by the way, has a kid of her own. Can you believe it?"

"My, I didn't know that," said Sainsbury with surprise and being further drawn in by the redneck. "And, yes, Filomena is a charmer, just a different kind of charmer than you, Marilyn."

"Well anyway," Marilyn continued, "I thought she was uppity when I met her during registration at the beginning of the semester, but now that I'm getting to know her, I see she's very different. It's a 'take a walk in my shoes' kind of experience, I suppose. Filomena's actually kind and gentle, even if forthright like yourself. It's so peaceful and fun being with her; I wish I could spend more time with her, but she's kind of tied down with Rachel, her little one. And boy, she's pretty; she drives the guys crazy. But how come the little kid? She's sure knowledgeable, but maybe she lacks some street smarts. Maybe we should put that in the mission statement for the Metro: street smarts."

"You don't lack street smarts yourself, Marilyn, but I do have to leave it at that. I asked you to come in today because President Beame suggested that I have a word with you. He knows I was a bit of a rebel myself in college, and although he did not want me to reprimand you for organizing the protest, he wanted me to urge you to use caution in case anyone tries to take advantage of you."

"Thanks, ma'am. I will," said Marilyn as she prepared to leave.

"Phew," exclaimed Sainsbury privately when Marilyn had gone. "We learn something important every day."

***

Having informed Johnson that she would accept the graduate assistantship and work on the improvement plan for the Midleton school board, Filomena was greeted cheerily by Price when she arrived at the school district office in the Midleton town hall on the following Monday as scheduled. Once she was introduced to the staff in the main office, Filomena met with Price alone for coffee in the boardroom.

"As you can see, Filomena," said Price, showing her around and handing her a copy of the draft improvement plan and a thumb drive that contained it in digital form, "this is the collection of materials we relied upon in drafting the plan."

"May I record any notations I may have on the digital copy of the plan?" asked Filomena.

"Of course," said Price. "It's only about 50 pages long, excluding the appendices. There are still some sticking points to be resolved by the school board, and these are indicated in the document as it now stands. But where I would most welcome your assistance is with the treatment of curriculum matters in the draft plan."

"Yes, I understand. Dr. Johnson explained that to me."

"Dr. Johnson might also have explained that our original intention was to finalize the plan at our last school board meeting.

We were keen to get it to the feds well before the December 15 deadline. Unfortunately, at that meeting, there were objections that we had not anticipated. Wayne Singleton, who is running for the vacant congressional seat in the special election, and the chair of the Metro board, Butch Conners, were strongly opposed to the plan. By the end of the meeting, the general feeling was to delay everything until the December meeting. But Mr. Blair and I now think it might be a good idea to move more quickly and to do so in two stages." Price was careful not to convey that the real reason for acting quickly was to get around likely opposition by Conners and Singleton's foot-dragging. "If all goes well, we could submit whatever we have ready for approval at the November board meeting on the 18th, and the remainder at the December meeting."

"So, I had better get going on this right away then?"

"Well, yes and no, Filomena," said Price, sounding like Professor Kelly. "It would be unfair to put you under that pressure on such short notice. We were thinking that if we make our first submission to the feds before the end of November, we could always amend it by submitting the section on curriculum at a later date, as long as that also arrives by December 15. So, sometime before the December meeting of the school board would be the time to aim for. Shall we say December 5?"

This sequencing of submissions sounded odd to Filomena, but she let it go without saying so. Not putting the treatment of aims and curriculum at the beginning of the process did not sound like a good idea, even to a novice such as she. Later, she would also notice that there was almost no attention given to classroom teaching in the plan, an omission she believed Dr. Kelly would find troubling.

Although early December was set as a deadline for Filomena's contribution, Price also asked her to submit her initial reactions to the curriculum aspects of the plan by the end of the following week, so that they could be presented to the advisory group of Blair, Johnson, and Burnett before the upcoming November school board meeting. Price wanted to ensure they had a sense of the changes that would likely be recommended by Filomena.

***

"OK, folks," Kelly said as he began class the next day. "Even though we are already into November, I need to bring us back to that early question of the educated person. When we explored it last, I suggested that if the government or school boards pay teachers' salaries and require children to go to school, they must have something particular in mind that they wanted them to learn. Why would they spend the money if 'anything goes?' So, to repeat it, my question is not so much what they want to teach young people, but what *should* they teach them. That is, what is the proper content of an education if students are to be considered educated? Put differently, what is an educated person?

"Now, when I asked that question before, Miguel said he didn't think it was a fair question because it's based on the assumption that there is such a thing as an educated person, to which I replied that I'd like to address the question anyway because of the issues it might raise. So, now that I am bringing it up again, what do you all think?"

To Kelly's pleasant surprise, hands were raised right away.

"It's not an assumption, as Miguel thought, if countries and communities everywhere aim to give their young people a good education, and they do," volunteered Christine, having worked out her thoughts on the matter to her satisfaction over the past several days. "I was reading the chapter by Hirst that you asked us to read, and he said that the reason we should study academic subjects is that they not only give us knowledge, but they enable us to think. We cannot think except through the disciplines of knowledge, he said. We need to study a range of them because they provide different information and require different kinds of thinking. After that reading, and upon further reflection, I believe that education is knowing a broad range of subjects and understanding how to do the thinking involved in them. That's what makes a human being; that's what makes for an educated person or a good education. If we get a job afterward, all the better."

"Yeah," observed Miguel unenthusiastically, "I remember that reading too. Actually, I thought that guy said the forms of knowledge, not the disciplines, but no matter. I disagreed with him anyway. He said there were only seven or so forms. I think there are more than that. And I still think car mechanics or mechanics of any kind is one of them. Urban development is another, and there are so many others. That guy didn't…"

"Next, you'll be adding home economics," interrupted Anette with something between a sneer and a frown.

"Sure, why not?" said Miguel. "I like to eat—might as well learn to cook, too. Anyway, that was a good class in school to have some fun with."

"I didn't need to learn to eat in school, and neither did my husband. And we have good taste," replied Anette in a huff.

"I think Anette raises a pertinent point," said Kelly. "Is home economics of any value in making you a better person besides teaching you how to cook and eat? Does it have any value beyond that?" he continued, as if serious. "What do you think, Anette?"

"It has no place in school. I'm not surprised schools are dropping it from the curriculum, even for girls," came Anette's confident assertion.

"But should men not learn to cook too?" asked Kelly.

"My husband has learned, and he's a good cook. He didn't learn it in school, but at home, before we got married. Now I teach him the finer points," replied Anette.

Christine had been waiting patiently for her turn to speak, so Kelly allowed her to have a say. "My daughter is a dietitian" began Christine, "and she found it very helpful to her higher education to have studied home ec in school. There was much material in her course of studies that reminded me of the kinds of things I learned in my own home ec classes, although it was sometimes called domestic science back then."

"If you want to include it as a part of vocational or tech school, I suppose that's OK," said Anette, "but that doesn't mean it should count for general education. As a young woman, I found it demeaning."

At this, Miguel's interest was piqued by the possibility of having a disagreement with Anette. "Are you saying that if it's useful, it shouldn't be in gen ed? Surely nothing should be in gen ed unless it *is* useful. That's crazy talk, Anette."

Christine was also unhappy with Anette. "I'm sorry to say this, Anette, but if you found home ec demeaning to your womanhood, I have to seriously question if you fully understand what it means to be a woman. Of all the subjects in the school curriculum, home ec is the one most dedicated to issues of particular value to girls and women and the lives many of them will lead as mothers and homemakers. This is not to say that men cannot be homemakers or caring fathers, or that young girls should not aspire to be engineers, doctors, or professors. It's high time we took the study of women's experiences and gender issues seriously in school. They have real educational value and great potential for the discussion of questions crucially important to all of our well-being. We should also settle on a better name for home ec. Maybe call it 'home and wellness studies' or 'health and wellness.' I believe there's a moral aspect to this, also."

"Go for it, Christine," said Miguel. You know, maybe I was wrong to dismiss home ec earlier."

"And why might you have been wrong, Miguel?" asked Kelly.

"I think I was wrong because now I can see that not only does it contain useful knowledge, it contains knowledge that is essential for all students, in other words, a base of knowledge that is part of gen ed. I mean, we all need to know about good health and good health habits. Maybe that's what my mom means when she keeps saying to my brothers and me, 'Don't they teach you anything in school about taking care of yourselves?'"

"Professor Kelly, I must object," announced Anette, skirting the issue and out of sync with the class discussion. "I don't appreciate being singled out for people to disagree with me in this class. Especially by people who can't speak properly."

Acknowledging what she said but not wishing to be rebuked by Anette for appearing to come to her defense, Kelly decided to bring the discussion back a few steps. "Christine, what did you mean when you said that it was about time we introduced the study of women's experience to general education?"

"Well, our class discussions and the readings have gotten me thinking. Much of what we study in school, like geometry, science, and history, and in college, subjects like philosophy and politics, are largely built around the lives of men and their interests or achievements. This is not to say that women cannot be scientists, philosophers, or historians; it's just that these are subjects that were largely built up by men who were interested in the kinds of things that historians write about, that scientists and business people have an interest in. Their work revolved around these matters. Home ec is different. It is focused on stuff that women have traditionally thought about and worked with, things like homemaking and looking after children and teaching them good health habits."

"What's wrong with studying things men are interested in?" asked Mark.

"I didn't say that. Besides, there's more to it than that," added Christine, putting Mark's question in context. "While home ec is a sort of record of the knowledge that has been amassed—mostly by women—about the things their lives and experiences have been built around, this knowledge is just as essential for men, that is, for being an adult who is able to look after yourself—just as scientific knowledge built up by men is relevant for women too. And there's nothing wrong with everyone studying that."

"I agree," said Serena. "We talk a lot about equal opportunity for women in the workplace, but if women are to have an equal standing there, men will need to be able and willing to do things in the home to pick up the slack. I know that a lot of men do and that they do possess those skills, but I mean all men and every day."

"Able is one thing, willing is another," declared Miguel, as if he were beginning to change his mind again. "Not many dudes I know will buy that."

"Just remember, Mr. Macho," said Anette, "some women can do it all. Professional women, at least."

Although there was an interest in keeping the discussion going, Kelly indicated that time was running out, and he wanted to address a few more issues before the end of the class period. So he began, "One of the most compelling questions that has arisen from our discussion is regarding the place of practical education built around social and personal matters in our lives, that is, as distinct from practical knowledge and reasoning found in tech or engineering and other forms of practical education."

"Could you give us some examples?" asked Jean.

"Of course. Examples of what I call practical education of a social or personal kind would include education in how to take care of ourselves as regards our health and well-being, civics, media and communications, interpersonal relations, and general issues of wellness," Kelly explained. "Some of these areas of study might fall under a broadly conceived program in home economics or wellness education, however it's labeled. But others probably wouldn't, including aspects of environmental education and many forms of political education. Another example that I should mention is service education; the kind of matters it deals with cover a wide range of possibilities, including but also ranging beyond social and personal matters," Kelly added. He pointed out that such matters were dealt with differently in various school systems across the country and the world. This revealed that there was more variance in how they were valued than was the case with the standard academic subjects.

With no time remaining for further discussion, he said, "OK. I think we're done for today."

As students slowly filtered out of the classroom, having spent more time writing in their notepads than was usually the case, Mark had a question for the professor. "Professor Kelly? Can I sue someone in the class for being a patronizing know-it-all?"

CHAPTER 12

Thinking there was no immediate hurry to approach Kelly with questions arising out of her meeting with Price, and realizing that several more issues might pop up once she studied the Midleton schools improvement plan more carefully, Filomena resisted the urge to call him right away. When she spoke briefly with him following the next class, she asked if they could meet for a quick chat—though hoping for a slow one—the following week. Kelly was agreeable, and they decided to fix a time later.

But before any of that, Filomena would be seeing Marilyn to hear an update on her meeting with Sainsbury following the student protest on campus.

***

A few days later, the two got together over coffee before class.

"Marilyn, I can't wait to hear more about your meeting with Dr. Sainsbury. I know you couldn't get into it on the phone, so how did it really go?"

"It was great. She sends you her regards, by the way. And I found out more than I expected," said Marilyn, who seemed to specialize in finding out things. "As it turns out, it was the president who asked her to meet with me; they wanted to give me a heads-up about not getting caught off guard by the wrong people after the protest and all that."

"What do you mean, 'a heads-up?'"

"Well, I mentioned Edwards and his outburst at the committee meeting, which Dr. Sainsbury saw for herself, of course. After I thanked her for having me on the committee, I explained that I thought I'd hate it but actually found it fun except for Edwards. I said to her that he's no ad for gen ed, and then added that she shouldn't have him out front trying to sell anything."

"You said that? Did you really?"

"Sure, I did. I also made a crack that he's no well-developed human being, in my view. He might have a well-developed beer belly,

127

but that's about it I said. She even giggled at that, although I could see she tried not to," Marilyn said, laughing out loud herself.

"Marilyn, you surely didn't say all those things to Dr. Sainsbury. You do realize that she's the vice president of the university, don't you?" exclaimed Filomena, laughing incredulously. "And what did she say to that? Or did she just throw you out?"

"I'll tell you word for word what she said, because besides my dad, nobody has ever said it to me. She said, 'Well Marilyn, you are a charmer.'"

"My God, Marilyn, you are magic!"

"And just as importantly, Filomena, she said that you are a charmer too! Now, how about that? Two charmers for the price of none," said Marilyn, followed by another giggle.

"This is too much, Marilyn," said Filomena. Noticing that time was catching up with them, she continued, "Unfortunately, we've got our classes to attend shortly, but let me tell you about my weekend. I got a job. It's not very demanding, but it pays and I love it. Can you believe it?"

"Golly! The VP is right; you are a charmer. How did you manage that?" asked Marilyn.

"It was simple. Dr. Johnson offered me a fellowship if I would do some work for the Midleton school district on their curriculum plan."

"Yeah, for you, that's not a job at all. Just a source of income!"

With that, they were off to class, plodding their separate ways through the wind and rain.

***

"Good morning, everyone," said Kelly as he entered the classroom with a hand towel draped over his arm. "Let's take a few minutes to dry off and pull ourselves together. This weather makes you want to live in a cave, like you-know-who in our readings!"

Following Kelly's recap of issues that he brought up in several previous days' classes, and before he could dive into the discussion topic he had planned, Filomena raised her hand. Issues she was dealing with in connection with the Midleton school board improvement plan had raised some curriculum questions in her mind, and she thought the class would be an excellent place to hear them discussed.

"Professor Kelly," she began, "before we discussed home economics and related issues in a recent class, the topic of the forms of knowledge in one of our readings came up. I was hoping we could discuss that a little further."

"Do you want to get us started, Filomena?"

"Sure. I agree to some extent with Hirst's forms of knowledge idea, but it reminds me too much of our form courses and area studies here at the Metro. And I agree with Miguel that there are more than seven forms or ways in which we think and know, but I don't think practical subjects like home economics and engineering are all that are needed over and above math, science, and reading if we want an appropriate balance in the curriculum. I think history and art are important, for example, and in college, philosophy. Where do subjects like music, drama, and dance fit in? They are sometimes the object of popular criticism and even ridicule, but are they important to a gen ed curriculum? Whether or not these are disciplines or forms of knowledge, I think they make one a more educated person, although I'm no longer sure exactly what that means."

"Thank you, Filomena. In response to what you say, let's examine how we got to where we are today," said Kelly, turning to what he had planned for that day's class. He talked about the evolution of the idea of a general education, tracing it back to Plato's concept of the philosopher king, Cicero's writings on the orator, the emergence of the *studium generale,* and the seven liberal arts and sciences that accompanied the rise of the university in the Middle Ages, much of which the class had read about over the previous weeks. Kelly laid this groundwork in anticipation of introducing his own alternative idea of a general education. He even brought Newman's reliance on a core of required subjects into the picture before saying a few words about the reading from Mortimer Adler that had been assigned, Hirst's forms of knowledge, and the approach to general education at the Metro.

As Kelly elaborated along these lines, referring to how the idea was understood at the levels of both college and schooling, several students expressed agreement with the concept of general education as they understood it, seeming to agree that one could not be considered an educated person if general education was not a part of their schooling or college education. Yet many of them were outspoken in their dislike of the form courses and area studies model adopted at the Metro, even if several were impressed by what Adler had to say.

Kelly continued, "Newman and Adler believed in a core of essential subjects that were vaguely akin to the form courses and area studies at the Metro. Although I have strong reservations about how we apply our model here at our own university, and I dislike how the idea of a general education has come to be overly glorified by many, I do believe that the idea of a core has some merit. And while I personally favor a reconceptualization of the idea of the educated person, I do not wish to dismiss the contributions of anyone dating all the way back to Plato and Aristotle."

Before ending the class session, Kelly also wanted to tie a few ideas together, beginning with the forms of knowledge raised by Filomena. "You will have noticed that the idea of the forms that got us started today has some broad similarities to the medieval concept of the seven liberal arts and sciences, as well as to the Metro's general education model, which covers quite a span of time. You will also have noticed that the emphasis in these cores is on what are often called academic subjects that are essentially theoretical in character.

Altering his approach a little, Kelly continued, "I should say, I find it noteworthy that these subjects are generally considered a prerequisite to further studies in professional areas such as law and medicine. This is true at many universities today, and it was also true of the medieval university where one had to spend time studying the arts and sciences before gaining admission to the professional schools of theology or divinity, law, and medicine. Even more noteworthy for me, while the arts and sciences are considered a prerequisite to more advanced courses—as are the form courses and area studies here at on campus—the idea of integrating these studies with practical subjects or professional courses in general education is widely rejected in practice. This point became clear at the most recent meeting of COGEM, even though one of our university associations and other groups have recently begun to advocate for such integration.

"I have one final point I need to make, so please bear with me," said Kelly keeping a close eye on the clock. "I've just mentioned that there is a general unwillingness to integrate the teaching of liberal arts content and professional content in our universities, although I favor such integration myself." He then asked if anyone had heard of a man by the name of C.P. Snow. No one had. So he continued,

"Well, C. P. Snow gave a celebrated lecture at the University of Cambridge in England back in 1959, which he later expanded into a book called *The Two Cultures and the Scientific Revolution*. In this work, he argued that the two main intellectual traditions or cultures of the western world—by which he meant the arts or humanities and the sciences—had difficulty understanding each other. This, he believed, poses a grievous threat to our continued well-being. Snow also appeared to suggest that those in the humanities were at a greater loss than the scientists. Educationally speaking, this mutual lack of understanding could be translated to mean that each of the traditions needed to be better informed of the knowledge base of the other. Now, in the 21st century, some 60 years later, I believe we are making just as grievous an error by separating out theoretical studies from practical studies, that is, the arts and sciences from the professional studies, for example." Then, uncharacteristically raising his voice, he continued with emotion and passion. "For crying out loud, the world of theory resides in a world of practice. They cannot be disentangled!"

"This is interesting, Professor," said Jean cautiously as Kelly regained his composure. "But I have to wonder where you stand on all of this yourself. Now that you've said there are features of gen ed that you like and have had us read so many writers that support the idea, I'd like to know more about what your reservations are. I can't imagine how most of us could disagree with Mortimer Adler, or how you could possibly improve on his philosophy."

"I agree with Jean," said Anette. Almost immediately everyone joined in asking Kelly to give them a fuller account of his own take on the idea of a general education.

"Come on, Prof. Cough it up," said Miguel, attempting to lighten the mood. After some laughter and finally an agreeable thumbs up from Kelly, who seemed to have run out of words, they realized with dismay that once more, time was up.

***

As he got started on the next day's class, and back to his usual form, Kelly asked if anyone objected to having a Metro student visit with them the following Tuesday. There being no objections, he explained that because of what he had in mind for the next hour or so, it would be best if everyone had the opportunity to make a little class presentation.

"No, this is not a pop quiz. It's more like a pop presentation. We have done it in class before, so there's nothing new here. To be specific, what I'm asking you to do is just what you asked me to do toward the end of our last class. And there are two parts to it. In about two minutes, please tell the class: (1) What you like or dislike about general education and (2) How you would improve or change it for the future, if at all. You can address the topic either at the level of schooling or college or both. Just be clear about the level you have in mind.

"Also, I'm handing out a sheet of paper to each of you with a place at the top for your name, and five or six boxes printed on it. I'd like you to pick five or six points from what you hear in the presentations, and evaluate them in a short sentence or two. I'll pick these up before you leave, and will return them to you with a checkmark on them at our next session.

"OK. I think we're nearly ready. Who would like to go first?" asked Kelly. "After that, we'll go in alphabetical order by surname?"

Jean volunteered to go first, just beating out Christine for the honor.

When everyone had presented without any major commotion and following some discussion, Kelly collected the sheets of paper, telling the students they were free to go a little earlier than usual that day. Having left in the papers in his office, and with a little more time at his disposal, he and Filomena then went for coffee together in the student center cafeteria to talk about her work with the school board. As they walked and chatted, both comfortable in the other's company,

Filomena explained how her first meeting with Price had gone and that she was asked to provide an initial report by the end of the week.

"That all sounds good, and it looks as though they have some real work for you to do. I'm especially interested in the meaty parts," said Kelly as they sat down.

"There are a few challenges, but only one serious one that I can see at this point," said Filomena, newly aware that there was a side to Kelly that she had not felt before his little display of passion in the classroom the day before, which somehow made him all the more appealing. "The lesser ones include matters such as misspellings, grammatical weaknesses, and, to my surprise, little or no mention of teaching method and not much of a sense of the available curriculum literature on general education. I think I can handle those matters, so I don't want to take any of your time going into detail on them unless you wish to."

"I'm happy for you to keep going, Filomena," he said.

"OK, then let's look at the most serious challenge, as I see it, for this might well determine the value of everything else. It looks like the school board will be making their submission to the federal government in two stages, although I'm not sure that's allowed. The second stage is the curriculum portion of the improvement plan, the part they have asked me to look at."

Following a pause, as if intimating that the challenge was more than just a minor flaw, she continued, "Seemingly, no one aside from the superintendent considered the curriculum to be crucial to the entire project, so they focused on construction and maintenance of school buildings, budgets, union contracts, district organization, and several other such matters. Now, these administrative considerations are surely important, but by downplaying or overlooking the curriculum, I think they've put the cart before the horse, as my grandfather would say. What do you think?"

"I think you're right, Filomena, although I have not seen the documents myself," said Kelly with a degree of resignation, as if he had seen this kind of thing happen before. "Assuming your assessment is correct, and I'm sure it is, that's a fundamental error. Yet, sadly, this is often how school boards treat these things. They don't bring a clear education perspective to bear on these matters. People would rather have the CEO of a corporation or even a celebrity on the board than a few experienced educators with proven professional knowledge."

"My goodness, Dr. Kelly, that's not very good news. What do you think I should do?" she asked with obvious concern.

"First, Filomena, at least outside of class, please call me Pat or Patrick J or even Paddy," he said, bringing a smile to her face.

"I sure will, Pat or Patrick J.," she said enthusiastically.

Returning her smile, he added, "I think you have the makings of a good initial report for Dr. Price. You probably won't be able to correct the obvious error of putting the cart before the horse, but that's really out of your hands. I would be sure to make careful mention of it in your report, however. Itemize your other concerns and how they might be rectified, given the appropriate time to do so."

"Thank you so much. This is really helpful. I know you have a meeting to attend, and I don't want to bother you any further with this right now. I feel prepared to draft a report of my initial reactions for Dr. Price, but if you could cast your eyes over it, I would be very grateful."

"That's a good idea. I'd be happy to read it," he said, believing it to be another way for them to stay in touch outside of class.

"Writing up the report shouldn't take very long because I already have a rough draft outline made out. Would it be OK if I sent it to you this evening? Once I hear back from you, I'll forward it to the superintendent, as she requested."

"That'll be fine," he said. after which, with palpable reluctance, they slowly made their way out of the cafeteria and went their separate ways.

***

Filomena was determined to get her report to Kelly for his comments that evening. Following dinner, and with Rachel tucked away in bed, she set to work on writing it up. In fact, what she sent to Kelly, aside from the emoji, would be little changed from the rough draft she had prepared in advance of their get-together over coffee. She simply expanded and refined it, and sent it off to him before midnight.

Kelly replied promptly, early on Friday morning, suggesting minimal changes. So, with confidence, she sent the report on to Price, who called back, asking if she could come in to meet with Blair and herself later that afternoon.

***

Upset at Conners for having Beame take him to task him over his mistreatment of Filomena and Marilyn at the COGEM meeting, and at Beame, for the attitude he adopted when he called him into his office to follow up on the matter, a riled up and brooding Edwards got on the phone to Conners later that morning, wanting to know when he was going to get a move on with Sainsbury's dismissal.

"She's got to go, Butch," exclaimed Edwards angrily. He did not hide the fact that he and his buddies were getting impatient.

"I know, Joe. I feel your pain. I am trying to wrap this thing up today."

"Let me know how it goes," said Edwards solemnly.

"I will, but first I need to have a word with Dick Blair, chair of the Midleton school board, to see if I can win him over to the idea."

When Conners called Blair immediately following his conversation with Edwards, Blair decided not to take the call and avoid a misdirected harangue from Conners. Besides, with new and inviting possibilities opening up for advancing the improvement plan, he was far keener to focus on what could be done to expedite the advancement of that project. Should Conners persist in trying to reach him by phone, Blair would couch these thoughts a little differently for Conners's consumption.

Having been egged on by Edwards and irritated by not reaching Blair, Conners impetuously decided it was time to make his move. By early afternoon, members of the Metro board had received a summons to a special meeting on November 25 to consider the dismissal of Sainsbury.

"OK, Joe, I've done it," Conners said when he called Edwards to give him the news. "I've called for a special meeting of the board to advance the dismissal project. You should have it in your email by now. Thanks for the push, old chum. It helped to get me over the line. Boy, this will bring Beame to his senses and get that uppity shrew off our backs once and for all," Conners opined to Edwards, who was the first to be told of this action on the phone.

CHAPTER 13

Within half an hour, Beame was on the phone to Conners.

"Butch, I am out of town right now, but what has gotten into you? I'm already inundated with text messages, and I've got more than this to deal with right now," said Beame almost breathless in anger and frustration.

"Look, Jim. I told you I was going to do it, so what the hell are you so strung out about?"

"It isn't just me that you need to be worried about; you'll have half the goddamn board gunning for you over this, I can promise you. Judging by some of the messages I've received, you'll be lucky if you're not the one to be sent packing!"

***

Back in the Midleton school district boardroom, and having only just seen the email from Conners, Blair was more than a little distracted by the news when Price introduced him to Filomena that afternoon.

"It's nice to meet you, Filomena," Blair greeted her, clearly preoccupied with the email from Conners.

"And you," said Filomena.

"Mr. Blair and I want to thank you for coming in today, Filomena, and for your report on your initial reactions to our draft of the improvement plan," said Price as she turned attention to the business at hand. "I have already arranged to have a copy editor revise the report as you suggested, and Mr. Blair and I are still inclined to move forward in our effort to get the non-curriculum phase of the submission sent off following our school board meeting next Monday."

Blair was still stuck on the message from Conners, but forced it out of his mind to focus on the task before him. "We are very interested in your observations on the curriculum phase of the plan, Filomena, and we would like to discuss that more fully. We would also welcome any assistance you can provide as we set about rewriting that part of the plan itself."

Happy to elaborate on what she said in her report, Filomena reaffirmed her view that dealing with the curriculum phase of the improvement plan would be the logical starting point for the entire document.

"Even if the board agrees to send on one part of the submission right away, I believe we should rewrite the curriculum section as if starting the full document from scratch," she said.

Although both Price and Blair would have wished to hear otherwise, they were prepared to accept Filomena's view of the matter and asked her what she thought that meant for the writing of the curriculum section.

"I'm happy to begin drafting it, if you like," said Filomena.

"Thank you," said Blair, "but could you give me a sense of what that means? What subjects will you be including, teaching methods, and that kind of thing, for example?"

"Certainly. I'll follow a format that has been used by many curriculum specialists. Before ever turning to the subjects in the curriculum, that usually involves a consideration of the school values with which you wish to align, and establishing the aims or objectives of the school programs. That will be followed by a review of which school subjects and other worthwhile learning opportunities ought to be included and how they might be best organized for teaching."

Turning to what would be the topic for the next meeting of COGEM as well as the next meeting of EDUC 401, and for which Filomena had already devoured the required readings and more, she continued. "A great deal of vigorous debate has swirled around the question of school curriculum in recent years, as new and challenging views on the content of general education are emerging. We must be cognizant of these issues when considering the composition of the curriculum in Midleton schools. We also ought to consider which pedagogical approaches should be explored. I should point out, however, that I did not see that aspect addressed anywhere in the plan. Lastly, it is important to include a discussion of testing or evaluation of learning at this point, although I know you have already built this into the part of the document you are planning to send on first." As she finished up, Filomena hoped that what she was saying made sense to Blair and Price.

Blair, she thought, seemed to experience some difficulty in keeping up, although no one made any mention of it.

"I think that's about it in general terms. I hope that was helpful," said Filomena.

"Thank you, Filomena," said Price enthusiastically while Blair let on that he too was quite impressed with the young graduate student. "If Mr. Blair is agreeable, I'd like you to begin developing the curriculum portion of our plan. You have an excellent grasp of the issues, and we are glad to have you on our team." Turning to Blair, Price added, "I think it would also be helpful if we could invite Filomena to attend the next meeting of the school board, if she is free."

"Yes, of course," said Blair, seeing as Price thought so.

"Evenings are tricky for me, Superintendent Price, but I'll see what I can do. I'll let you know as soon as possible," said Filomena hopefully.

As it turned out, Filomena's babysitter, who was only called upon infrequently, was able to oblige. Filomena was ready for anything when she arrived for the school board meeting on the following Monday evening. And anything was on the agenda when Conners and Singleton arrived unexpectedly.

***

As members of the school board chatted in small groups while waiting around for others to arrive, Johnson was commiserating with Filomena regarding Edwards's behavior at the recent meeting of COGEM, and he caught the attention of Blair.

"It was embarrassing to see how disrespectful and out of order Edwards was, especially to students," said Johnson.

On overhearing their conversation, Blair joined them. "Is that what led to the protests on campus?" asked Blair. "I'm so sorry to hear that, Filomena. I didn't realize you were involved at all."

"Yes, somehow I found myself caught in the middle of it, Mr. Blair. I'm grateful for how well Dr. Sainsbury handled the rather boisterous affair."

"Yes, Valerie was outstanding. She really showed what a capable leader she is in that appalling episode," said Johnson. This time, Johnson caught the ear of Conners, who had unexpectedly turned up for the meeting. He walked toward their group, fixing his eyes on Filomena and hoping to have a word with Blair. Unaware that he was approaching, Johnson continued. "Even those at the meeting who normally defend Edwards thought he was badly out of line. They agreed that Sainsbury handled the situation evenhandedly and skillfully."

Picking up on the tone of the conversation as he approached and recalling that Beame did not expect board members to welcome the prospect of dismissing Sainsbury without apparent cause, Conners moved away, uncertain of what it all meant for the upcoming special meeting of the board. Instead, he went to join Singleton, as he, too, arrived unexpectedly with a grin of expectant satisfaction on his face. Internal polling indicated Singleton would comfortably win the election following a strong endorsement from the party leader and the unwillingness of the electorate to put two and two together in evaluating his trustworthiness. Singleton had already left word of his good news with TVViews and Radio YOY, in time for their evening news broadcasts. In return, they would be expected to let their audience know that Singleton was, of course, fulfilling his responsibilities to the constituency by attending the Midleton school board meeting.

As the meeting got underway, it became clear to the chair and the superintendent that their desire to submit a phased version of the improvement plan would meet opposition. Nonetheless, they felt they had little choice but to go ahead with their proposal as intended.

Shortly after Blair opened the proceedings, Singleton rose to speak and drew a round of applause from members of the public in attendance. Several of these were party loyalists, putting up a show of strength for their man.

"You can be sure we live in a great country when a candidate for public office can attend a school board meeting the evening before an election," Singleton began in self-congratulatory mode.

Chair Blair quickly put a stop to this.

"I'm sorry, Mr. Singleton, but you are out of order. Please take a seat," he said. "We need someone to second the minutes."

Next, Blair moved to the chief item on the agenda and invited the superintendent to detail the revisions made to the plan since the previous meeting of the board. Price explained that, following further consideration of the matter and broader consultation with members of the community, it was her recommendation that submission of the improvement plan would take place in two stages. Phase II, the adoption of which they proposed that evening, would address administrative and management issues, including construction and maintenance of school buildings, budgets, and union contracts. Phase I of the plan would address the curriculum, which had not been given sufficient additional consideration to date, she added. To clarify, she emphasized that Phase II would be submitted first.

When Price finished her presentation, Singleton was on his feet again to imprint himself on the proceedings and to get his statement into the minutes of the meeting.

"Mr. Blair, ladies and gentlemen," Singleton began, "you can be sure we live in a great country when a candidate for public office— me, in this case—can attend a school board meeting the evening before a historic election. And, uh…" he stammered, trying to splice in the next segment of his prepared remarks, "… my attendance tonight speaks volumes about the support I have attracted in the community over the past several weeks for my opposition to the rush to relinquish local control of schooling to the federal government. Now we're being told by Superintendent Price that she needs more time to hear from the Washington crowd which subjects we need to put into our curriculum. Well, I can tell her what we need: we need the basics. That's what Midleton has always stood for, long before Superintendent Price joined this proud school district," he said to cheers of support from his followers in the sizeable audience.

At the mention of basics, Conners rose in support of Singleton. "It's time we came to our senses and put a stop to socialists and liberals infecting our young people. It's bad enough that we've got this kind of thing going on at the Metro, and if I'm going to put a stop to it there, you can be damn sure I won't stand for it in Midleton schools."

Then, pointing to Price, he demanded, "Math, reading, writing, American history—not social studies—and in high school, physics and chemistry. That's it, Superintendent. This is not rocket science. We don't need Washington and leftist curriculum specialists sticking their nose in our business, training the young to despise our great country, and thinking they know what's best for us. Let's not politicize this."

Once again, it fell to Burnett to address the critics of the proposed improvement plan.

"Mr. Blair, Superintendent Price, ladies and gentlemen, I'm an architect. I'm not a socialist, a liberal, or whatever catchy label anyone wants to pin on me. I'm not even a politician. But I am a Midletonian who loves our town and our country," he began. "I, too, have studied math, reading, writing, American history, physics, and chemistry." Standing up and looking toward Conners and Singleton, who sat alongside one another, he continued. "I've also been to Washington, and I have even read some books by educators like Mortimer Adler, a great American. His ideas are not those of a crazy socialist, I can tell you, and he believes that we need to rethink American education by focusing on the curriculum. All of our public schools need an improvement plan, and it's about time we got on our way with it. So, I move we adopt the recommendation of Superintendent Price without further delay." Then, catching sight of the local TVViews reporter in his periphery, he raised his voice and finished with zeal, "The kind of plan we need is a balanced and fair plan. We recommend; you decide."

This did little to expedite matters other than open the way for a noisy and divisive shouting match, with accusations of pandering mixed in with allegations of infidelity to principled causes, generating the most forceful denials and counteraccusations.

Although they missed the punch-up in one section of the audience as temperatures were raised, the drama was caught on camera by TVViews and was relayed live to the studio.

It was bewildering stuff for Filomena, who sat in the audience bemused and wondering if the schoolchildren should take over policymaking in Midleton schools.

Eventually, as the energy subsided, Blair managed to have someone second Burnett's motion to accept the recommendation of Superintendent Price.

To no one's surprise, the motion was defeated. The TV Views cameramen left the room as some people shook hands, and the meeting was adjourned. As the members left the room, Filomena had a quick word with Price, who asked if she could continue working on the improvement plan.

Filomena also departed and was joined by Johnson, who thanked her for attending the meeting. "Just another day in the trenches," he observed, as he walked with her to her car.

CHAPTER 14

Having finally gotten hold of Blair after the board meeting, Conners tried to explain the reason he wanted to speak with him earlier: He wanted to clarify the supposed miscommunication concerning Sainsbury's dismissal, hoping to play off his proposal to consider the dismissal of the vice president as a simple error. "I only became aware of the confusion my email to board members caused when Jim called to ask what was going on. It's this goddamn secretary of mine," he maintained.

Being well accustomed to political denial talk highlighted on national television during the Mueller investigation and the presidential impeachment process and experienced in dealing with gaslighting double-talkers, Blair did not believe a word of what Conners had to say. Displeased with Conners's contribution to the debate at the school board meeting, moreover, a not-so-gentle rebuke was in order: "But why did you not send out a cancellation memo right away, Butch? That might have set us all at ease. Some of us might even have believed you."

"Yeah, that's what everyone's been saying. It would have been nice to hear that from you when I tried to call you. It's a bit late to hear it now," Conners added, shifting the blame. "Anyway, I'll send it out first thing in the morning, but this is not the end of the debate about gen ed at the Metro. You heard from me tonight how I feel about the basics, and that got strong support. You can bet it'll be the same at the Metro board when I get it back on the agenda there."

The call for a special meeting to consider Sainsbury's dismissal was passed off as a mistake by Conners's secretary and was retracted in an early-morning email sent by Conners to Metro board members the next day. According to the email, Conners merely wished to place a *special item* on the agenda of the next meeting (not call a special meeting) of the Metro board. The intent was to have a more thorough consideration of the continuance of Sainsbury's Committee on General Education and the Major, not the continuation of Sainsbury herself.

After the email went out, there would be no more talk from Conners about the vice president's dismissal. His effort now would turn with a greater sense of urgency to the termination of COGEM.

For this reason, the email also said that since the original special meeting was already scheduled for Monday, November 25, that would remain the date for the meeting at which COGEM was now to be reconsidered. Sainsbury was invited to speak again at the meeting if she wished to make a "more compelling argument" on behalf of her committee than she did at her previous appearance; otherwise, it was "likely doomed."

Having been informed of this, or most of it, by Conners and been further filled in by Beame as soon as he heard about it, Sainsbury was already looking forward to what she might pick up in the way of ammunition for her case to the Metro board from Kelly's next presentation to COGEM. This would take place a few days before that fateful board meeting.

***

When Marilyn accompanied Filomena to Kelly's class that day, she was looking forward to the proceedings and felt somewhat prepared for it, having already heard what Kelly had to say when he first attended COGEM. When Kelly asked her if she wished to say anything once he had introduced her to the class, her reply was vintage Marilyn.

"No, thank you. I'm only here just to cheer."

With that done, Kelly held up some of the papers the students had handed in to him at an earlier class meeting and indicated he would use them as a sort of backdrop for what he had to say. "As you know by now, I am reluctant to merely lecture, preferring to facilitate a conversation, an exploration and exchange of ideas. Yet a lecture seems to be what you would like me to do regarding the idea of a general education, so here is my plan for today."

Reminding the class he had already drawn attention to some of the attractive features of a general education as it is widely portrayed, he promised to address the topic by looking critically at the position of Adler, whose little book, *The Paideia Proposal*, had caught the imagination of the public at large and which the class had already been reading. Adler's ideas were also agreeable to the parents of many of the students, as was expressed in the papers they had submitted. Based on their reading of Adler, several in the class also found his position to their own liking. As Kelly explained, Adler was closely associated with *Encyclopaedia Britannica* and the Great Books program, and he was well-known to the public from his many appearances on PBS.

"Perhaps the main features of Adler's position and its broad appeal," Kelly began, "is the attention he gives to what should constitute the content of a general education, which for him is largely a core of traditional academic subjects, including math and science, history and geography, social studies, a second language, and drama and the arts. He emphasized that all should acquire what he termed the 'skills of learning,' such as reading and writing, and be exposed to Socratic teaching, which promotes understanding of ideas and values. There is little that is unusual about this in the mainstream literature on general education, be it at the level of college or schooling.

"To be clear, I am not saying Adler includes everything that may be essential, and, just as importantly, I am not saying I agree with his argument or reasoning. On the contrary, I believe his argument is erroneous and misleading, and this is one of the reasons his curriculum proposal is deficient, especially in comparison with other writers, such as Dewey and Paulo Freire, who we are also reading in this class. Adler is not sufficiently sensitive to the pedagogical dimension of schooling as they see it. As you know, in previous classes, I explored the positive features of the idea of a general education. I will now focus on some of its failings by looking at key aspects of Adler's position." Kelly paused to inquire if anyone had any questions. There being none, he continued.

"I would first emphasize Adler's failure to build the curriculum content and the teaching methods he advocates upon careful consideration of what he calls the three objectives of schooling: the preparation of students for work, for citizenship, and for personal development. He wants you to believe that he does that, but he actually falls very far short of doing so. He made no attempt to carefully examine what such preparation entails. He did not, for example, analyze the kinds of knowledge, skills, and attitudes that make for becoming a good citizen or achieving success in the workplace.

"Consequently, he failed to critically explore what such preparation would suggest for the selection of curriculum content or subjects. So, as is commonplace in traditional approaches to general education, he simply fell back on the standard subjects and intellectual skills one typically associates with general education, mainly assuming or just accepting that they adequately prepare one for what he considers the callings of life," said Kelly. "Nor did he include preparation for being a member of a family among his objectives for schooling, which could be considered a further weakness in his position."

"May I ask a question?" said Jean, raising her hand.

"Please do," replied Kelly.

"But surely, his are the right subjects. Is that not what colleges and schools all over the country do? Besides, what other kinds of curriculum content or subjects are there, anyway? I still think he's right," said Jean.

"I'll respond to that point more fully in our next class, Jean, so maybe you can raise the point again then. It might be more helpful if I do so while developing my own alternative position, which you have all asked me to do. And which I promise I will get to."

"May I ask a question too, Professor Kelly?" asked Marilyn to everyone's surprise.

"Of course. And I hope you're not just asking if it's OK for you to leave," Kelly said as Marilyn chuckled.

"Not at all. My question is, why do so many people agree with Adler, and why does he argue the way he does? Is it just to sell more of his *Encyclopaedia Britannica*?"

"Thanks, Marilyn. Those questions are both fair and difficult to answer. It's my guess, and I say guess because I have no reliable evidence, that it's not just to sell the encyclopaedia. I think he believes he's right. He seemed to have a fairly dogmatic approach. One of his early books, as an example, was called *How to Read a Book*. To be fair, the title sounds more presumptuous than the contents. As to why so many people believe him or think that way, maybe it's 'groupthink,'" added Kelly half-jokingly.

"That's what I say, Professor, and I said as much to Dr. Sainsbury when I went in to see her the other day. We were chatting about why gen ed gets rave reviews from some folks," Marilyn said to Kelly's surprise.

"You actually said that to the VP?"

"Yeah, and she asked if I could expand on the point," said Marilyn, straight-faced. "I said I thought it was a form of brainwashing."

"Well, this is good to know," said Kelly in his own mind, as he tried to gauge the distance that existed between Sainsbury and himself on the topic he was going to address at the next meeting of COGEM.

"How dare she tolerate you saying that, since she's the one in charge of gen ed at the Metro?" declared Anette, unsure of what to make of Marilyn.

"But she's also the one who established COGEM, you know," Marilyn replied.

"You should hear what my math professor, Dr. Edwards, thinks of that. He's a big advocate of gen ed," came Anette's retort.

"I know, believe me. I've met the man," said Marilyn.

Not wishing it to come to a shouting match, Kelly said there were just a few minutes left in class, and he wanted to add to what he was saying about Adler before time ran out. "I've explained what I think of Adler's approach to general education, but I have said nothing about how I might develop a different position from his. That is what you have asked me to do, and now that I've provided some relevant context, that's what I'll cover next time."

When class was over, Kelly went to have a word with Marilyn to follow up on her conversation with Sainsbury, and he asked Filomena if she could wait for a few minutes because he wanted to ask her about the latest developments regarding the school board's improvement plan.

"It's good to see you, Marilyn," said Kelly. "I enjoyed your input to the class discussion. Tell me, did you get any sense from Dr. Sainsbury as to what she thought of your brainwashing comment?"

"After I elaborated a little on that point, the conversation moved in a new direction. She didn't give much away, but the VP did say I was a charmer before it was all over," Marilyn added with a laugh.

"I think she's right about that," said Kelly.

"She said the same about Filomena too. So, what do you two think of that, now?" she added provocatively, catching the attention of both Filomena and himself, as he was turning to Filomena to inquire about the improvement plan.

"Well, Filomena, how are things at the school board? Are you a member yet?" Kelly asked, trying to deflect attention from Marilyn's remark.

At that, Marilyn excused herself and was on her way with a wave and a smile.

"Things are not going as the superintendent had hoped, I'm afraid," said Filomena, almost blushing. "The proposal to submit any part of the plan was voted down, but Superintendent Price would like me to continue working on it anyway. The meeting was quite a rowdy affair, I must say. It was almost as bad as Edwards at our committee meeting, just without the profanities. Contrary to expectations, Singleton and Conners were in attendance, and they dominated the discussion."

Filomena then went on to speak of Conners, and how she found his behavior odd as people were standing around and chatting before the meeting got started. "He made a beeline toward my group, which included Dr. Johnson and Mr. Blair, as we chatted before the meeting got started. But then he suddenly moved away when he overheard Dr. Johnson say he thought the VP handled the situation surrounding Edwards's abhorrent behavior at the COGEM meeting very well. Mr. Conners then went to join Singleton, who was just arriving."

"That's odd," said Kelly, not really knowing what to make of it. "Anyway, I hope nothing was said or done to bring your involvement with the plan to an end." He felt the urge to put his hand around her shoulders, but resisted.

"On the contrary," she reminded him. "I'll be working on the next revision, which will get started without delay. I hope we can have a chat about it when I've got my part underway."

"I'd love that."

"By the way, you should know that Mr. Burnett, who is on Superintendent Price's side in all of this, brought up Mortimer Adler and seemed to agree with him. He even called him a great American," Filomena cautioned.

"I don't know Burnett, but I'm not surprised to hear that. A great many people view him favorably." Changing the subject, Kelly said, "I wonder what is going on with Valerie Sainsbury. She led me to believe that she would call me for a chat about what I'm planning to say to COGEM at our next meeting. As you probably know, she's asked me to make a presentation to the committee. But I've heard nothing from her lately. That's why I wanted to speak with Marilyn just now, after what she had said in class. I don't know if you know this—and maybe I shouldn't say it, so please keep it to yourself—but Conners tried his darndest to have Sainsbury fired."

"Oh my God," exclaimed Filomena. "I hope it's not because of Marilyn and me."

"No, his distaste for her predates your involvement. If anything, you two might have gotten in the way of his intentions," said Kelly. "Anyway, you didn't get to talk to Conners at all in connection with the school board plan, right?"

"That's right, although I did think his behavior was rather odd, as I told you."

"Yeah. I don't really know Conners myself. But I do believe that he and Edwards are old buddies, and they seem to be of the same mind on many matters," said Kelly as they began to move out of the classroom to make way for the next class coming in.

"He also sided very strongly with Singleton at the school board meeting, and he seemed to be very chummy with him too. I'm sure you heard that Singleton won the election the other night," said Filomena.

"Yes, I saw that. We'll see how it all works out. Anyway, I think I'll give Valerie a call to see what's up with her," he said as Filomena fidgeted for her car keys. She thanked him for inquiring about her work on the improvement plan, and they parted ways.

***

Kelly's planned statement for the upcoming meeting of COGEM was not foremost in Sainsbury's mind, as he learned when he called her.

She had just heard from Beame that Conners's plan to pursue her dismissal had been dropped and would not be resurrected.

"My dismissal is now off the table, I believe. It seems as though Conners figured out a pretext for getting himself out of the jam he caused with that. In any event, it's welcome news, I must say. But the board meeting that was called to consider my termination will now be asked to consider the termination of COGEM instead."

"You're kidding me. I thought the committee was secure at this point."

"Apparently not. It survived the first hearing, but now we have to face a second go-around. But I'm beginning to think that Conners is losing credibility among Metro board members, so I'm hopeful."

"Well, Valerie, I'm sorry to hear of the ongoing trial of COGEM, but I'm relieved that at least the threat of your dismissal is a thing of the past."

"Me too. On a happier note, I'm very much looking forward to your next presentation to COGEM. Maybe I can pick up something to bring to the committee's defense for the Metro board meeting. By the way, I should warn you that it can be rough and tumble with some of those COGEM folks, especially if Edwards decides to act the ignoramus."

"You mean it's just an act? I always thought he was the genuine item."

"Yeah, true. It's not quite as bad as Murryfield U in there, but I think it's best if you don't stand on ceremony. Mix it up with them like you did last time. You'll be a target anyway since you're an invited hometown speaker."

Changing the subject, Sainsbury added, "By the way, I believe someone is now writing a lengthy *exposé* of Murryfield U. That'll be a humdinger, I bet."

***

"Thanks for checking in, Marilyn," said Associate Dean Wang when she dropped in to see him in his office in the business school that afternoon. "What's the news from your committee?"

"Do you know this Edwards creep?" Marilyn asked by way of response.

"Not very well. I just know him from serving on the university curriculum committee, which he thinks is his baby. He has been the secretary of that committee for years, long before I got here. He's always struck me as a self-important blowhard. But tell me, how creepy is Sainsbury? I don't know her very well, either, but between you and Edwards, I trust you are keeping her in check."

"I like Dr. Sainsbury, but she has not really shown her hand yet. She's very astute. She clearly doesn't care for Edwards, but then again, I don't know who could. I certainly won't be taking sides with him."

"You don't mean you'll be on Sainsbury's side if she advocates for this 'less is more' stuff that I hear she talks about? I know you don't care for the current gen ed regs, but I don't want you backing anything that would mean changes for our school, Marilyn. We've got things pretty well set up for us as they are, and we don't want change. Change is for left-wingers, Marilyn, unless it's good for business, of course."

"Who told you about 'less is more?' It wasn't Edwards, by any chance?"

"Yes, he did bring it up in the faculty lounge one afternoon. It didn't make much sense the way he talked about it."

"He isn't fit to talk about that, Dr. Wang. He hasn't got a freakin' clue about what it means. He doesn't make much sense of anything, it seems to me. I mean, properly described, 'less is more' could be advantageous for the major in the business school. I could take more courses and that kind of thing in surveillance services, for example, if I had fewer fluff requirements in gen ed. Delve deeper into my major for greater understanding. My friend Filomena tells me that's important, and she's a strong supporter of gen ed."

"Well now, Marilyn, don't you think our faculty has enough teaching to do without having to teach more courses in surveillance services and the like? We're pretty much full up as it is."

"I don't feel full up, Dr. Wang. I'd like 'less' gen ed stuff and 'more' surveillance services if you see what I mean. Just think of what more surveillance services content could mean for my major."

CHAPTER 14

Wang was, in fact, beginning to get a sense of what it could mean.

"Thank you, Marilyn," said Wang, beginning to change his attitude. "Maybe I should go chat with Dr. Sainsbury and feel her out about all of this. And do check in with me again. I'll be interested to hear what you learn."

When Marilyn left, Wang began to consider the possibilities in how Marilyn viewed the 'less is more' notion, and he thought he should explore it with the vice president before it came to the attention of his dean.

***

Sainsbury was more than a little curious as to why Wang wished to meet with her about COGEM. He was the only person outside of arts and sciences to ask for a meeting in that connection since the last committee meeting. Hopefully, Marilyn had not gone running to him to complain.

"Thanks for seeing me," Wang said to Sainsbury on his arrival to her office the following morning.

"The pleasure is mine. How can I be of help?"

Wang began with an unsettling introduction. "I've been chatting with Marilyn, who serves on your committee. When she agreed to serve, I asked her to check in with me from time to time, which she did yesterday."

"That's good to hear," said Sainsbury cautiously.

"She informed me that your committee has talked about what she calls 'less is more.'"

"That's true. We have discussed that idea in part to get the discussion going."

"Marilyn seemed to think it could be used to promote additional course work in her major, which rather took me by surprise. I wondered if you have any thoughts in that regard."

"Nothing that I have emphasized or have even given much thought to."

"But you have given it some thought?" he asked, trying to figure out how much credit he might be able to earn by intimating that his upcoming suggestion was entirely his idea.

"That's right," she said, unsure of what he was getting at.

"I would like to suggest that you push the idea. I see great potential here for upgrading both our undergraduate and graduate programs. If we were allowed greater space in our undergraduate programs, for example—space now occupied by what many of us in our business school see as unnecessary gen ed courses—we could surely improve what are already outstanding programs by enriching them with more advanced content," he said with enthusiasm. "This would give our undergraduate students an even better educational experience, further improving our school's reputation. But there would also be other benefits; with the additional faculty needed to implement this proposal of mine, we could similarly upgrade our graduate programs for correspondingly desirable outcomes at the graduate level," he said, continuing to press his case.

Sainsbury's reply was predictable. "While it is certainly a laudable idea, Dr. Wang, we don't have the financial resources to support hiring additional faculty in your area."

"But you surely would with a little reallocation of resources. With a reduction of courses and faculty devoted to unpopular subjects and remedial gen ed courses such as Arithmetic Around the World, funding would become available for this purpose. It's a no-brainer, don't you see?"

"Let me say, this, Dr. Wang. If it's so obvious, as you suggest, why don't you come along to one of our committee meetings and bring it up there to see what reception it might find," said Sainsbury, not wishing to be the one to draw the wrath of the arts and sciences people for even raising the idea in committee. "In fact, we're meeting this afternoon. As you know, I have invited all members of the faculty to attend this meeting of the committee, where I am asking Dr. Patrick Kelly from the Department of Curriculum and Teaching to make a presentation. He is a highly regarded scholar with expertise on the topic. He has written widely on general education, and his upcoming book deals with the role of the major."

Sainsbury's unwillingness to outwardly express a favorable view toward Wang's suggestion notwithstanding, after he left, she too began to see some advantages in the notion, and she wondered what Kelly would have to contribute on the matter.

CHAPTER 15

As members of COGEM gathered in the university council room for the much-publicized November 22 meeting, there was an air of anticipation; this was no ordinary meeting of the committee, since all faculty members had been invited to attend and Kelly was asked to make a formal presentation, much as would a keynote speaker at a scholarly conference. As an added attraction, the image that had been conjured up on campus by Edwards' recently embellished notoriety ensured a well-attended event. Eyes would be trained on Edwards as much as on Kelly.

Once the usual introductory formalities were attended to and the minutes of the previous meeting were adopted, Sainsbury clarified that the gathering was mainly a meeting of COGEM and that the order of proceedings would be conducted accordingly. Having already thanked Kelly for agreeing to make a presentation and indicating that there would be a Q&A session to follow his talk, she also said that Kelly was open to taking questions during his presentation as well. She then invited him to speak.

"When I previously spoke of general education before this committee, I refrained from the use of curse words, and I shall attempt to maintain that approach today," he began to the amusement of some. "I also endeavored on that occasion to review the historical evolution of the tradition of a liberal or general education, and to highlight what I believe are its strengths. With that on the record, today I shall aim to develop an alternative stance to what is the prevailing view and widespread practice. I will not dwell on what I consider to be their weaknesses, although it may be necessary to advert to some of them.

"In formulating my own views on general education over the years, I am following in the footsteps of a handful of others who have gone beyond a mere critique of existing practice by venturing into the uncertain territory of suggesting an alternative way of conceiving or imagining general education. This builds upon my critique of general education, which, while implicit in what I will say here, is made quite explicit in several places that I will be pleased to share with any of you if you'd like to follow up on that. In expressing my alternative stance, which differs in fundamental ways from widely held practices and idealizations, I shall nonetheless adopt the commonly held view that the primary purpose of general education is to empower the individual person to attain his or her full potential compatible with living harmoniously with others in a community of fellow beings.

"Having said just that, forgive me if you think I have nothing to add to widely held views and promotional talking points for general education as the pathway to personal development, since this appears to be an objective shared by all." As the nodding of heads around the room indicated, many were satisfied with this take on general education. "Of course, I do believe I add something new and challenging, for many of the lofty claims to foster the full potential of young people that are found in college mission statements and the like are misplaced and misleading. I can show that be restating a little differently what I have just said.

"When I expressed my view of the purpose of general education as empowering the individual person to attain his or her full potential compatible with living harmoniously with others in a community of fellow beings, there appeared to be a good deal of agreement on that point. But now, let me express that view in a way that might not be found quite so agreeable: I view the purpose of general education as enabling the young to deal successfully with what Mortimer Adler terms the 'callings' or 'vocations' in life that are common to all of us. Adler identifies these as the call to work, to citizenship, and to personal development. Others use different language, but appear to have much the same idea in mind."

With these words, there came an audible sigh of incredulity from the gathering, and many hands shot up.

"That's outrageous," said a professor from ancient classics, not meaning to be rude but feeling unfairly put upon. "What does general education have to do with preparing our students for work or for anything, for that matter? General education has no such ulterior ends. General education is an end in itself."

Kelly nodded in thought. "If that is so, then why is it widely claimed that general education programs are the best preparation for life, for further studies, and for entry to the professions? That association was central to the idea of gen ed as it began to emerge with the rise of the university in the Middle Ages." When this was greeted by a protracted silence, Kelly went on, "To make matters worse, this claim that general education is the best preparation for life is a suspect claim in the first place."

"What do you mean it's a dubious claim, Kelly? Is this not why we are here?" came a question from someone else that cast as much doubt on the point of the first question as it did on Kelly's point.

"It's suspect because little, if any, sustained effort to establish and carefully characterize what 'preparation for life' requires of us is found in the promotional language advocating for general education today. There is no exhaustive analysis of what is required as a preparation for the vocations of living common to all people, as Adler put it. It is necessary to examine these callings or vocations and what they require by way of education before rushing to lay out a program of study and then running around trying to sell it to an unsuspecting public."

"I can't accept that," responded an older gentleman.

"And why not?" asked Kelly.

"We all know what's needed, just as we have over the centuries," said this man, adding that he was from economics. "This tradition that you denounce goes all the way back to antiquity. Maybe you need to brush up on your history, Professor Kelly."

"With respect, sir, the mere fact that the tradition dates back to antiquity does not show that it has examined the educational implications of the callings or vocations in life common to us all. But let's not get bogged down on the historical dimension of this, if you don't mind," suggested Kelly, and he returned to his presentation. "In looking forward rather than backward, I wish to share a more speculative phase of my thinking, what I label a 'theory of progressive general education.' Maybe such a theory has not yet been widely articulated, but it is emergent.

"I recognize that the word 'progressive' is a naughty word in some circles, but it's also a proper characterization of the position I adopt relative to general education. It embodies two principles of progressive education as it came into existence in the early decades of the 20th century."

"You're beginning to sound like John Dewey all right," said the man from economics, as if to denounce such an association.

"Yeah, that's Dewey, the Trotskyite," came another voice expressing agreement with the economist.

Without objecting to the banter and pressing ahead, Kelly explained that the word 'progressive' and the theory he was advancing "welcomed active and participatory forms of 'experiential learning' and are sensitive to the perceived needs and interests of students. Understandably, progressive general education is not nearly as well defined as the traditional theory. Yet, as I say, various expressions of it are increasingly represented in the scholarly literature."

Unsure if those in attendance had much familiarity with this literature, even if Filomena had, and aware of the resistance being expressed, Kelly altered his approach a little. "OK, let me make a generalization. The conceptualization of progressive general education is coming together around a notion that is anathema to traditional thinking, that is, it favors the inclusion of practical knowledge and reasoning within the idea. In one of his books on curriculum, John White underscored what he terms the 'primacy of the practical,' and argued that we ought to approach thinking about the curriculum by viewing the student as an agent rather than as a knower."

With this, the chair of the English department, Professor Gordon Cameron, felt the need to set the record straight, and raised his hand as if for permission to speak. "I don't mean to interrupt, Professor Kelly, but surely human beings are knowers. If they were not, why would we have universities? Why would there exist our proud tradition of a liberal arts education, to which English literature contributes so wonderfully, even if much of it has now been lost or should I say, worse still, discarded by our deplorables?"

"Hi, Professor Cameron. It's good to see you. but I'm afraid I don't accept what sounds like a right-wing talking point about good literature being lost. I keep falling over it every time I visit our library and the campus bookstore," said Kelly. "As for the other matter you raise, no one denies that human beings are knowers. The point here is that we can approach a topic or problem from different perspectives. Just because one may view a political issue from a Nationalist perspective, as someone like Frank Mobilo would, does not deny that there is a contrary Patriot perspective held by someone such as the newly elected congressman Wayne Singleton. Similarly, we can approach general education by viewing learners as persons with capacities and interests in doing and making and not merely reading and reflecting on issues; or to be more extreme, activists as distinct from contemplatives. There is more than one way to live a life, so why privilege the contemplative over the activist? Better still, perhaps, why not try to accommodate a range of perspectives, which is my personal inclination?"

With no rebuttal from Cameron, Kelly continued. "A distinction made in higher education over the years between the so-called liberal arts and sciences and practical or professional studies such as medicine and law has also been called into question of late. Rather than perpetuating their independence from each other or separating out such different forms of knowledge from one another, their interdependence is now emphasized by some. This not only as it does occur in the research sphere, but also in teaching and general education itself."

"You don't have to have a med school to be a university," interjected Edwards. "And are you trying to say that the Metro should have subjects in our business school integrate with arts and sciences? Not here, sir! No way!"

"I think you've missed the point, Joe," said Kelly, but instead of directly engaging with Edwards, he continued with his planned line of discussion, believing it was still pertinent to Edwards's remark. "In the traditional idea, a distinction is drawn between liberal and professional education because practical knowledge associated with the professions was considered contrary to the notion of pursuing knowledge for its own sake. What I am saying is that this is now questioned by authoritative sources in higher education in favor of the view that in general education, there are benefits to be gained from integrating liberal arts and science subjects with the professional or practical, and vice versa."

At this, Torino raised his hand to speak with Edwards at his elbow. "Who are you kidding, Professor?" he began, Edwards-like. "As leaders of the union on this campus, Dr. Edwards and I keep our eye on all of these authorities, as you call them."

"Yes," added Edwards, "we know well what they have to say."

"Tell me, then, what do you make of the position that the AAC&U takes on this matter?" asked Kelly. "Or some of the research supported by the Carnegie Foundation?"

"You tell us what you think," replied Torino uncomfortably.

When Kelly began to move on, Edwards added his two cents. "There you go again, Professor Kelly, passing the buck."

Implying she wished that Kelly would be allowed to make his presentation without trivial interruptions, Sainsbury pointed out to the surprise of almost everyone that the AAC&U and Carnegie have been strong proponents of greater collaboration between departments in the arts and sciences and professional schools for some time, and then gave way for Kelly to continue.

Departing from his script, Kelly said, "Personally, I go even further than that and reject the assertion that practical knowledge and reasoning is unfit for inclusion in a program of general education. As I view it, students who are not exposed to practical learning are deprived of the benefit of encountering knowledge and understanding that can be gained only from some level of involvement in practical affairs—and which, every bit as much as a classical liberal arts course of study, has no ulterior goal in mind. Consider this: If you saw a child trying to gain his or her balance on a bicycle, would you assume that child was learning to ride a bike to become a professional cyclist? Or would you conclude that the child simply wanted to know how it's done and how to perfect the skill? And could that insight and skill development be acquired from merely reading about it or submitting to a lecture on it? When educational authorities fail to recognize the point I'm making, I believe they do students a grievous injustice that is the result of an incomprehensible oversight in traditional theorizing on general education."

"That's ridiculous, Professor Kelly," protested someone with more than a hint of disbelief. "Surely you cannot mix conceptual learning with practically oriented content. Maybe you can mix arithmetic and woodwork in a vocational or tech school, but not in a seat of higher education. Cicero would be turning over in his grave."

"On the contrary, I would argue that Cicero, for whom oratory may have been viewed as the highest form of intellectual activity, was an early advocate," replied Kelly. "In fact, as I understand him, all liberal arts as he put it, were viewed as an aid or ally to the professional knowledge of the orator. He believed that drawing on history and classical literature enabled the orator to enrich and embellish his language and to sway his audience. I even wonder if that is where the AAC&U got their idea," he added half-seriously.

There being no response again, Kelly pressed on. "As I pointed out earlier, few efforts have been made to formulate a fully comprehensive statement of progressive general education. So, I will now point to some salient aspects of what a holistic view and the thinking behind it might look like. Such an education would incorporate practical knowledge and reasoning essential to gaining a fuller understanding of the world we live in. It would accept that the education of the whole person encompasses goals of emotional, moral, and spiritual formation, alongside narrowly defined intellectual formation. It also would reject the view that such all-around formation means pursuing merely useful ends. Instead, I suggest, it would enable us to attain more successfully than a conventional academic approach the universally agreed-upon goal of general education, that is, personal fulfillment. These are the values of progressive general education. So, I conclude that a person who is educated to deal with the vocations or callings of life is a person of many-sided or all-around development based upon exposure to a broadly based curriculum that is entirely liberal in character, even as it includes practical knowledge and skills along with theoretical or academic knowledge."

"But surely that's a contradiction," said Cameron, speaking up again. "How on earth can you have a general education that draws on both liberal and practical knowledge and still claims to be 'education for its own sake?' You've lost me already, Professor Kelly. Now I'm thinking we inhabit different universes, and I'm inclined to stay in Metroland."

"Now we're getting somewhere," burst in Edwards, thinking he needed to agree with the chair of English but not making much sense. "I've said it many times: Half of the tripe we get in here are blank slates. As Yeats said, our job is to fill 'em up. That's just what our form courses and area studies do!"

Taken aback, Kelly responded, "Yes, I am aware that there are those among us who believe our students are in some cases, blank slates or empty vessels needing to be filled up. Those who believe this, like Joe here, disagree, of course, with one whose work Joe celebrates out of one side of his mouth while rejecting it out of the other. For, it was none other than William Butler Yeats who wrote that 'Education is not the filling of a pail, but the lighting of a fire.'"

Moving on, Kelly decided to use these words from Yeats again to introduce his next point. "I also argue for an additional requirement in general education, for which the words of Yeats provide a helpful backdrop. This is the recognition of a pedagogical dimension—some might say a psychological component—often overlooked in traditional theorizing. In rethinking general education, it is necessary to view learners not as empty pails on entering school or college classrooms but as persons of varying experience, and know-how or practical knowledge. This experience surely reflects different cultures and value orientations. Since a good deal of what our undergraduates know exists at a commonsense level, it may not be as well organized as it could be. Yet, as Dewey would argue, this is but the starting point from which such commonsense knowledge is to be nurtured. Such nurturing toward and integration with systematized knowledge or theory as it exists in the academic disciplines, for example, is the responsibility of well-prepared teachers and professors."

"Are you saying that the kids who come to the Metro are empty-headed dullards?" asked Torino.

"Stay quiet, Vic," said someone. "You've lost track again."

"Thank you, whoever said that," responded Kelly as he returned to his prepared remarks once more.

"Now, I don't mean to be offensive in what I have to say next because it relates directly to our approach to general education here at the Metro: I reject outright the imposition upon all students of a one-size-fits-all, predetermined, monolithic curriculum format. Sadly, this is present in both theory and practice today, not to mention the absurd heights to which it is elevated here at the Metro. In recognizing the imperative of the pedagogical dimension to which I've just alluded, I join with progressive educators and seek a new way forward, a way that calls for a more nuanced understanding of the curriculum content of a general education. It recognizes and accepts the diverse experiences that students bring with them. It acknowledges that, at least in some respects, a curriculum for one may need to be quite different from that for others."

As Kelly stopped to drink some water, Sainsbury had a question. "If we cannot lay down a curriculum before we know our students, does that not make formal education in schools and colleges almost impossible? Yet we do seem to meet with success even with our current practice."

"I recognize that this poses quite the challenge," Kelly acknowledged, "so let me take a stab at responding to your question. As you know, the standard question regarding the curriculum of a general education has and continues to be, 'Which subjects do we include and why?' In progressive general education, as I view it, that question is replaced by this one: 'How should teachers, professors, and the curriculum respond to the particular needs of different students?' For sure, detailed answers cannot be provided to this question in the abstract or without knowing those for whom it is intended. Yet this does not mean that we cannot work around this reality, for that is what it is. I argue that it is possible to develop guidelines or curriculum parameters to steer us, not one-size-fits-all, inflexible pigeonholing. Most of our students are probably already following such self-selected guidelines when they choose their majors, realizing what their own experience, interests, and talents are telling them. And of course, individualized academic guidance from professors can be of great help here too. But that is not how we approach our general education requirements, at least here at the Metro, and for me, that remains a problem."

"OK. This will call for a great deal of planning and personalization of the curriculum, I fear. But I think I can live with that, at least for now. Thank you, Dr. Kelly," said Sainsbury.

"And with that, I think it's about time for me to wrap it up, anyway," said Kelly. "So, in conclusion, let me add this: Admirable past achievements of traditional liberal education have enabled many to grow toward intellectual excellence as it has been traditionally defined for purposes of general education. I say this truthfully and not merely to pander to those of you who favor the traditional view. Yet I must add, these are limited achievements, confined as they are to a narrow and inadequate concept of intellectual excellence. On their own, they do not enable us to attain our full development as human beings, or as Freire put it, our vocation to become more fully human. To attain this ideal, Freire believed that we need to engage in reflective action for the betterment of all. Accepting the key features of more progressive general education, this fulfillment is to be achieved through praxis, that is, through reflection and action to change the world for the better. In this way, the learner is capable of naming (or changing) the world, and not merely reading the word or observing the world. If this can be achieved by rethinking general education, the social and educational consequences may be very considerable. So, with that, I'll say thank you for your time and attention, and let's go, Metro!"

Predictably, reaction to Kelly's presentation was mixed. The student members of the committee, many of the younger faculty, and a good sprinkling of more senior faculty stood to applaud. The disgruntled kept their heads down, waiting for the Q&A session to follow.

Once the Q&A session got underway, Jackson was the first to speak from the floor. "Thank you, Pat. That was illuminating. I hope our committee will transform some of your ideas into recommendations, and that we will all have the opportunity to implement some of your ideas in our programs and in our teaching," she began. "As a political scientist, I would love to work with faculty outside and even inside of arts and sciences. I could see myself working with faculty in the schools of business and engineering, and I would welcome collaboration with the curriculum and teaching or urban planning departments, for example. And while this may be of great benefit to the programs we offer, as well as to our students, I can see that another benefit could be a greater sense of camaraderie among faculty. Our athletic teams promote that to a degree, and this could be another way of doing so."

Next to speak was Jennifer Armstrong, chair of history. "Thank you for your excellent presentation, Pat. I welcome the fresh perspective you bring to the discussion of general education at the university. Yet, I'm also a bit of a traditionalist. I mean, I do believe that along with math and science, literature and the humanities in general still have a great deal to offer our students. Not to mention the classics. So, I'm a little concerned that you appear to play down their contribution."

"It's not so much that I wish to downplay their contribution, Jennifer, but I do not wish to overlook other potentially valuable subjects and learning opportunities," began Kelly in response. "When you look at the literature on general education, especially as it is treated in higher education, there is a strong tendency to do just that. Besides, the curriculum structures we find in many of our universities are such that even permitting a modicum of curriculum innovation and novel subject integration is a serious challenge. The more established subjects in higher education, such as math and the sciences, and maybe even history, don't need much support from me in this circumstance."

"Hi, Dr. Kelly, I'm Maurice Trudeau, a recently appointed assistant professor in modern languages," began the next person to speak. "Along the same lines, I am surprised you had little to say about modern languages and the value of literature and the arts in general."

"Thank you for making this point, Maurice, but I would respond in much the same way as I did to Jennifer," said Kelly. "I would add, the structures I just referred to also minimize opportunities for students to explore possibilities that we who are aged enough to be on faculty can't even conceive of in a rapidly changing world. We cut off these opportunities from many of our students by our overreliance on constraining structures."

"Hi, I'm Peter Zaleyev. I'm in linguistics, Professor Kelly, and I agree with Noam Chomsky that we are all born with inherited capacities of mind, with an innate knowledge of grammar, but that we need to nurture those capacities just like our innate capacity to walk upright requires that we are nurtured in doing so. So, my question is, how do you address that challenge from a progressive standpoint if it is up to the student to determine what he or she is to learn?"

"Hi, Peter. I'm not in a position to argue with you about the views of Professor Chomsky. But I take issue with your understanding of progressive education because I do not see it as leaving it up to the students to determine what they are to learn. Dewey, for one, believed it was the role of the educator to aid the young to become citizens of a democratic society and to grow in the knowledge, skills, and understanding of such a society insofar as their capacities enabled them. Just because he believed that the educator ought to take cognizance of the experiential level of young people in aiding them on this journey is not to be taken as saying that the student should call all the shots. In my view, those who fail to consider the experiential level of the learner ought to be the object of criticism. Dewey became a punching bag for those who disagreed with his social and political leanings, but this does not mean his educational views were deficient, any more than Rousseau's politics meant he was mistaken in his understanding of child development. Despite his disagreements with Dewey, Adler was astute enough to see this and chose to dedicate his book, *The Paideia Proposal*, to Dewey, Horace Mann, and Robert Hutchins."

Anxious to get another word in, Edwards rose to his feet once more. "I have a question, not just a softball comment about this pie-in-the-sky Dewey romanticism, now that you've brought it up. Actually, I have several questions. What you say about the Dewey crowd does not mean we should be hand-holding or allowing students to decide what they want to learn. It's we, professoriate, who know what they need, not them. Rigor is more important than coddling. Math, history, the sciences—that's what the kids of today need, not social studies from commies and socialists like your friends Dewey and Freire. Next, you'll want feminist theory calling the shots. The Metro isn't a kindergarten, you know."

"Joe, we've got to present material to our students in a way that they find interesting and meaningful, in a way that they can enjoy it and cope with the challenges it presents. If that's coddling or just a load of feminist baloney, then I'm all for it," said Kelly.

"But that's what our gen ed does. We've identified where all these kids should be, and we've laid out where they've gotta go next. It's all there in our form courses and area studies, sir. Besides, we do make allowances," said Edwards, warming to the exchange. "For example, we allow science, math, and engineering majors to fulfill some of their English requirements by taking Technical Writing 101 instead of Literary Analysis 101 or The Poetry of Shakespeare," he added boastfully.

"My God," interjected Filomena, uncontrollably aghast. "That's an abomination. Don't you realize that's a complete abdication of the very idea your form courses and area studies model pretends to uphold? What on earth does technical writing have to do with the appreciation of literature or seeking to understand the ideas and values it reflects upon?"

"Well, Miss Smarty-pants, you are back, I see. Just remember that your argument is not with me. You should take it up with one of the organizations concerned with distribution requirements for gen ed courses, where I learned of it. We check our sources carefully, you know," said Edwards, completely failing to grasp the point of Filomena's objection. Following a quick consultation with Torino, he explained that it was by checking such sources that they came up with their form courses and area studies model. That was also how they came up with the phrasing for the handbook they 'published' on distribution requirements for general education at the Metro.

"So, let me ask you, Joe," began Kelly.

"Which reminds me, Dr. Kelly," said Edwards, cutting him off, "it really does disturb me to think that lefties like you are in the business of educating our future teachers, people like this supposed grad student who I know is in one of your classes. You are living proof that Hirsch is right when he says the cultural left has come to dominate our schools."

"Before you set another student protest in motion, Joe, let's get back to your form courses and area studies approach to general education. When you interrupted me, I wanted to ask: Why do so many of our students find our general education requirements to be such a burden, as you say they do?"

"You mean the burden should be on us to individualize the curriculum for each kid?" responded Edwards, deflecting. "As I said, the Metro isn't a kindergarten. We don't have that kind of time around here. You do realize there are deadlines, right?"

Kelly responded, "So, we insist that everyone takes one course from Math 101 or 102 or 103 and another from English 101 or 102 or 103 and the like. You realize that this is why we have 15 sections of Math 101 and English 101, and so on each semester. And we have highly qualified professors teaching so many 100-level courses, they don't have time to teach advanced courses. These advanced-level courses are the kind that students need to have a real major, where they can feel academically challenged and motivated to explore further. And here you are, trying to tell me you're not running a kindergarten!"

"Instructors for our intro courses are well qualified, for sure, and anyway, some of them are even associate professors," said Edwards. "They are also adaptable to our gen-ed conditions, and they know how to provide the requisite learning experience, I might add," replied Edwards, who had clearly not expected this line of questioning, and veered off the point.

"And," Kelly added, "at the same time, we have highly qualified faculty members frustrated at not being able to teach courses at levels that a true and more individualized major requires, and from which they would benefit if they could teach them. Getting back to the nub of the issue, Joe, why can't there be more flexibility in your model? That could allow courses that qualify for general education to better reflect the major that a student chooses. Some universities do that. And so what if that means there is greater variety in the courses that students choose to fulfill their general education requirements?"

"So you want a kind of gen ed that is not really gen ed at all, is that it?" asked Edwards. "I mean, how can it be gen ed if it's different, or to use one of your fancy words, individualized for everyone. That's a contradiction, can't you see?"

"Well, if it is, then maybe general education is not the way to go. Maybe the error lies in thinking one size fits all."

"So, you propose having a university that has no gen ed. You mean we should be a tech school?"

"I don't mean that at all, not that there's anything wrong with tech school. I just believe there must be more than one way of being a university. Universities did evolve over time, you know. There is no preordained straitjacket into which they must fit. Not all are or ever were the same."

"If I may, Dr. Sainsbury," Wang interjected, "before we leave the topic of multiple sections of Math 101 and English 101 and the like, I wish to return to the issue raised by Dr. Kelly, where he questioned the practice of teaching endless sections of entry-level courses. We permit these courses at the cost of frustration to the faculty who have to teach them and who are then unable due to lack of space allowed for the major to teach more advanced courses that would enable our students to be competitive with graduates of universities elsewhere in the world. Colleagues of mine believe these universities bring their students to more advanced levels in their majors. I am familiar with graduates of British universities, where I am regularly asked to be an external examiner. These British students have spent almost all their time in university studying just one or two subjects."

Not noticing the frowns on the faces of faculty members seated behind and around him who felt uneasy at the thought of universities from another country somehow being ahead of the Metro, and just as uncomfortable at the idea of calling for change, Wang continued, "I realize that the British model has been the subject of some criticism too, but maybe there is a middle way or another alternative to how the Metro does it, a way we could restructure faculty hiring to cut down on the number of faculty hired to teach endless sections of Math 101 or English 101 and the like. We could use the monetary savings to enable those of us in the business school or any other department to hire more faculty to teach a greater number of advanced courses for our majors. Does your thinking take you down that road, Pat?" he asked, provoking more than just frowns of unease.

"Take it easy there, folks," objected Cameron, jumping in before other department chairs could, fearful that their departmental fiefdoms may be endangered, and as the unease in the gathering became tangible. It was as if the hallowed university council room itself were under siege by such an irresponsible notion. "Ideas such as those intimated by Dr. Wang," said Cameron in the affected fashion he reserved for such occasions as this, "are not for promulgation previous to judicious scrutiny and scholarly debate; they are not for unreflective enunciation in a place so revered as the university council room. We have our values and venerable traditions to which we hue. Of course, these include the traditions of English literature in all its grandeur. We also hold dear the traditions and values of the trivium and the quadrivium. We can look backward as well as forward."

Deriding in his own mind the drift of Cameron's remarks, Kelly wished to respond to Wang's point, and he did so before others could express further outrage. "What you raise here, Dr. Wang, are issues I treat at some length in my forthcoming book. Undoubtedly, this question poses a challenge to the way that colleges and universities across the country conduct business today; the Metro is not alone in this. And yes, I believe that these issues deserve serious and urgent reflection by faculty in all disciplines and at all levels, and without a doubt, they ought to be considered in a committee such as this one. They also have significant implications for graduate study, for faculty research and funding, and for the overall stature and research orientation of our university. Thank you for raising the point and for drawing it to the attention of the faculty at large. We need to think urgently about these matters."

"As a member of our board of governors, I'd like to raise a point," said Edwards's pal Torino when Kelly finished speaking. "All of this kind of talk is fine and fancy," he began, "but I'm in anthropology, and we only get to offer three courses to the gen ed program. So how can anthropology offer more courses and hire more faculty if we are going to cut back on the number of gen ed courses undergrads are required to take? I mean, we need more students or we will lose faculty members. It is time we got our ducks in a row and cut out all this nonsense about less is more," he said, although no one had yet raised that thorny issue.

As he did so, Dr. Sainsbury thought it was time to draw the proceedings to a close. They had been in session for almost three hours and it was past dinner time for most people. She did not want the event to invite a tiresome airing of simpleminded commentaries or to be dragged into a shouting match about whatever cropped up as the focus faded further and tummies began to rumble.

When Torino objected, Sainsbury suggested that he raise the matter at the Metro board of governors meeting. Remembering that she was hoping to gather new and helpful perspectives to put on display there, such a question from Torino could enable her to vanquish all opposition when Conners again brought up the matter of dispensing with COGEM. By drawing on Wang's suggestion (which he took from Marilyn), impressionable board members would have an opportunity to see how forward-looking she was. The sooner Torino opened up such an avenue for exploration at the Metro board meeting, the sooner she could demonstrate how indispensable COGEM had become.

To Kelly's surprise, Sainsbury also indicated she had further questions around the issue she raised earlier because she was not convinced of the applicability of Kelly's response in a university context. She suggested scheduling a private meeting between them to tease out the matter before too long, and then she declared the meeting over.

***

Later in the evening and wishing that she too could meet privately with Kelly to tease out some matters of a much different complexion, Filomena was reduced to electronic communication. Upon checking his email before calling it quits for the night, Kelly found a message from one of his students. "Dear Pat or Patrick J.," it began, "I was very proud of you this afternoon as you made your wonderful presentation to COGEM. I am so blessed to have you as my professor, and now, I feel, as my friend and someone special. XXX Filomena."

***

The next day, a Saturday, Sainsbury met with Lukas, the secretary of COGEM, to draw up a lengthy set of minutes from the meeting. She sent them on to Conners, this time by email at his insistence, as well as to all members of the committee and the Metro board. In an attempt to present a balanced and comprehensive account, the report contained a summary of the main points of Kelly's presentation and of the Q&A session that followed.

Sunday morning, Conners called Edwards to gripe. "What to do you make of this report on the COGEM meeting, Joe? You were there, I take it? Does it really need to be this long?"

"She's full of it, Butch. She makes it up if she has to, anything to push her agenda. What else can I say, except that Kelly's almost as bad, pandering to the kids and their soccer moms with his progressive drivel. Nothing of substance, but he does manage to drag the kids along with him."

"It's easy to say that to me, Joe. Just be sure you're ready to go after Sainsbury at the board meeting tomorrow, and don't leave it all up to me like everyone did last time. And be sure to tell Torino and your other buddies that we need them to weigh in, too," said Conners, showing his customary agitation.

CHAPTER 16

"Excuse me, Mr. Conners," began board member Stanley Kirk, interrupting Conners as he introduced Sainsbury to the Metro board meeting in the same rough-and-ready fashion he had employed when she first addressed the body. "You're out of order. To my regret, I allowed this matter to slide when you introduced Dr. Sainsbury in a similarly unprofessional manner at the last meeting of the board."

"Be seated and be quiet, Mr. Kirk, or I will have you escorted out of here," demanded Conners. To his alarm, other members of the Board began to object to his aggressive attitude. The memo regarding Sainsbury's dismissal had left its mark, and the members were now less willing to toe the line for Conners.

Joe Smothers spoke up. "If you throw out Mr. Kirk, sir, you can also expect yours truly to leave with him. Who knows who else will join us; maybe we'll set up a shadow board. This is no star chamber, sir."

"Well said," came a deep voice from behind.

"Dr. Sainsbury, you may proceed," said Conners in a fluster, thinking it the best way to restore order.

Shortly after she began to speak and order had been restored, Conners interrupted her. "Excuse me, Dr. Sainsbury, but there is one more matter that I need to draw attention to before you go on. It has to do with protocol…"

"Let it go, Butch," someone said quietly near the front of the room.

"Let's have it out, you mean," responded Conners.

"Mr. Chair, can we please move on?" urged Kirk.

"Hear, hear," came another voice from the floor.

Sensing the mood was leaning in her favor, Sainsbury decided to move ahead while Conners fumbled and appeared to concede the point.

"Since you neglected to inform the members of the reason you invited me here today, Mr. Conners—perhaps 'instructed' would be a better word—I'll fill in that blank for you," began Sainsbury only to be interrupted again by Conners.

"They know why you are here, ma'am," snarled Conners.

"I'll fill in the blank anyway by quoting from your communication to me. It may provide context for the members. It read as follows: 'As Chair of the Board of Governors of Metropolitan Atlantic University, I wish to know why Arnie Smatter of Radio YOY believes the Metro's general education program is being disrupted. You are ordered herewith to explain this at the next meeting of our board, where the termination of your Committee on General Education and the Major will be considered.'" Sainsbury revealed.

She continued, "That is pretty much the same question Smatter himself asked me on his radio show some time ago. On that occasion, to my horror, Mr. Smatter was accompanied in his mobile broadcasting truck by Dr. Joe Edwards, who also happens to be a member of this body. By the way, that truck is parked outside our building again today. For all I know, Smatter might be hooked up to Dr. Edwards to hear what is said at our meeting."

"Search him!" came the deep voice from the back of the room.

"Oh, get on with it, ma'am," ruled Conners, pounding on the dais where he was perched.

"In that case, Mr. Conners," Sainsbury suggested, "it might make more sense to invite Mr. Smatter in here to answer the question you've asked me, that is, why he believes that the Metro's general education program is being disrupted. Failing that, maybe Dr. Edwards can take a stab at it. My guess is that he's the one who put Smatter up to the question in the first place."

"Again, get on with it, Dr. Sainsbury," Conners ordered, still trying to restore a semblance of normalcy to a decidedly abnormal meeting.

"I can best 'get on with it,' sir, by explaining that rather than aiming to disrupt the Metro's general education program, my aim is to revitalize it, to improve it. And I ask for the agreement of this body to engage in a dialogue here and now, rather than listen to a one-sided and uncontested presentation of my view.

"As to why I am here at all: As we speak, COGEM is examining the question of whether our general education program should be reconceptualized to meet the exigencies of our day and beyond, and if so, how we should accomplish that goal. No decisions have been reached, but since I appeared before this board last, we have made progress along two fronts. The first regards how we wish to define the purpose and content of general education at the Metro, and the second addresses its possible reorganization and the realignment of faculty at the undergraduate level. The committee will also consider the consequences that this might have for the university's graduate programs and faculty research."

"So, what then?" inquired Conners.

To the annoyance of Conners, Smothers wanted to speak. "If I may, I'd like to ask Dr. Sainsbury what she means by the realignment of faculty, and what possibilities and opportunities she sees for our graduate and research programs."

"Mr. Smothers, I've asked this woman here to answer for her disruption of gen ed at the Metro," said Conners.

"But, sir," cut in Sainsbury, "addressing the question of disruption—and it is no more than a question—necessitates considering the issues raised by the gentleman." She then turned to address Smothers before Conners could respond. "These are excellent questions, Mr. Smothers, and simpler for me to speak to than trying to figure out why Mr. Smatter hallucinates that my goal is to disrupt the Metro's general education program."

When her comment raised a chuckle all around, Sainsbury grew more confident that many of the members were already on her side. "Regardless of the form the redesign of general education takes, the possibilities for research opportunities and faculty realignment at the undergraduate and graduate levels still exist. And you are correct, Mr. Smothers, it is important to discuss this matter right now."

"Sounds good to me," came the deep voice that seemed to have qualities of bilocation.

Overlooking the exasperation that the scowling red face of Edwards expressed, Conners thought it best to let matters take their own course for now. With this, Sainsbury decided it was opportune to relay the issue raised by Wang at COGEM, since Torino seemed to have no intention of bringing it up. By introducing the issue at a board meeting that included only one or two department chairs, she could avoid the backlash it was sure to generate in a more hostile faculty meeting, where a higher number of department chairs would be ready to pounce. She could also earn credit and admiration from those board members attracted to what appeared to be her executive and even corporate-style leadership qualities.

Although the demeanor of the chair of English conveyed his unease, knowing as he did what was to follow, Sainsbury continued, "At our most recent meeting of COGEM, as I relayed in summary fashion in my mandatory report to this body, we had a balanced discussion surrounding the possibilities for faculty realignment and a fuller realization of research opportunities on campus. It was gratifying to see how the decision to form COGEM in the first place was conducive to exploring issues pertinent to our mission as a go-ahead institution in our state and region. Some members were especially interested in considering whether we could restructure faculty hiring. One member suggested it would be possible to reduce or altogether eliminate the number of faculty hired to teach multiple sections of introductory- and even remedial-level courses unbecoming the Metro's high standard of education. The savings obtained in this way, he suggested, could make it possible to attract and hire highly qualified faculty, enabling us to teach more advanced courses for our majors and graduate students. It's also likely that such a move would support a higher level of research productivity and make us more competitive when pursuing research and development grants," Sainsbury added, believing she was on safe ground.

"What wonderful energy!" exclaimed the CEO of Mid-State Industries, one of the companies in the region. "This is the very kind of thing our stockholders and corporate friends are attracted to. I dare say we would be willing to provide research monies for this kind of initiative. This could be big for the Metro, for the state, and for our region."

"I agree," chimed in Bartley, president of the Midleton Savings and Loan Association, who was well-known as a member of the Midleton school board, and who was serving his 11th term on the Metro board. A stalwart member of multiple boards in the community, his word carried weight.

"Take it easy there," demanded the chair of English who had already shown his strong, traditionalist leanings at the recent COGEM meeting. "We are a university, not a for-profit business nor a front for neo-liberalist crusaders."

"Besides, sirs" added Torino, finding his feet before big brother Edwards could, "while this may sound like a good idea to some of you off-campus members, where do we get the funds to support hiring more faculty?"

"Wise up, Torino," snapped Smothers. "If you simply cut down on hours and courses for college-wide elementary-level gen ed courses, you'd have the savings available to hire more productive folks. It's simple!"

Wishing to remain highly visible on what several board members were beginning to view as a favorable dimension of faculty reorganization, Sainsbury thought it prudent to elaborate. "We could also avoid losing our best faculty, who grow weary from teaching at a more mundane course level," she said to general expressions of agreement. "We stand to attract more upwardly bound faculty who prefer to teach at advanced levels and engage in community-responsive research." She concluded on a note she hoped would appeal to all sides, "in a way, these are welcome cost considerations that have nothing to do with neo-liberalist ideologies."

While Beame was satisfied to see the discussion take its own course, Conners and Edwards had not anticipated this development and were at a loss for how to respond. For his part, Conners could not be perturbed by the prospect of greater prestige for the university. Yet his designs for the elimination of COGEM were clearly not being advanced or even heard.

Preoccupied with scuttling COGEM, and seeing little opportunity to focus the discussion on the range of topics for which he was prepared, Edwards decided to make a move. "All I hear in this discussion, if it can even be called that, is talk about faculty hiring and research. My friends, according to the highly touted Cardinal Newman, who is now considered a saint, I am told, a university is a place of learning and teaching. It is not primarily a center of research. I have yet to hear anyone show how research improves student learning at our Metro. Let me say, then, the basics are the basics, be that in school or university, and the basics include math and reading and science. There is a core of knowledge that everyone should have, and we know what it is at the Metro. Does anyone here have a better idea, and can anyone show why we need COGEM?" he asked of a mostly disinterested audience.

"I've attended all the meetings of COGEM held so far, and I've not seen a better idea than what we now have come up yet," added Torino, too chastened by the reaction to his earlier contribution to add anything else.

Disregarding Torino, Blair rose to speak. "As chair of the Midleton school board, and as our distinguished chair knows, the Midleton board has been engaged in a similar debate over the past year or two, and I have to say that whatever the outcome will be, it has been a worthwhile and dynamic discussion. That being the case, I see no reason to question the existence of COGEM. A university ought to be a place for discussion and debate, and every so often, it is desirable to examine ongoing practice in light of changing circumstances. As for the student members on that committee, I've come to know one of them since she signed on to help us draft our district improvement plan, and she's just a terrific kid. So, I say, well done, Dr. Sainsbury and committee, and I look forward to learning more of your progress in the future."

"Hear, hear," added Smothers to further nods of agreement.

"I can't agree with that," objected Edwards, trying to adopt a civilized tone. "I see many good reasons to question the existence of COGEM. Of course college kids want to change things to make it easier for them to get a degree; that's why we need to restrain them and get them on the right road to the future. And we've got plenty of kids on that committee. Some are instructors themselves, who are children in their thinking." Hitting his stride and showing more coherence and self-control than usual, he continued, "I've been reading up about gen ed. I follow the work of the Core Knowledge Foundation that Vic and I admire so much, and that man whose name I can't recall just now, who did such a great job of taking down the wayward blogger when she lost her bearings and drifted left. As for Mr. Blair's suggestion that every now and again, we ought to examine ongoing practice, I have news for him, and here I cite the great Robert Maynard Hutchins. He rightly believed that eternal truths never change; the core of our general education program represents eternal truths. To which I add, right on Robert Hutchins, and stay on course, Metro!"

"Yes, there are eternal truths," agreed Cameron, "and I applaud our erudite and distinguished mathematician for having the courage to say so. I was fortunate to be at the University of Chicago to imbibe the delights of the Hutchins-Adler era and their Great Books Program. President Hutchins and his ever-so-learned colleague, Professor Adler, may not grace our corridors and places of learning today, but if they could, they would agree that changing circumstances are no reason to alter our approach here at the Metro, for we have truth on our side. Although the great men had departed the university before I arrived at U of C, they were like fathers to me. I improved significantly both as a student and a person, I am told, as I participated in the demanding general education course they developed that was based on the 'Great Books of Western Civilization.'"

"My wife is Asian, and it seems to me Chicago could have chucked in a few great books of Asian civilization too," said Kirk with a smile of satisfaction on besting the chair of English. "I bet you eat Asian," he added, "but do you ever read Asian?"

As the energy in the room began to fade, and thinking he might have better luck at putting an end to COGEM at a future date, Conners begrudgingly thought it best to draw the meeting to a close, which he did without objection even from Edwards, who seemed to be thinking along the same lines.

"Good job, Valerie," said Beame to Sainsbury as they crossed paths after the meeting.

Meanwhile, Conners sought out Blair. "Hi, Dick, you're just the man I was looking for," he said when he finally got him to himself. Making no reference to Blair's words of support for COGEM, he had a different and seemingly petty goal in mind. "By the way, Dick," he said casually, "that kid from COGEM you've got working for you—I thought if I could join the small group that Price has working on the Midleton improvement plan, I might get a better idea of what's going on with COGEM itself. Do you think I could join you?"

"It's a very informal group that the super has just put together piece by piece as the need arose, Butch," Blair said, startled.

"Good. It should be easy for you to arrange then, eh?"

"Well, I'll have to talk with Margaret. She plays stuff pretty close to the vest, so I wouldn't be too sure," said Blair, feeling uncomfortable with Conners's pushy attitude. "Anyway, we don't meet again until after Thanksgiving."

"In that case, maybe I'll just pop in to see her myself," said Conners, feeling rebuffed.

***

Blair was right in his estimation of Price's reaction when he called the next day to inform her of his conversation with Conners. Being protective of both Filomena and of her "first claim" on her, she was reluctant to accede to Conners's request. She certainly was not going to act before speaking about it in person with Filomena, who was popping into the office later that afternoon on her way home from campus.

"Have you met Butch Conners, the chair of the Metro board of governors?" asked Price after greeting Filomena that afternoon.

"No, I haven't met him, but I know who he is."

"He's asked to join our informal working group."

"I'd be curious to meet him, I must admit," said Filomena.

"Why is that?"

"Well, the students on COGEM don't have a great opinion of him, nor does Dr. Kelly, if I guess right. I thought his behavior at the last school board meeting was rather odd," said Filomena, thinking to herself, "what is this all about?"

"He certainly was not favorably disposed to our proposal that evening, for sure. The problem is that if we want to maintain a good relationship with the Metro, I'm reluctant to object to his request." Hearing nothing further from Filomena, she added, "I'll have to think about it some more, I guess."

***

In the end, recognizing that Conners was a friend of Wayne Singleton, who was now a congressman, and therefore worth having on one's side, Price did invite Conners along to the next meeting of the working group.

Like a dandy, wearing a casual jacket that matched his suntanned complexion and sporting his pebbly bison leather moccasins, Conners turned up for the meeting looking to befriend Filomena, who had escaped his embrace on the evening of the school board meeting. Having introduced Conners and Filomena to each other, and before Conners was able to ingratiate himself to her, Blair asked Filomena if she could update the group on the work she'd done on the curriculum plan since they last met.

Filomena had already sent a draft of her presentation for the working group to Kelly, and he had signaled his general approval, so she felt comfortable enough to present it to the group, even with Conners staring at her. "Something unexpected arose as I was working on this. A second-grade teacher at Westside Elementary School heard from a student in my EDUC 401 class that I was working on the district improvement plan, and she contacted me. She knew that my professor, Dr. Kelly, is quite progressive in his thinking because she had taken one of his graduate courses. Having read some scholarly work on critical pedagogy, such as *Pedagogy of the Oppressed* by Paulo Freire and a book by Duncan-Andrade and Morrell, this teacher asked me to take a look at the social studies element she had built into her reading and writing program, and then requested that I observe them at work. Well, I was astonished at what I saw when I went to visit. These children, only seven or eight years old, were engaged in social-political action integrated with their literacy education program. It was service-learning and literacy education all at once. The teacher told me she had read an article in the *Elementary School Journal* of a similar approach in an Australian school that was very well received. So she decided to give it a try."

"I'm sorry, but I've had enough of this, Filomena," objected Conners, interrupting her, having concluded she was not his type. "Here we go again with Deweyan sentimentalism and socialist ideology taking over our schools. Not a word about computers or leaving kids unable to read and write and ill-prepared for the workplace. They just become troublemakers like that Marilyn tramp and those other placard-bearing ruffians in the Metro a few weeks ago."

"Come on, Butch. Please remember that you're an invited guest of this group; let's keep things civil. Let Filomena continue with her presentation," said Blair, showing his annoyance. "Please continue, Filomena. I'm interested in what you have to say."

"For the record," Conners responded, "I had to write to that lassie after I saw her on TV. Professor Edwards was right about her; she is a waste of space, all right."

Patently ignoring Conners, Blair again invited Filomena to continue.

"Well, the extraordinary thing about the class I observed— and I trust you will find this of interest, too, Mr. Conners—I was an English major in college and would probably be considered somewhat of a traditionalist or conservative in curriculum matters, but it was clear that these children were advancing by strides in their reading and writing. On top of it all, they were developing self-esteem and leadership skills in community development. They even succeeded in involving the town council and the mayor in their project. With the help of their teacher, they sent a proposal to the town budget committee for assistance with their project to clean up a blighted section of downtown.

"Yet that was only a detour from my main work on the improvement plan. I also completed a draft of the aims and objectives section of the curriculum part of the plan. This follows to some extent the way Mortimer Adler tried to set about designing his course of studies, but I modified it based on Dr. Kelly's critique of Adler."

"Yes, I've heard of Adler from Professor Cameron. Can you move this along?" interjected Conners again.

"But have you examined his work closely, as Dr. Kelly has?' asked Filomena, astonished by Conners's rudeness.

"Yes, I've heard of Pat Kelly, too. Please keep going, I don't have all night," added Conners uncomfortably.

Blair wasn't willing to be as diplomatic as Price, and was loath to put up with Conners's boorish behavior. "What's the rush, Butch?

I thought you wanted to be here. You're welcome to cut out early if we're boring you. Please go on, Filomena."

Filomena obliged. "Well, putting aside my visit to the elementary school, my work on the plan sets out overall aims and objectives for the district in a way that can be modified by teachers at different grade levels," said Filomena a little assertively, conveying to Conners that, while polite, she was no pushover. "Next, I identified a range of content that could be used to meet these aims and objectives. This would have a significant weighting of traditional subjects. I also left space for creative teachers to build in other forms of learning, such as those I witnessed at the elementary school. I also made some general proposals for other kinds of hands-on activities for student learning and creative teaching. I should add, however, that if the district is to move in that direction, it will call for ongoing in-service education, guidance for our teachers, and buy-in from the teachers themselves. Lastly, I've just begun to identify the kinds of teaching or pedagogy that could be employed in these kinds of programs, and the forms of assessment that might be suitable. I have not yet finished that part."

"Thank you, Filomena. That's an impressive presentation that you've made, and in such a short space of time," said Blair.

"I must say, I have to agree with Mr. Blair," added Price, who was cut short by Conners.

"Well, young lady, if you're not beginning to sound like a curriculum expert already, a fledgling left-winger who wants to put teachers in charge of what they should be teaching, no less!" began Conners. "We don't need your opinion when it comes to what Midleton kids need in school, and I don't think a young one like you has much to teach a man of my experience about this stuff. We people who are a little bit ahead of you were taught the basics in school, and we're doing pretty well, as you can see. No need to change that. Despite the malarkey from the U.S. Small Business Administration, the small business I used to run in Philly was really quite large and was seeking a listing on the Nasdaq before I agreed to give it all up and come back to serve here at the Metro. All of which means the improvement plan doesn't need any work on the curriculum side. So, Margaret, if there's nothing new to add to the curriculum side of the improvement plan, is there really any need to bring it back to the board?"

"I wasn't finished speaking to Filomena, Butch, when you interrupted me," began Price, turning to Filomena. "Filomena, I was going to say that I agree with Mr. Blair. You've laid out quite an agenda for the district in what you have offered. Unfortunately, I don't think we will be able to complete everything you've touched on in the time remaining before the improvement plan must be submitted," she added before Conners cut in again.

"There you go again. So, what's the bloody use of her presentation to us, then? Just a lot of our valuable time wasted sitting here and being lectured to by this kid. It's easily known, my little lass, that you've been infected by this Sainsbury woman at the Metro. You're on that harpy's Committee on General Education and the Major, I believe," said Conners, his temperature rising.

"May I inquire, Mr. Blair, how Mr. Conners knows I'm on that committee?" asked Filomena.

"That's Chairman Conners if you don't mind, young lady," snapped Conners.

"But you haven't answered her question, Butch," Blair put in.

"Does it matter, Dick? I just know. That's not against the law," he said, standing up and getting ready to leave. "Look, I've got to go anyway. I don't see much point in my being here," said Conners as he left the room, more agitated than usual and leaving Filomena in no doubt as to what his true intentions were.

After Conners had gone, Blair and Price made it clear that Conners would not be invited back to any more of their group meetings. Johnson, who had remained quiet up to this point, agreed and was clearly upset by Conners's behavior. With the unpleasantness behind them, they all focused on exploring how much of Filomena's presentation could be included in the plan, and how much should be used as a part of their regular and ongoing district improvement activities after the plan was submitted. With a few new guidelines arising from this discussion, Filomena was asked to finalize the curriculum section of the improvement plan, which would then be blended into the existing draft. This final version would be sent to members of the school board for its next and final meeting of the year, to be held on December 11, which was just about a week away. There, it would be voted on again before the December 15 deadline for submission to the feds.

***

"Hi, Wayne. Butch here," Conners announced on the phone to Singleton a little later that evening. "Listen up, Singleton. We've got a problem, and it's bigger than I thought. I've just come from a small group meeting on the district's improvement plan. We need all hands on deck."

"Just a minute," said Singleton, who was having a beer in the local along with a handful of constituency workers and was caught off guard by Conners's sense of urgency. Leaving his group for some privacy, Singleton explained that he didn't have much time to talk. "Just give me a quick rundown. I know we've talked before about what might be needed to scuttle the improvement plan. We can go public with it, if necessary."

"It's not just the improvement plan anymore, Wayne, and it's not just Petty Officer Price. Boogeman Blair is in on it too. Look, the super has run her course, my friend. She's got to be pushed out, and we need a guy in there, a team player," he said excitedly.

"Have you spoken to Arnie about this? He's usually good for getting things out there."

"We need to *do* something, not just sit around talking about it like at the freaking school board meetings," said Conners before launching into his account of the meeting he had just come from.

"What do you mean, 'we gotta do something,' Butch?" inquired Singleton.

"If we can quash this improvement plan, maybe Price will move on and we'll be rid of her. Getting on the radio with Arnie as you say, might be a good place to start," agreed Conners, out of ideas himself.

"Yeah, that usually works. I need to get back on the air with Arnie anyway; maybe we can do this together. I'll give him a call and see what I can set up. Will you be free to get to his studio tomorrow?" Singleton asked. "I'll be able to get some constituency people to help too, I bet. And of course there's always the parents."

"I can be free tomorrow. Early suits me better. Just let me know when you get a time from Arnie," said Conners, satisfied with his day's work.

***

To no one's surprise, Smatter was keen to have two community stalwarts of a friendly political persuasion appear on his radio program.

"Good morning, fellow Midletonians," he announced early the next day as the morning commute was getting into full swing. "This morning, I have two of the best men in town for you. Nothing but the best from Arnie, as you know. With me this morning is newly elected Representative Wayne Singleton of the Patriot Party, along with the distinguished chair of the board of governors of the Metro, Mr. Butch Conners. Well, tell me, boys, what news can you make for me today?"

"It's not the best of news, at least not yet," began Singleton. "Midletonians, we've got some bad news for you today."

"What's the problem?" Arnie asked.

"It's the Midleton school district—they want to peddle teacher-led, sentimental education again, which I thought we had got rid of with our last Patriot president," said Singleton.

"Before we go any further with this, boys, let's take a quick break."

> For the finest of wine,
> Simply go to online
> Sent from Sam Kirby's store
> Right to your own front door.
> THAT'S KIRRRRRRBY'S!

"You were about to add, Butch?" prompted Arnie.

"When it comes to the Midleton school board, we need to listen to Wayne Singleton, a man who knows what it's all about. Right now, they've got a kid from the Metro directing business over there. She thinks she's a conservative, poor thing," said Conners. "Though I must admit, she's a pretty filly, for sure."

"You mean she's a 10, eh?" asked Arnie.

"Oh, she's a 10 all right, but just from the ears down. She did seem kinda smitten by me, though who could blame her?" said Conners.

"So, is she just a student from the Metro? Do they pay her?" asked Arnie.

"Yeah, they pay her from my budget, if you can believe it," replied Conners.

"Surely you can put a stop to that."

"Rest assured, Arnie, I'll be banning that kind of thing, but I can't control the school district office or the school board by myself, not to mention that brain-dead superintendent. The Price woman, you know. You remember, she stumbled on to your show one day. We're going to need good folks in the community to speak up, to take sides on this," Conners added.

"I suppose this is where you come in, Representative Singleton. How can we at Radio YOY contribute?" asked Smatter. "You know we stand for traditional values, law and order, and community solidarity here at Radio YOY."

"I was just coming to that, Arnie," began Singleton. "Until now, in our battles with the school board over this improvement plan that the superintendent wants to submit to the feds, we have not called on the public to do much for us. But now it's time to let the parents in our community know that their kids' futures are on the line. Our tax-paying seniors can show up too."

"Of course, Wayne. Count Arnie in too," offered Smatter.

"Butch and I will have organizational details ready in 36 hours, and as always, my staffers will be working hard to get the word out and provide support, you know, car-pooling and the like," said Singleton. "You could help in a big way, Arnie, by giving us coverage through your show. You can reach everyone, you know. That's your thing as we all know."

Singleton was not finished. "In times of need, solidarity is what counts. We on the school board stand with tradition, and this time will be no different. So, folks, please listen up and help out."

As the chat dragged on without any clear indication of what exactly was being planned, even if it did sound like a protest of some kind, callers to the show expressed support and asked for directions. Should they make out placards and posters? Could the kids come along? Would there be coffee and donuts?

Then came a surprise question.

"Should we bring our guns?" asked an older guy.

"It depends," said Conners, feeling some pressure and unwilling to stick his neck too far out.

"It's OK to be angry," added Singleton. "Maybe we can have a fiery speaker or two to create a rallylike atmosphere, with flags and T-shirts mixed in with the signs."

With the conversation drifting toward topics considered inappropriate by his advertisers, Smatter decided to call a halt to the interview and suggested that his guests could figure out further details of their protest off the air. Turning to Singleton and Conners with a nervous smile unseen by his listeners, he bade them farewell with a line he picked up on a late-night TV show.

"Thanks for being my guests. I really appreciate it," he said as the *Kirby's* ditty was faded in.

***

Oblivious to the goings-on at Radio YOY and still trying to play catch-up following the Thanksgiving break, Kelly wasted no time in getting class started a little later that morning.

"In a previous day's discussion," he began, "I identified some weaknesses in Adler's position on general education, and I indicated that I would develop my own alternative view by responding to that position. That's what I plan to do today.

"Since we've had a bit of a vacation, let's start with a short recap," he began as the class settled down. "Having said the objectives of schooling are to prepare students for work, citizenship, and personal development, Adler failed to critically examine what such preparation would suggest for selection of curriculum content or subjects. Instead, announcing that 'the best education for the best is the best education for all,' he told us what he believed were the best subjects. These happened to be the subjects typically found in traditional theories of general education, and from which the best students allegedly received the best education."

Having said this by way of recap, Kelly continued. "Although there is much more that I could say by way of disagreement with Adler, I think it best if I move forward now to present the main features of my alternative ideas, as you all asked me to do."

He spent the next half hour spelling out the core elements of his alternative view, while making it clear that there were some differences in how it would be applied at the college level and at the level of schooling. Much of this was adapted from his presentation to COGEM for a classroom setting. When he finished speaking for longer than usual, there was silence while those students who remained attentive gathered their thoughts. When people did begin to speak up, the issues raised related to their own needs and circumstances, to the needs of children they would be teaching, and to what they thought about the courses they themselves took to meet the general education requirements of the Metro.

Jean was first with her hand up. "OK, Professor, I think I follow your argument, but I still don't understand what other subjects there are besides the ones identified by Adler. I raised that point earlier and until I know what these are, I still think he's right."

In response, Kelly said, "In my view, deciding on the content of the curriculum involves first asking what it means to be prepared for the broad challenges that are usually encountered in the course of our lives. Only then are we in a position to identify suitable subjects or possible curriculum content. What is required might not always take the form of traditional subjects, although basic math and reading appear to be necessary as preparation for much of what we are called upon to do in the course of our lives."

Kelly then indicated that he wanted to discuss other possible forms of curriculum content beyond the standard subjects, and encouraged the class to think outside the box. "Such content might be relied upon to supplement or even replace existing content when it appears better matched to objectives of schooling, such as those identified by Adler. I'll start by talking about health education, although one could make a similar argument based on, say, 'wellness education,' 'environmental engineering,' 'urban development,' or 'media education,' most of which are ignored by Adler. But just to be clear, while Adler does mention knowledge about our health as part of his broader course of studies, it is seen only as an addendum that may be lectured on or, and I stress, be 'instructed about.' Yet, his more prized subjects are to be the object of discussion, not mere instruction or narration. So, not only does he pay little attention to subject matter such as health education, but he demeans it further by implying it is not worthy of discussion and so can be downplayed in a 'real' or 'serious' course of study without undue concern.

"But the reality of health education and other such subjects, including physical education, worthwhile civic education, consumer education, and other practical subjects, is that they bear directly on how we live our lives as individuals and as members of a family, a community, and a workplace." Then, developing the point he made in his presentation to COGEM, he explained that these were forms of curriculum content that enable students both to think and behave in ways not always found in traditional subjects, such as history and physics. They not only inform students about the world, he explained, but they also provide them with opportunities to deal with real situations in the actual world they live in. Recalling how he had described it in his COGEM presentation, he said he rejected the belief that practical knowledge and reasoning are not fit for inclusion in a program of general education. Reading from his notes for the COGEM presentation, he continued, "Students who are not exposed to practical learning are deprived of the benefit of encountering knowledge and understanding that can be gained only from some level of involvement in practical affairs. Failing to recognize this does students a grievous injustice, and is an incomprehensible error in traditional theorizing."

Rather than jumping right into answering Jean's question with a mere list of subjects, Kelly then asked Jean what she believed preparation for work required.

"That's a difficult one," she answered.

"Surely, it's not that difficult, Jean. You know how to work. What does it demand of you?"

"Well, I do my schoolwork and sometimes do some work for my mom around the home, but I've never had a proper job, so I really don't know," she protested.

"It's not that I don't trust you, Jean, but I don't think that's true. We've all worked at something without having a paid job. What was required of you when you helped your mom at home?" he then asked while others looked on and wondered how they would answer these questions themselves.

"I suppose I did what she asked me to do."

"Such as?"

"Set the table or empty the dishwasher."

"So, you'd follow directions, right?"

"Yeah, I suppose."

"Would you ask questions?"

"Sure, I would."

"Such as?"

"Why don't you ask Jonathon—that's my brother—to set the table?"

Hoping for a different kind of answer, Kelly just chuckled and said, "I see. So you would assert your rights?"

"Yeah, I'm no dummy."

"Thank you, Jean. Anyone else want to give examples?" Kelly asked, turning to the class.

"I worked summers at the YMCA," volunteered Serena. "Following directions is key, in my opinion. Sometimes the directions are written down on the notice board, so you have to read them or even go looking for them, maybe check them out on the computer, if you know how to use the tech in that particular YMCA. Sometimes the directions are spoken from a boss, so you have to listen and know which questions to ask so that you have all the information you need. And sometimes the person in charge might not be so nice, and you have to watch your P's and Q's."

Once several students had given an array of examples, Kelly asked if there were any common features among them.

"Yeah," said Mark. "No one seems to be too excited about working. That seems to be common."

"That's not what I'm saying, Mark," replied Serena. "I actually like to work. Besides keeping me busy, it gives me a sense of purpose, something to be committed to. I suppose some people find work tedious or uninteresting. And, of course, there is such a thing as slave labor, which is gross, if you ask me."

"Another thing, you have to know the rules, and you have to be careful with union agreements and that kind of thing," Mark added. "And if you want to keep your job, you've got to do things properly. You might keep your bedroom messy, but you've got to do it right at work. Maybe that's why I don't care for it."

"You also need good communication skills, at least you do at the YMCA," said Serena. "You've got to do more than just follow directions; you have to think for yourself. As a teacher, for example, I might have to figure out the best course of action to take with a particular class without being given specific directions. And if the instructions given to you are morally objectionable, you might just have to quit, like I wish some people in politics would do."

Kelly intervened to ask how well prepared for work the students were based on what was provided at school, and how the class felt about Adler's position that one of the objectives of schooling was to prepare students for work.

"It's like this, as I see it," Miguel said, "I suppose some of the subjects we learn in school, like basic math and literacy, give some preparation for work. I guess they also give some preparation for personal development and even for citizenship, Adler's other two objectives for schooling. But, and this is a huge 'but,' those basics are not where the real challenge lies in being prepared for work. You need a whole lot more, like Serena said, such as attitude, disposition, commitment, communication skills, and if your work brings you in contact with members of the public, you certainly need to know how to handle people, including the nasty ones. I learned that when I worked in a retail store one summer."

"OK, then," asked Kelly. "So, tell me, to what extent are these varied kinds of knowledge and skills taken care of in Adler's curriculum, or even in general education at the Metro or in your own high school program?"

"Well, as I just said, Professor Kelly," responded Miguel quickly, "I do believe that some of the gen ed stuff, like the basics, helps in most places of work. But there's nothing in Adler that I can see that addresses the real skills and attitudes needed to work alongside colleagues, deal with members of the public, understand unions, have a positive attitude, maintain a strong work ethic, and that sort of thing. That's really crucial stuff, and its completely left out of gen ed. Call it street smarts or work smarts if you want to." Then, with delight and hoping for a thumbs up from Kelly, he added, "See? I've just coined a phrase!"

"But, Miguel," said Anette, "surely many kinds of work require specialist knowledge beyond the basics. I mean knowledge that a lawyer or an engineer or a teacher is required to know—that's essential in professional working situations. I do agree that there is a whole lot more beyond specialist knowledge, and you mentioned much of this. From observing Professor Kelly, I would add the importance of evaluating situations and making judgments, and from seeing my husband at work, I would stress sticking to a demanding task until it is completed."

"I do agree with you about how Professor Kelly and your husband need to make judgments and so forth," responded Miguel in a rare moment of harmony with her. "And as regards specialist knowledge being needed by lawyers, doctors, and teachers, I agree that is necessary too, but surely that falls under the umbrella of professional or specialized education, not general education."

"That's great," said Kelly. "So, let me switch now to inquire about the two other objectives that Adler laid out."

Filomena saw an opening to make her input. "As regards preparation for personal development, I find it difficult to say that anything that's on the curriculum, either in school or college, is not supportive of personal development, and... at least potentially. And one could probably say that is also true for much of what is *not* taught in school. My main challenge now, after taking this course, is to decide which and how many of the subjects we typically find in a school curriculum are sufficient or necessary. They might have some value for what we call intellectual development. But now I can see there is more to personal development than the intellectual side, narrowly understood as cognitive development. There is the emotional, the spiritual, and even the physical and perhaps other forms of intelligence. And along with the question of the curriculum, there is what Professor Kelly calls the pedagogical dimension.

"So, I am finally beginning to think that there is far greater merit than I first thought in the notion of the vocations or callings we all face, such as the need upon us all to work and to be good citizens, to respect and care for others, to relax and have fun, and to listen to and nourish our bodies as well as our minds. For example, if knowing how to relate to others is an important part of working life and civic life, then perhaps we should examine what these vocations require of us, and then consider what knowledge, attitudes, and skills are needed to prepare students in these respects—around which we ought to build the curriculum. To be truthful, as Professor Kelly has said, in *The Paideia Proposal* Adler does not address at all what is actually required of us in responding to the vocations in life to which he says we are all called."

"I understand your point, there, Filomena," said Jean, "but don't literature and the arts address many of the emotional and spiritual dimensions of living? At least, that's what my literature and art professors and my teachers in school said. They also raise ethical and moral questions, as does history. I mean to say, it was Hamlet who said, 'To be, or not to be, that is the question.' Surely that is a real moral issue for us all, and I don't know if it's a question you'd face in the workplace."

"I wouldn't bet on that, Jean," replied Filomena, "but I'll leave that question aside for now. Getting back to the contribution of literature in preparing us for life—which is sometimes put forward by advocates of traditional general education as being the core of general education—I'm beginning to have doubts about its efficacy and all that is claimed on its behalf. Or, more correctly, all that is unjustifiably claimed on its behalf. I do accept that scenarios or virtual realities created in classical literature, for example, can provide one with opportunities to reflect upon various moral and other challenges that fictional characters might have to deal with, challenges that cannot always be replicated at will in real life. Yet, as is stated in one of our readings, while literature might be a good way to observe the world, it is less good as preparation for participating in the world, taking action, or doing and making things, even simple things like how to exercise or complex things like how to care for children or carry out intricate tasks as members of a team in the workplace. Having had to translate *De Senectute* by Cicero in high school and read *As You Like It* by Shakespeare in Middle school, I'm not sure anymore if that cuts it."

"And what about the contribution of the arts?" asked Kelly.

"I feel differently about that," said Filomena. "Of course, who am I to say, but I marvel at how creative and open-minded so many people in the art world are. Some students in art education really impress me with their originality, as do art majors when I go to see their work at student art exhibitions on campus or discuss social and political matters with them. They really do see things imaginatively and creatively. Without any disrespect to Anette and her lawyer husband, I just wish we had more people with art degrees than lawyers in Congress and in politics. I mean, can you believe what that senator just said in response to protest marches going on across the country? 'One thing above all else will restore order to our streets: an overwhelming show of force.'

"So, what, if he was a lawyer," interjected Anette quickly.

"My point still stands," said Filomena before continuing. "Even though I am a literature major myself, I still think the art people I know are the most creative and imaginative. It would be nice to see necessary life skills, knowledge, and attitudes identified, and then the question asked: What can art contribute to enabling young people to grow in attaining them? That question could be asked of a wide range of subjects. I realize that this is what Professor Kelly advocates, but we do not seem to approach curriculum making for general education in that way at all. It's a pity, I think. If we did, maybe we could dump much of what we require students to study. It reminds me of a famous curriculum book that Professor Kelly recommended I read in connection with my work for the Midleton school board. I think everyone would get a kick out of it. It's called *The Saber-Tooth Curriculum*. It's fictional, but it really conveys why we need to look at what living in the present day requires young people to learn. Today, for example, we do not need to spend a great deal of time teaching young people how to fish by hand or follow directions in our cars by reading the stars at night instead of our GPS devices. I'm planning to recommend it for reading to the members of COGEM."

"There were a few notable attempts to adopt such an approach to curriculum development in this country over the years, Filomena," Kelly interjected, "but they were not well received."

"I can understand what Filomena is saying," said Jean. "But for me, the problem with seeing subject matter in that way is that it views literature and the arts merely as subjects that are valued for their usefulness, not for the joy that they provide."

"But, Jean, that's not quite what I said," replied Filomena, "What I said is, I don't see why we can't approach literature, music, and all of the arts both for their usefulness and for enjoyment, and, I would add, for the knowledge and 'understanding of ideas and values' they provide. If Professor Edwards could coin a term for that, he might call it 'smart-arts.'"

Following a bout of laughter and cheering that followed the wisecrack, Kelly realized that class time was almost up and he intervened to say so. In wrapping up, he explained that by now, the class had heard him express his own views on what was now being referred to as his alternative idea of a general education. "I wish we could continue to talk about the issues we have been discussing that need more time, but I will need to move on from this point in our next class since we are also nearing the end of the semester and there are one or two other matters I would still like to bring to your attention. As an aside, I also wish I could get the funding for a research and development project that would scrutinize the demands made on us by working life, life as a citizen, life as a member of a family, and so on as a basis for examining what they suggest for educational programs intended to prepare us for what Adler refers to as callings or vocations of life."

***

Mention of guns and protests on Radio YOY the day before was enough to spawn the headline, "Shotgun Deal 'n Donuts" in the *Midleton Morning Mouthpiece* the next day.

"We've all heard of shotgun marriages," the news report began, "now we've got something that everyone can avail of—free donuts! It's going to accompany the protest at the upcoming meeting of the Midleton school board and foreshadows good things that are in store for Midletonians."

The final sentence of the accompanying editorial in the *Midleton Morning Mouthpiece* read, "By the sounds of things to come, it would appear that once again, our town and college elders have the best interests of community stability, law and order, and good education in mind."

Since there was no explicit connection made between the protest and the school board meeting by Conners or Singleton, or even by Smatter, in the course of their radio interview, all three were astounded to read of it in the morning paper.

"Let's go with it, Wayne," said Conners on the phone to Singleton, having just seen it, even if he objected to being referred to as an elder in the accompanying editorial. "This way, we'll be sure to catch the attention of the board members, and it'll put even more pressure on them to see things as they should be seen. Price might even resign then and there and solve that issue for us. Yeah, let's go with it!"

***

Although he did not have a class to teach, Kelly was back on campus for a meeting over coffee with Sainsbury in her office that day. Sainsbury wanted to discuss the issue she raised at COGEM regarding his view that it is possible to develop flexible guidelines or curriculum parameters of general education to address the tasks encountered by everyone in living life to its fullest.

"While this might be suitable in considering the shape of general education at the level of schooling, especially in the earlier years, I am not convinced of its usefulness for the Metro," Sainsbury explained once they got together. "I mean, by the time our students arrive at the university, they have surely learned how to deal with many of the challenges of living, in one way or another. I knew how to look after myself before I left middle school. By the end of high school, their education must be broad enough to cover the general knowledge requirements for meeting the vocations or callings of life, as you call them. Surely, by the time they get here, they are more or less ready to indicate or even choose the subjects they want to follow in college. Do we really need to adopt a framework or measure of the kind you refer to, which might have been useful enough at the level of schooling?"

"What you say is a common understanding," said Kelly, "but it raises more questions than it answers. First, have those who finish high school really had a sufficiently broad education as regards the challenges of living in the 21st century? Are they really ready for college or the world of work in all its novel and challenging dimensions? Are they really ready for participatory democracy beyond voting once every year or two? Just look at some of the people we elect to high office. This is to say nothing about their readiness to competently participate in a range of everyday activities, from healthy living to environmental awareness to communications savvy to caring relationships and emotional well-being. For some of these students, even living on campus and away from home is a challenge. Of course, there is no guarantee that conventional education can ever cater to all of these requirements, but I'm pretty sure academic schooling on its own will not.

"Turning to the second set of issues you raise: If, as you say, our students are ready to indicate or even choose the subjects they want to follow at the university level, why the heck do we need 15 sections of English 101 and Math 101 and why do we need the form courses and area studies that Edwards and his people keep pushing?" Kelly said.

"Well, you know that I have strong reservations about the way we handle general education at the university today. In fact, that's one of the reasons that I established COGEM in the first place," said Sainsbury. "But back to your first point, even if we can create some measure of a good general education that prepares young people for living in the real world, and if I grant, even for the sake of argument, that the notion of the vocations of living suggests a sort of measure of what is required to attain that goal, how on earth can anyone or any institution cope with accommodating all the particularities that this would raise if we add in your call for the greater personalization of programs to respond to individual needs?"

"This might be more complex than figuring out how to get to the moon, for sure, Valerie. But at least it might help us recognize the enormity of the challenge."

"True. Now, Pat, I realize you spend much of your time analyzing these questions, and that is helpful. But as a university, as a society, we need to do more. I've got some thinking to do."

"Yes, we all have thinking to do, Valerie. But I don't believe you should unduly burden yourself with concerns that might not properly fall within your remit," said Kelly.

"What do you mean?"

"Well, I'm not sure anymore if, in the 21st century, it's the role of the university to focus on providing general education. That may have been a reasonable concern when universities first came into existence in the Middle Ages and when those admitted were sometimes in their early teens and did not have much in the way of formal schooling as we now understand it."

"That's a fair point I hadn't considered," said Sainsbury.

"If I may add something that I have not yet fully fleshed out—I'm beginning to think that the role of the Metro ought to be focused on what comes after general education, that is to say, specialized or advanced and professional studies, as is the case in universities elsewhere. Wang touched on this point when he spoke at COGEM. Sure, we do not want to create a world of unconnected specialists, and maybe some common elements ought to be included in all advanced programs of study for undergraduates, but I would not correlate that with general education as it is now commonly understood. I am increasingly of the view that the provision of general education—if that's even the correct concept— ought to be dealt with before students begin their university education, a point I shall be discussing shortly in EDUC 401."

***

While Kelly was attempting to get to the bottom of the conundrum of general education with Sainsbury, getting out the word of the planned protest at the upcoming meeting of the Midleton school board was progressing apace. The effort was aided by news reports on the *Midleton Morning Mouthpiece,* the TV Views around-the-clock advocacy programs, and the many reminders by Smatter on Radio YOY. In addition, circulars were delivered to all households in the district, and Conners had his secretary fill in her time by preparing directives for organizers tasked by Singleton to run the ground operation; she sent other missives to Smatter, to keep the pressure on him and to help him weaponize his radio broadcasts to assist the cause in any way he could. Singleton was also busy working his social media connections.

The upshot of all this activity was a refinement of the messaging for grievances related to the school district improvement plan that Conners and Singleton objected to. Unfortunately for the cause, these improvements rarely reached protesters, who were creating homemade posters advocating for a wide range of often conflicting goals, such as more time—and in some cases less time—devoted to advancing the athletic programs of different schools in the district.

***

Citizens less taken in by the messaging were also paying attention, like Marilyn, who was glad to have a friend on the inside to keep her up to date on the goings-on in the district office and on the school board itself. Offended by the way Conners treated her at the small group meeting, it was actually Filomena who encouraged Marilyn to keep an eye on the protest.

"Marilyn, he was so rude that I actually showed some displeasure with his behavior, almost to the point of being rude myself," said Filomena when they got together for lunch one day during the build-up to the protests.

"He's not fit to be the chair of the Metro board. I'm going to say that to Dr. Sainsbury next time I speak with her," said Marilyn, getting worked up about Conners. "I'll say it to his face if I get the chance. He should be fired."

Filomena almost let it slip that Conners had tried to have Sainsbury fired, and although she didn't come right out with it, Marilyn seemed to get the message.

"I'm not only upset about Conners's behavior toward you and the VP, Filomena. Along with that weasel, Singleton, he's provoking unrest and egging on anyone who wishes to protest the upcoming school board meeting without thought of the consequences. That's not appropriate behavior for the top representative of our beloved Metro," Marilyn said with resolve. "I'm going to go along to watch the protest. Would you like to come with me? I can get some more friends to join us, and we'll have a good time, maybe even turn it into a bit of a counterprotest."

"Thank you, but I'm going to be at the board meeting, remember? But I do urge you to attend to see how Conners behaves if nothing else."

"Golly, I forgot about that. By the way, I also meant to tell you about the virus that's coming. Have you heard?"

Filomena had heard nothing.

"Anyway, here's the deal for the school board meeting: You report to me on what happens inside the meeting, and I'll report to you on the happenings outside. Is that a deal?"

"It certainly is."

CHAPTER 17

Back in class and halfway through the second to last regular week of the semester, Kelly focused on the pedagogical aspects of his alternative idea of a general education, to which he had devoted some attention the previous day.

"OK, folks, it's time to get to the point," he began, throwing a curveball. "Does anyone agree that the idea of a general education—as distinct from the idea of an educated person—is a misleading idea to begin with?"

"What? Why do you say that?" asked Jean, puzzled. "I thought that's what made an educated person."

"Me too," added Serena.

"It's like, this," began Kelly. "Earlier this semester, I said that everyone learns differently and that everyone is at a different point in his or her education."

"So why do we put people into classes, then?" asked Jean.

"Maybe it's because we don't believe this to be the case, or maybe because it would make schooling prohibitively expensive if we had a highly individualized or personalized teaching approach. But look at it this way: If all students are at a different point in their learning—not to mention individual interests, preferences, likes and dislikes, and special talents—could it not be argued that each student should ideally be offered a different selection of curriculum content?" asked Kelly.

"What does that mean for the notion of the common school?" asked Anette. "Isn't this a significant part of the history of education in this country?"

"That's a good point, Anette," said Kelly. "Yes, the idea of the common school has been important in our history, and I would not want to say otherwise, especially as regards many of the common values around issues of morality and democracy that it seeks to teach. But I'm not sure that this means the values need to be taught to everyone in exactly the same way or at the same time."

"But some of the values that schools taught throughout history were the preferences of certain powerful groups," said Miguel, referring to the difficulties that Horace Mann encountered in Massachusetts when some groups resisted his move toward the common school.

"Also right, Miguel," said Kelly.

"But Professor," said Filomena, anxious for him to finish the suggestion that maybe general education was a misleading concept, "I agree with the idea that everyone learns differently and that everyone is at a different point in his or her education, but I'd like to hear more about why you think that maybe general education is a misleading idea. Since I'm a strong believer in general education, I'd like to figure out for myself if this suggestion is sustainable and if I'm going to be forced to change my point of view."

Kelly began, "It may be important that people have certain common or shared knowledge and values, but how can one argue in favor of general education if we have individual needs and talents that ought to be nurtured? And what if it means, as it did for Adler, that general education should be essentially the same for everyone? So, if general education means essentially the same course for all, then without much greater clarification, it needs to be challenged as a misleading and unhelpful idea. When I say misleading, I mean it can lead us into defective forms of schooling, such as 'one-size-fits-all.' When I say unhelpful, I mean it may lead us to ignore individual talents and special needs, and all of what that implies."

"So, what form does the clarification you call for take?" asked Filomena.

"That may seem like a simple question, but it calls for a sophisticated answer. I'm not sure how well positioned I am to provide it, as I am still grappling with it myself, but let me take a stab at it anyway.

"Since you were there, Filomena, you know that this is how I presented the idea to the university faculty when I spoke recently at COGEM. If one cannot design in advance a suitable course of studies for all, since the needs and abilities of students are so individual, and since to be truthful, we do not sufficiently know the students for whom it is intended, maybe there is no such thing as a universal idea of general education that ought to be provided to everyone. That is to say, even if we have and can justify an idealized view of all the knowledge, skills, values, and attitudes that everyone needs in life, many students may already possess significant portions of that when they get to school or college. Besides, maybe different people have different needs for knowledge depending on where they live or the cultural expectations of their community. So, if all of this is true, we are presented with a new challenge. We have previously asked the question, 'What subjects should we include in the curriculum of a general education and why?' Maybe the question we should be asking is, 'How should the curriculum respond to the particular needs of students, and how individualized as opposed to general should it be?'"

"That's interesting, for sure, but much of what you say is still based on supposition and questions."

"Well, I did say that I wasn't satisfied that I have an answer, only that I was thinking the matter through. That's often the first step in arriving at answers to novel questions. And that's why I need you and you need me to keep having these sorts of conversations."

"Thank you, Professor," said Filomena to Kelly, and then quietly to herself, "Gee, that's more than I was expecting!"

While Kelly's remark did not go unnoticed by some, preoccupied with his own thoughts, Miguel spoke up. "Professor, you do realize this isn't a graduate class, right?"

"But Miguel, you sound more like a grad student every day, and you seem to be enjoying it!"

Unaware of the little stir he had caused, Kelly looked at his watch and, as often happened, said, "Our time is up."

CHAPTER 18

The end of the semester was closing in fast, so Kelly got started straight away in class the next day. "I'd like to examine a point we touched on last time, one I believe doesn't get sufficient attention. Consider the following: Would it make schooling too expensive if we had more individualized instruction? Would that just be a waste of money?"

"Wouldn't that depend on whether it was more effective or not?" asked Christine. "If it were more effective, we then could consider the question of cost and whether it is worthwhile. But if it were not more effective, perhaps it's not even worth discussing."

"How do you define effective?" asked Miguel.

Kelly elaborated. "Good question, Miguel. Let me put it this way: If it allowed for more classroom discussion and less lecturing by the teacher, what would you say?"

"Well, Freire said that education is suffering from 'narration sickness,' and I agree," Serena said. "But lecturing is helpful too. The discussions in this class can be exhausting, and you seldom give us a straight answer, just more questions. Professor Kelly, if you'll forgive me, I'd hate to be your wife!"

Filomena was about to say something but decided not to. So, Kelly asked yet another question. "Leaving marriage and relationships out of the equation, let me change the subject a little: Would you prefer to call me professor or instructor?"

Jean answered quickly. "I wouldn't want to be a liar and call you an instructor. There's very little instruction in this class. I might be thrown out of the university if I lied and called you an instructor, and I want to get my degree before I leave the Metro."

"I would prefer it if you were an instructor. My husband thinks you're derelict in your duty," said Anette loudly. "That way, you wouldn't be invading my private thought processes and poking around in my brain, looking for the way I think. You might even give us something to write down in our notepads," she said, pointing to an empty page.

"Maybe I should resign then," said Kelly, gathering his belongings and heading for the classroom door.

"No, please don't," went up a chorus of voices as several of the students went to prevent him from leaving.

"OK then, I'll stay for now," he said as he returned to his spot at the lectern. "Yet," he continued lightheartedly but serious, "Maybe there is a legal dimension to this. It's not as though I think I've betrayed an oath like doctors take, that is, to do no harm."

"Lawyers take an oath too, you know," inserted Anette.

"My concern is that maybe the Metro and other universities have betrayed their unstated oaths to serve their students properly," claimed Christine when Anette had finished interrupting. I just love the discussions we have, and I always learn a great deal from them."

"I don't get it, Professor," said Mark.

"Here, let me show you," said Kelly, turning to his computer and projecting up on the screen behind him a number of course descriptions on the university website, which also showed which 'Instructor' was teaching each course. "That's not all,' he added, "I get constant messages informing me that this group or that is offering a seminar on how instructors can provide their students with greatly improved educational 'experiences.' And, so, the word gets out. You've probably heard it yourselves on campus: Professors are instructors. Ask a course-related question in some campus offices, and you're likely to be asked, 'Who's your instructor?'"

"That reminds me, Professor," said Christine. "When you were recently discussing the weaknesses of Adler's position, you pointed out that one of the ways he belittled certain areas of study was that he said there should be 'instruction about' health in school. But when speaking of the main subjects in his proposal, such as history and the teaching of ideas and values, Adler wanted to have a discussion. He even used a phrase like 'Socratic questioning or teaching' when referring to those subjects."

"That's correct, Christine," said Kelly, pleased that someone was elaborating on the point he wanted to make. "So, if your professors are supposed to be 'instructors,' is it any surprise that many of you come to me saying that you mostly have instruction in your courses?"

"Spot on, Professor," said Miguel with two thumbs up. "It's about time someone spoke truth to power. I couldn't have put it so succinctly, but I've been annoyed by sitting through dumb lectures for the past several years and wondering why I was not just given tape recordings of lectures and told to soak 'em up. And believe me, I hope that online learning doesn't magnify this bloomin' problem. I don't need to attend Harvard or even one of the colleges at the University of Oxford where Newman hung out, but I sure have come to value the kind of back and forth discussion we have in this class."

"I agree," said Filomena. "To say nothing of Professor Kelly, I just love this class. And to add what Miguel just said, it might be of interest to everyone that as part of our work on COGEM, I had reason to check out what Newman had to say about this matter and would you believe, he went so far as to say that there were at least some occasions when students discussing topics among themselves, even without a professor present, could be educationally beneficial."

"So, could we save some bucks if you only came in every second day, Professor?" Miguel asked Kelly.

"As long as the bucks don't come out of my pocket, I'm OK with that," said Kelly with a chuckle. "Unfortunately, we need to refocus here. It's almost the end of the semester, as you know, and we need to get back to business. When considering whether your professors should be called instructors, Christine pointed out that Adler used the word 'instruction' to convey the mere passing along of information to students, and that this contrasted with classroom discussion. If a university is best understood as a place for the discussion and exploration of ideas, that could indicate that the word 'instructor' is the wrong one to use when referring to professors. I would add that using that term in this way suggests that the job of the professor is simply to pass on information."

"But surely there is a place for the passing on of information, even in a university setting," suggested Serena. "When professors do both lecture and foster discussion, that's when I learn the most."

"I am inclined to agree with you there, Serena," responded Kelly. "This is a complex matter, having many angles to consider. There is certainly a place for the passing on of information, but the complaint

I receive from students is not that there is too much discussion, but that there is too much lecturing and information-giving and too little conversation. Research studies also point in that direction. Using the word 'instructor' may contribute to this. Perhaps it's part of a legacy we inherited unwittingly."

Kelly waited to see if anyone else had any questions, and when there were none, he continued. "I now want to add a somewhat more abstract point. To avoid a misunderstanding, let me start by saying that I support faculty development programs on university campuses. On the whole, I believe they provide an important service, and I have occasionally worked with them. However, I recently received an email from such a program at another university that was offering assistance to 'instructors' in delivering a high-quality experience in their classes." Making light of the situation, he continued, "While I welcome all the assistance I can get—and that includes you guys in class who contribute so much—that statement contains a misleading implication. Would anyone like to wager a guess as to what that might be?"

"Is it the notion that professors 'own' their classes?" asked Levi. "I mean, if any of the beautiful female students in this class— who surely find me the most attractive guy in the room—came to me and said, 'Would you like to come for a drive in my car?' I would understand that she owned the car. But what if it were a rental car?"

"What the heck, Levi?" said Miguel. "Why beat around the bush? Just jump in, man!"

"I don't see any such offers, Levi, so let me just jump in myself. Time is running out here. In this class or any of my classes, I don't believe it is my responsibility to deliver a high-quality experience. Now, before you all go ahead and tell me that, for sure, I've already demonstrated that, I want to go in a different direction. I might be able to deliver information, as can a book or a recording or even a movie, but it's only you, yourselves, that can 'have the experience.' And it is by you having such experiences that you grow in knowledge and understanding, I believe—as did Adler, by the way. It is the discussion or back and forth conversation, either between you and me or among yourselves, that enables you to have such experiences. That is why

I like to get you all in on the action here. It's not intended to punish you."

"But I can also have a worthwhile learning experience if I just hear you lecture, as you do once in a blue moon," said Jean.

"Once again, Jean, I must agree," said Kelly happily. "As I said earlier, this is complex stuff. Yes, one can have a learning experience from lectures and even from textbooks. While that is an important form of experience, it is limited and does not embrace the full range of learning experiences that a good education enables. And because it is limited, Adler advocated for the use of Socratic questioning to supplement what is gained from lectures, textbooks, and the like. Clearly, I agree with him on that. I would add that promoting the growth of understanding and appreciation of knowledge and the associated forms of critical thinking that Socratic dialogue facilitates—and not merely form courses and area studies—is an aspect of education that a university should prioritize."

CHAPTER 19

By the day of the final school board meeting of the year, Price and the district office staff were well aware of what was afoot regarding the planned protest. The revised improvement plan with Filomena's modifications had been circulated. Understanding the role that Radio YOY might play that evening, the superintendent had also alerted the Midleton police in case the protesters became a threat to members of the school board or to school property. In the interest of safety, Filomena was informed that she could opt out of attending the meeting, although she indicated that she would be there. This was partly because Marilyn, who wanted first-person feedback from the board meeting, had encouraged her to be brave. The protest was planned to begin at 4:30 p.m. so that it would be in full stride as the members arrived for the 5:30 p.m. meeting, and be over and done with before complete darkness set in.

As those who were gathering on the green outside the district office awaited school board members to arrive, the scene was colorful if noisy. It was a welcome spectacle for the photographers and out-of-town TV crews that were eager to make hay as the sun shone on a fair December afternoon. Several placards read, "This is the People's School," but others were less tasteful. Donut stands and soft drink vendors were busy serving children, making the best of their opportunity. A series of firecrackers went off, causing a mild degree of panic. A group of teenagers with electric guitars and drums erected a set of makeshift loudspeakers and played amateurish but enthusiastic music until the appointed speakers for the occasion came to the microphones set up on the temporary speakers' platform. Holding a copy of the Goodies 2020 Act over his head, Conners took to the stage to introduce the keynote speaker, his son, Jake. With Singleton surprisingly nowhere to be found, and before all the planned speeches concluded, a second round of firecrackers rocked the crowd, louder and more intense than the first. This sent parents and children scurrying for cover under the trees that surrounded the gathering place behind the district offices, where some fly-by-night salesmen had set up shop to hawk this, that, and the other.

When the firecrackers quieted down and dusk arrived, attention was drawn to a small aircraft overhead sporting a sizeable, colorful sign attached to its tail that read: LIBERATE MIDLETON! At this time what looked like a passenger in the aircraft was getting ready to jump. After he jumped from the plane, and as his parachute opened up, emblazoned upon it were the words, "I SAY NO SURRENDER." Although the chute opened in plenty of time, the windy conditions and the jumper's hesitance to exit the plane threw him off course, causing him to come crashing down into the tallest of the trees around the office building and the rambunctious crowd below. He was stranded on high for a good 20 minutes and unable to untangle himself. By the time the fire brigade came to his rescue, the daylight had passed and policemen were busy rounding up rowdy protesters and those seen throwing beer bottles at school board members entering the building. The sirens of ambulances arriving to tend to the injured had replaced the confusing exhortations of the speakers, who had left the platform. As fire fighters were readying to rescue the parachutist, the spotlights beaming upward from the fire engine showed in vivid color that it was none other than Singleton. His arms flailing and expletives heard from quite the disatance, he was hanging upside down from some fragile-looking branches and somehow trying to hold on to his trousers. All that could be seen of the remnants of his parachute were the words, "I SURRENDER."

While the policemen eventually restored order outside the building, it was a different story on the inside. Several of those bearing arms who had arrived for the protest had made their way into the meeting, leading some board members to wonder who was in charge. Several quickly donned the bulletproof vests they brought along, just in case. As Blair attempted to call the meeting to order, Conners objected to starting the proceedings without Singleton. "Maybe he'll drop in later," said Blair, anxious to press ahead.

With Singleton still not present, Conners spoke again before the official proceedings began. "It is clear that the people of Midleton, many of whom have gathered outside, strongly oppose this plan and its submission to the feds. We must send a clear message to the leftist commies in Washington that we will not allow them to seize control of our fair district. I demand we reject this ludicrous plan now," he shouted, waving his copy of the Goodies 2020 Act for all to see.

"Take it easy, Butch," began Burnett as Conners sat down, and as it seemed the official meeting had actually started. "I see no evidence that all the Midletonians outside favor the rejection of the plan. All I saw on my way in were a handful of placards to that effect and a member of this very body hanging upside down from a tree with the words 'I Surrender' draped around his neck. I also received thumbs ups from many of those present who know my position on this. Maybe your message wasn't as clear or inclusive as it needed to be, Mr. Conners, and maybe Singleton himself is trying to convey that he has changed his mind. How else could one interpret that banner high in the treetop?"

Sensing the tides turning, the small group bearing arms moved to the back of the boardroom, and they marched out. At that, Blair finally succeeded in calling the meeting to order. By now, as the meeting proper just got started, members were getting worked up. The divisions among them were clearly evident, and various extraneous matters were brought up for debate. Conners tried in vain to push through his 'Komputer a Kid' proposal. Following a discussion of literacy on the middle-school curriculum, a proposal insisting that four hours of phonics per week be added to the program was also rejected.

Eventually, Blair got around to the main item on the agenda, and he invited Price to introduce the improvement plan. This she did by explaining the revision made since the previous meeting and urging the members to adopt it without delay. At the time, it appeared that this was an unrealistic proposition, given how riled up the members had become by now.

Irritated by the rejection of his Komputer a Kid proposal, and absent the 'steadying hand' of Singleton, Conners leaped to his feet to lead the charge against the improvement plan. Before long, his presentation descended into an offensive and sexist attack on Price rather than a denunciation of the plan. "Ms. Price is a lowlife who attempted to sully the name of our distinguished and highflying representative in Congress, Wayne Singleton, falsely alleging he is a hypocrite on the on sacred airwaves of Midleton's own Radio YOY. Unlike Mr. Garrison, who was superintendent of schools when I was a kid here, Price conceals her true identity by insisting she is 'Dr. Price.' How could a harridan like her be up to the task of being our super here in Midleton? She's fake news. Just like her 'improvement plan.' It's all a hoax. Down with it!"

Reading the adverse impact of his words more quickly than Conners, Blair decided not to rein him in until Bartley indicated he wished to speak. "Thank you, Mr. Blair," began Bartley. "Mr. Conners, I was a friend of Ger Garrison, and you're no Ger Garrison. You don't even speak like Ger Garrison. I came here prepared to vote against the improvement plan this evening in protest against intrusion by the feds. Now I will be voting to accept the plan in protest against the protest, and I move that we vote on that forthwith."

"Seconded," said Burnett, jumping at the opportunity.

"Does anyone wish to speak?" asked Blair. There being no one since Bartley had already spoken for most of them, he called for the vote as tempers cooled, and visitors were asked to leave.

When the vote was taken and tallied, and against all expectations earlier in the evening, it showed that the improvement plan was narrowly approved by a vote of 8 to 7. The votes of all those present were recorded for the minutes and were given to members of the press who had waited around.

***

Working into the evening after he left the scene of the protest and the vote count, and recognizing the urgent need for damage control on behalf of Conners and Singleton, Smatter managed to arrange some exclusive late-night interviews on Radio YOY. Marilyn, who managed to "bump into him" at the protest scene, readily agreed to be interviewed, and led Smatter to imagine she would be supportive of those who had organized and took part in the protests. Marilyn tipped off Filomena that she would be interviewed on Smatter's show, and suggested that she listen in and make a recording if possible.

The interview would contain elements of the report she promised to Filomena on what was happening outside of the school district office during the protest.

"My first guest tonight is Marilyn, a stalwart young business student from the Metro who was happy to join those joyous citizens outside the district office as the school board was deliberating inside," said Smatter, attempting to sanitize the account of the protest for his radio listeners shortly after 11 p.m. "Marilyn, I believe you are a surveillance services major at the Metro. That must be music to the ears of Mr. Butch Conners, the chair of the Metro board of governors and former highly successful CEO of a small business out of Philadelphia. I'm sure you have much to learn from him in the way of services operations. So, tell me, why did you participate in support of his call to arms this evening, if I may put it that way, and what were the highlights for you?"

"The Metro is a great university," Marilyn began, "and our students among the best. Over the last week, I kept a close ear on your coverage of the planned protests of this evening's tumultuous event, organized by Mr. Conners and Representative Singleton. You sure did get the word out," said Marilyn, cozying up to Smatter and not wanting to anger him from the outset. "Let's reel him in gently, to begin with," Marilyn said to herself.

"Is there a great deal of admiration for Mr. Conners on campus? For that matter, how well do Metro students like my show?" asked Smatter with a smile on his face.

"To be truthful, Arnie—is it OK to call you Arnie?" Marilyn asked. "I notice other guests do that. You are so personal."

"Of course, Marilyn. That's who I am, Arnie Smatter, the host with the most."

"Thanks. I've never heard a bad word about your show on campus," said Marilyn, carefully omitting that she'd rarely heard any word about it at all. "But back to the protests—to be truthful, I thought Singleton looked like an ass hanging upside down in that tree. He can thank the fire brigade for lighting him up for all to see. That was highlight number one for me." When this drew an embarrassed chuckle from the Singleton promoter, Marilyn continued, "I must say, however, I did not approve of the men bearing arms any more than I did Singleton baring his you-know-what."

"Anything else?" asked Smatter abruptly, indicating nonverbally that he wished to move on to his next guest, who was expected to be more approving of Singleton and Smatter's own support for this entire misadventure.

"Yes, there are one or two other things," said Marilyn. "First, Conners should be fired!"

"That's enough, Marilyn," said Smatter, silencing Marilyn and ushering her out of the studio.

***

The next day, the *Midleton Morning Mouthpiece* headline read, "Rep. Singleton Misses Controversial Vote on School Improvement Plan." Showing disgust at the outcome of the meeting, and having excoriated the congressman, the editorial called for a recount. The paper failed to report that Singleton was hospitalized overnight, however, and he now wanted to know who had made off with his wallet and car keys.

Attempting to sing the praises of Singleton while buttering him up on his morning radio show early the same day, Smatter excitedly announced that the congressman promised a reward and a handshake for anyone who could turn in his stolen goods. The effusive praise was cut short by a caller:

"Can I kiss his ass, too?"

***

In Kelly's classroom that morning, there was a buzz of excitement before he arrived. Once again, nobody knew what to expect. Would he deal with the protest, and what about Marilyn's interaction with Arnie Smatter on Radio YOY, especially her call for Conners's dismissal?

What everyone did know was that Marilyn's performance on the radio the night before was all the talk on campus that morning. Her "heroic leadership and refreshing viewpoint" was featured as the lead news item in *The Metro Memo*, which showed a photo taken of her earlier chatting leisurely with the vice president.

There was no mention of the protest on TV Views.

Miguel had seen *The Metro Memo,* and in class, he gently set the ball rolling by asking Kelly if the Marilyn that appeared in the news reports was the same Marilyn that attended their class as a guest on a few occasions.

"Yes, that's our Marilyn all right, as can be seen in the photo," answered Kelly, who had seen the student newspaper. He then turned to Filomena to ask for an update.

"Last night after I got home from the school board meeting," Filomena began, "Marilyn called to tell me she would be on Radio YOY before midnight. Delighted by her performance and listening to her every word, I called her for a chat after I heard the interview. To my surprise, in our conversation, I got the feeling that she was more concerned about a virus that she said was coming than about the interview. Anyway, I'll be meeting her later today and hope to learn more about everything then. She seems to have the inside scoop on everything."

Kelly asked if anyone else had listened to Radio YOY. Several, including Kelly himself, had heard the interview because Filomena and Christine had spread the word. Jean and a friend had also attended the protest just to see what was going on.

"My husband listened in, but I was busy studying," said Anette. "He thinks Conners could be in trouble."

Christine said she was dismayed by what she heard.

Several other students in the class had also seen *The Metro Memo*, and a few even brought it to class with them on the off chance it might be used in a discussion.

When asked if that were a possibility, Kelly was open to it. "But first, I'd like to know if anyone would like to bring up the course readings or earlier discussions. That's usually what we do on the last day of classes."

That is not what the class was interested in. Everyone wanted to learn more about the protest and Marilyn's performance on Radio YOY.

"Professor Kelly, do you think Conners should be fired?" Jean asked Kelly straight out.

"That's a tough one for a professor to answer," said Miguel. "After all, Conners is kinda his boss."

"That's OK, Miguel," said Kelly. "But I do have to be careful here," and turning to Jean, he asked, "and why would I want him to be fired?"

"Marilyn said so on the radio. She also saw his performance at the protest, you know."

"You were at the protest too, Jean," said Kelly. "What do you think?"

"Oh, I agree with Marilyn."

"And why," asked Kelly again.

"So, here's Conners at the protest. First, he brings his son along to be the main speaker for the event, and he's only interested in selling computers. Talk about nepotism! Then, Conners asks for a round of applause for the gun bearers. And lastly, he brings the Metro into his argument for not passing the school board's improvement plan, telling everyone that the committee Filomena serves on is a hoax and ought to be terminated. Is this who we want to represent our university? I, for one, think not."

"Thank you, Jean, that's well stated," said Kelly.

"OK, Professor. Your turn. You said you listened to Smatter's broadcast. Should Smatter be fired?" asked Jean.

Christine intervened. "Ok, Jean. I listened too. Let's see if we can get this sorted out without calling on the professor's opinion. He won't be with us every time we face a challenge. For transparency's sake, I should say I listen to Smatter occasionally when I'm driving to class or wherever. It's hard to turn on the radio and not catch him spouting off about something. He's entertaining, if nothing else, and he was a big promoter of the protest the week leading up to it. In fact, the protest was concocted by Conners and Singleton on Smatter's show one day. I heard them planning it with Arnie's help. From the very beginning, they intended to get the people riled up. Last night, Smatter cooled on Marilyn as soon as she gave her unfavorable opinion of Singleton. When she said Conners should be fired, he silenced her completely. So, yes, I think Radio YOY should give Smatter the ax."

"That's fair enough," said Jean. "But who will cover the news if we fire the reporters? Should we get rid of CNN too?"

"I need to get another word in here," said Miguel. "Now, I must be clear, I didn't hear Smatter's show, and I wasn't at the protest. But I did read *The Metro Memo* when I got to campus this morning, and I chatted with some friends about it. It's no surprise that Marilyn thinks Conners should go. The editorial in the *Memo* also called for Conners to be fired, and they spoke very highly of Marilyn. Nobody seems to be standing up for Conners or Singleton. So here's my question: Where does all of this leave us on deciding what should happen next?"

A student who rarely spoke raised his hand, and Kelly invited him to speak. "Hi everybody. I'm Ali, and I sometimes write for *The Metro Memo*. I'm studying for teacher certification in communications as a grad student. I haven't spoken up very much in class because I missed some classes, but I am very interested in the professor's take on gen ed and I wanted to hear him out on this."

"Keep going, Ali," said Kelly, "I'm interested to hear your perspective."

"Well, Professor Kelly, I agree that it's essential to include the study of practical subjects in gen ed, like you suggest. Being in communications and interning for the *Memo* was an excellent experience of that kind. I certainly learned things I wouldn't have learned from lectures or reading or even from writing term papers. But to fully understand and form a sound opinion on what went on at the protest and during Marilyn's appearance on Radio YOY last night, you need to rely on more than observation and even participation. You need to apply critical analysis of the kind that one encounters in subjects such as history and politics, when well taught, as well as in your Socratic teaching. In other words, I think it's necessary to have a good old-fashioned liberal arts frame of mind. How does that link in with your idea of a good education?

"Good question," said Anette.

"May I speak, Professor?" asked Miguel.

"Please do," said Kelly.

"As you know, Professor, raising questions and critically examining evidence is supposed to be an important part of a rigorous intellectual education. I like what Ali said, so just in case you've had trouble coming up with final exam questions that would test the intellectual education we received in this class, here's one you might consider to evaluate our analytical skills: 'Based on your course readings, recently published reports, and radio and TV programs, critically consider the contributions of Butch Conners, Arnie Smatter, and Wayne Singleton to the quality of education at the Metro and the well-being of Midleton over the past two weeks.'"

"It needs refinement but I like that question, Miguel. By the way, have you been poking around in my cache of exam questions?" asked Kelly with a laugh.

Next, Kelly decided it was time for him to join the conversation. "We are running out of time here, so let me make a few closing comments," he began. "I agree with what Ali and Miguel have to say. So, in case I understated it during the semester, I'd like to clarify my position on the point they raise. As some of you know, I actually write about this topic in my new book, called *The Academic Major*, which deals with this point.

"I believe that one of the most important intellectual skills we can nourish in school and in college is the skill of critical thinking, and this is to take nothing away from ethical and emotional formation. Yes, some subjects like history provide ample opportunity for learning to debate and critique. In fact, almost any subject studied in depth—and especially one's major—in which students are academically challenged and encouraged to explore and, importantly, *evaluate* new ideas and possibilities, critically reflect on and discuss what is being learned, and creatively look into the future can be relied upon. But apropos the protest and Radio YOY, just consider the kinds of questions that could be examined and debated by looking closely at the events of last night if sufficient time were devoted to it.

"What are the conditions that led to the protest? What was the role and motivation of the key players, such as Mr. Conners and Representative Singleton, in bringing it about? How would you *evaluate* their performance? What were the contributions and the preferences expressed by various media outlets, such as TVViews, Radio YOY, and even our own beloved *Memo,* in the whole affair?

How would you *evaluate* their contributions? Why were so many people suckered in and willing to fall in line? And, importantly, what lessons can be drawn from it all, and what, if anything, should we as individual citizens do…"

Just before Kelly had finished speaking and as students were putting their hands up, the classroom intercom shocked everyone as it crackled to life with an announcement from President Beame that repeated several times: "Due to a critical public health emergency, classes are to dismiss immediately. Please leave in a safe, orderly fashion. Stay tuned for further updates."

Even though everyone was stunned at the disturbing news, the students quickly collected their belongings and began to leave. Kelly wished them well. As he looked toward Filomena, she blew him a kiss, which he gladly acknowledged with a thumbs up.

CHAPTER 20

At 6 a.m. the next day, Friday, December 13, 2019, it was officially communicated that all remaining classes for the semester were canceled, and the recreational center would be closed immediately. Final exams would take place on a shortened schedule the following week, with everyone using wipes, wearing masks, and practicing social distancing. Following exams, residence halls would be vacated within 24 hours. No meetings would be permitted on campus; all buildings, including the library, would be locked; and students, faculty, and nonessential staff would be barred from entry.

Sunset would arrive midday on December 20. No date was set for sunrise.

APPENDIX: QUESTIONS FOR DISCUSSION, SUGGESTED TOPICS FOR TERM PAPERS AND RESEARCH PROJECTS

QUESTIONS FOR DISCUSSION

- What is education?
- If you were to devise a program of general education for schools or colleges, what would be its defining features? Why?
- In a paragraph, describe what you see to be the essential features of Socratic teaching, and indicate how you would evaluate it.
- Do you favor the inclusion of home economics in general education? Why or why not?
- What is your stance on the place of religion in public schools? Why?
- To what extent, if any, should schools and universities act in loco parentis? Explain your thinking.
- What biases, if any, do you detect in *Gen Ed*? Justify your selection/s.
- How much of *Gen Ed* is a novel and how much of it is a scholarly treatment of the topic? Is it helpful in reflecting on the educational issues it raises?
- How would you rate Professor Kelly as a teacher? Why?
- The suggestion that we ought to focus on the learner as an agent rather than as a knower when planning the school curriculum comes from John White. What do you think of that idea?
- The idea of the forms of knowledge is treated in depth by Paul Hirst. What do you think of his idea?
- Who is the most interesting character in *Gen Ed*? Why?
- If you had to attend a week-long conference or spend a week at a beach resort with three characters in *Gen Ed*, who would you choose? Why?
- Which character do you dislike most? Why?
- What do you like or dislike about the treatment of the Metro in *Gen Ed*?
- How would you rate the humorous dimension of *Gen Ed*? Does it add to or detract from the central themes of the novel?

TERM/RESEARCH PAPERS

- Critically analyze Mortimer Adler's *The Paideia Proposal*
- Trace and critically consider the evolution of the idea of a liberal education from the time of John Henry Newman
- Critically analyze Jane Roland Martin's *The Schoolhome*
- Compare and contrast the educational ideas of Paul Hirst and Jane Roland Martin
- Create and justify your own concept of an educated person

REFERENCES

Adler, M. J. (1982). *The paideia proposal: An educational manifesto.* Macmillan.

Dewey, J. (1966). *Democracy and education.* The Free Press.

Freire, P. (2012). *Pedagogy of the oppressed* (M. B. Ramos, Trans.). Bloomsbury.

Kimball, B. A. (1995). *Orators and philosophers: A history of the idea of liberal education* (2nd ed.). College Entrance Examination Board.

Hirst, P. H. (1974). *Knowledge and the curriculum.* Routledge and Kegan Paul.

Martin, J. R. (1992). *The schoolhome: Rethinking schools for changing families.* Harvard University Press.

Mulcahy, D. G. (2008). *The educated person: Toward a new paradigm for liberal education.* Rowman and Littlefield.

Pediwell, J. A. (1939). *The Saber-Tooth curriculum.* McGraw-Hill.

Simpson, D. J. (1994). *The pedagodfathers: The lords of education.* Detselig Enterprises, Ltd.

ABOUT THE AUTHOR

D. G. Mulcahy is Connecticut State University Professor Emeritus in the School of Education and Professional Studies at Central Connecticut State University. He was formerly Professor and Chair of Education at University College Cork, Ireland. A registered secondary teacher in Ireland, he also held professorial appointments at the University of New Brunswick in Canada and Eastern Illinois University.

Mulcahy is a Past President of the New England Philosophy of Education Society and of the Educational Studies Association of Ireland of which he is a co-founder and current member of the executive committee. His research interests center on philosophy of education, curriculum theories, and educational policy. His books include *The Educated Person* (2008), *Knowledge, Gender, and Schooling* (2002) and *Curriculum and Policy in Irish Post-Primary Education* (1981). He has co-authored *Pedagogy, Praxis and Purpose in Education* (2015) and co-edited *Education in North America* (2014), *Transforming Schools: Alternative Perspectives on School Reform* (2013), and *Irish Educational Policy: Process and Substance* (1989). His research has also been published as chapters in over a dozen books and encyclopedias and as articles in journals in Europe and North America, including *Arts and Humanities in Higher Education, Augustiniana, Curriculum Inquiry, Educational Foundations, Educational Studies, Educational Theory, European Journal of Teacher Education, Innovative Higher Education, International Education, Irish Journal of Education, Irish Educational Studies, Journal of Educational Thought, Journal of Philosophy of Education, Journal of Thought, Revue des Etudes Augustiennes, Social Studies,* and *Studies in Philosophy and Education.*

Mulcahy has held a number of university administrative positions in European and American universities and has also served as external examiner for different universities and colleges. He has been active in curriculum development and in a consultancy capacity in professional development and the accreditation of schools and colleges in the European Union, North America, and the Caribbean.

He has served in an editorial and reviewer capacity for a number of publishing houses and academic journals.

Mulcahy has twice been awarded Fulbright Grants. *Gen Ed* is his first novel.

Printed in the United States
By Bookmasters